Canonical Texts

Selections from Religious Wisdom Traditions

Edited by Thomas Jerome Burns

University of Oklahoma

San Diego, CA

Bassim Hamadeh, Publisher
Michael Simpson, Vice President of Acquisitions
Christopher Foster, Vice President of Marketing
Jessica Knott, Managing Editor
Stephen Milano, Creative Director
Kevin Fahey, Cognella Marketing Program Manager
Becky Smith, Acquisitions Editor
Erin Escobar, Licensing Associate
Sarah Wheeler, Project Editor

First published in the United States of America in 2012 by University Readers, Inc.

Trademark Notice: Product or corporate names may be trademarks or registered trademarks, and are used only for identification and explanation without intent to infringe.

15 14 13 12 11   1 2 3 4 5

Printed in the United States of America

ISBN: 978-1-60927-053-7

www.cognella.com 800.200.3908

Contents

Dedication

For my daughters:

Clare Marie Wheeler
Kathleen Mary Burns
Bridget Agnes-Anne Burns
Colleen Margaret Burns

Preface

This volume is an attempt to bring together some of the texts that are central to the respective traditions they represent. In any such project there are tradeoffs, including the age-old problem of balancing breadth and depth.

I have tried to capture here the essence of a smaller number of works than do most anthologies, but to be faithful to the context in which they are written. It is important to have enough of a work to let it "breathe." It is thus, I believe, important to avoid (like the proverbial plague) having a bunch of disembodied snippets.

One of the guiding principles here is to come up with something that I would have liked to have had myself many years ago, when embarking upon this endlessly fascinating study of major religious traditions from around the world.

One thing students ask for repeatedly is basic readings—something giving a thorough grounding in enough depth to get a real sense of them, but not laden with obscure references that make no sense to them.

The course I teach is sixteen weeks long and we cover eight traditions. You can do the math, but I have found over the years that this level and selection of readings is about right for an upper-division undergraduate "survey" course in major religious traditions.

There is, of course, always the temptation to assign more reading and to brag about having "gotten through" copious amounts of material—the entire Mahabharata and Ramayana; the Pali Canon and the Lotus Sutra; the Confucian Analects and the Mencius, the Tao Te Ching and the I Ching all by the midterm! To those doing that, brag away. I prefer, even in a survey course, to stop long enough to drink, if not deeply, then at least enough to slake some of the thirst. We make eight such stops.

I have limited entries from each tradition to about 25 pages. While this would make it theoretically possible to read one in a single "sitting," I advise against that. Rather, think of reading poetry—and very rich and nuanced verse at that. "Speed reading" completely misses the point, as does reading in a distracted manner. I like to work through a few pages (give or take) at a time, and then go for a long walk or sit and think for a while—very *non*–21ˢᵗ Century I suppose, but I do keep hoping this will catch on.

The translations chosen here typically are older ones as well, many of which are now in the public domain. While there are, in many cases, newer and arguably more "accurate" translations available, I am drawn by the philosophy of an old poetry professor from my undergraduate days at the University of Maryland, Roderick Jellema. Rod helped me come to see that translations themselves have inherent value and poetry—a lesson I have carried with me, even these many years hence. The experience with these readings hopefully will be of the sort that draws the reader in, and gives a sense of the cultures of which the translations were part.

The people who have helped in this effort are numerous indeed, and I will mention only some of them here. Thank you to the people who introduced me to these ideas over the years in a variety of contexts. Many of my colleagues in Sociology and in Religious Studies are willing to engage in something beyond surface dialogue, and for that I am most grateful.

People in the community involved in interfaith understanding have made huge, albeit indirect, contributions. Lisa Connery and Richard Coberg have for years run a wonderful meditation group in Norman, Oklahoma. They, along with Father Jack Feehily, go above and beyond to promote religious tolerance and understanding. My friends in the Institute for Interfaith Dialogue, particularly Orhan Osman, Muhammad Cetin, Vahap and Nur Uysal have been most encouraging throughout. Friends at the Xenia Institute have been instrumental here as well, particularly Clint Williams and Chelsea Scudder.

I am grateful for my colleague and dear friend, Tom Boyd, for his wisdom and for being someone I can invariably count on for quality thought, good-faith discourse, graciousness, and humor. I am not sure what engaging in real dialogue with Socrates or the Buddha was like, but years of hanging out with Tom Boyd has been an experience that continues to remind me that the examined life really is something worth taking seriously. Tom and Barbara Boyd continue to contribute their irreplaceable energy to the universal oversoul, and to the Religious Studies program at the University of Oklahoma in particular.

Tom and Dara Fogel made helpful comments during the early stages of the project. The original plan had been for the three of us to collaborate on it. While this turned out to be a solo project after all, I am grateful for their input. I am glad Wil Scott encouraged me to develop this course many years ago now.

Tracey Fleming read prior drafts and made helpful suggestions throughout. Some of my prior teaching assistants have been helpful over the years in adding insights and feedback, particularly Brandon Pearson, Hoest Heap of Birds, Emily Pain, Shelley Herr, and J.D. Thomason.

I thank my students, former and current, for helpful feedback over the years. I have always regarded it as a privilege to try to live up to what it means to be a professor, and never one to be taken lightly.

The team at Cognella has been great. Becky Smith, Jessica Knott, Kevin Fahey, and Sarah Wheeler have been a pleasure to work with in bringing this project together.

Some of my own very favorite passages from each of the traditions have made it into these pages. I am hoping the resulting text is something that is not just educational, but is something you can savor.

Let us now turn our attention to some of the canonical texts of the world's wisdom traditions…

Chapter 1
Hinduism

From the Bhagavad Gita

The Bhagavad Gita, or Song of God, is considered by many to be the central Hindu text. It is part of a much larger literature from the Hindu tradition, composed of Vedas (older book of knowledge or wisdom) and Upanishads (later teachings or commentaries).

The Bhagavad Gita itself, eighteen chapters in length, is a relatively small but pivotal part of the Mahabharata, which is one of the longest epic poems in the world. While some people believe the Mahabharata to be revealed wisdom, handed down directly from God in the primordial past, historical scholars place its authorship somewhere around the Fourth Century, B.C.E. The song, or poem, probably was passed down as part of a rich oral tradition for centuries before that.

The two major characters in the Bhagavad Gita are Krishna and Arjuna. Krishna is an Avatar or incarnation of one of the manifestations of Vishnu. In the Bhagavad Gita, Krishna serves as chariot driver and advisor to Arjuna, the warrior. More broadly, Krishna is seen as the voice of God himself, advising humanity (as represented by Arjuna) throughout.

The story is recited by Sanjay, who has the gift of being able to see at long distances, beyond the physical realm. He is telling the story to Dhritarashtra, the blind patriarch. Unfolding over eighteen days, the Bhagavad Gita is a narration of the Battle of Kurukshetra, a dispute between two rival clans, the Kauravas and the Pandavas. A rich story that can be understood on a number of levels, almost everything in the Bhagavad Gita has a backstory and stands for something else.

Dhritarashtra's blindness and fate in the story stem directly from his Karma, one of the central themes of the Bhagavad Gita. In a past life, Dhritarashtra had been a king who upon taking a walk one day, sees a swan surrounded by one hundred cygnets, all swimming peacefully in a pond. For no particular reason other than to exercise his power, he has the swan blinded and the hundred cygnets killed. His fate in this life is not only to be blind, but to suffer an even worse fate. During the course of the battle, each of Dhritarashtra's sons is to be killed. Much of Sanjay's duty is to recount this horrible bloodshed to Dhritarashtra.

Another key aspect of the backstory is that there are three aspects of God in the "Hindu Trinity"—Brahma (the creator), Vishnu (the preserver) and Shiva (the destroyer). Vishnu plays a particularly important role in the Bhagavad Gita, through his incarnation as Krishna. The word Krishna in Sanskrit means "anointed one," and comes from the same linguistic root in the Indo-European chain as Christos in Greek.

While the words Christ and Krishna do have analogies, there are differences as well. While in Christianity, there is one Christ, in Hinduism, there are multiple incarnations over time of deities. Some of the best known of Vishnu, for example, are as Rama (as explored in another of the long epic poems of India, the Ramayana) and as Krishna (a focus of the Mahabharata, and particularly of the Bhagavad Gita).

The battle on the Kurukshetra plains pits Arjuna who is a prince in the Pandhava clan fighting against his relatives in the Kaurava clan. Yet the war is symbolic for the universal struggles we all face—those between people, and particularly within ourselves.

As the story begins and we move through the first several chapters, Arjuna asks Krishna to position his chariot between the two opposing armies of the Pandavas and Kauravas. A significant part of this chapter focuses on Arjuna losing his courage and not wanting to fight. This is underscored by the fact that Arjuna sees friends not just on his own side but on the other side—cousins and other relatives are there.

Krishna admonishes Arjuna, explaining to him how Karma interacts with another crucial Hindu idea—that of Dharma. Krishna tells Arjuna that he has a duty as a warrior to fight the war. If people die in that war, then so be it. Krishna tells Arjuna that he should be acting righteously, regardless of the results. In fact, to do the right thing is necessary for salvation. This is true regardless of the outcome.

Krishna tells Arjuna about his many manifestations and births. He presents himself as Arjuna's teacher and reminds Arjuna of the importance of having a wise and experienced teacher – a guru who ideally speaks with the voice and authority of God.

Arjuna is not totally committed yet. He tries to find loopholes, as it were. He pleads with Krishna to follow a path of renunciation. Krishna instructs him that it is better to follow a path of righteousness in action than inaction.

In Chapter 11, "The Book of Manifesting the One and the Manifold," Krishna does manifest himself with the radiance of 1000 suns containing all beings and material in the universe. Notably, Robert Oppenheimer, the architect of the Twentieth Century Manhattan Project, quotes from this chapter when he talks about the sheer power of the atom bomb.

Krishna then moves to other manifestations of power, including the power of devotion and prayer. This is followed by Krishna's explanation of the three modes or gunas of material nature. Following that, Krishna makes it an important distinction between divine and demonic natures. He emphasizes the necessity of renouncing lust, anger and greed.

In the final chapter, Krishna counsels Arjuna to move beyond Dharma altogether and surrender to him. In Hindu terms, this leads to Moksha or the final liberation. Like a drop *of water finding its true nature by surrendering itself to, and thus becoming one with, the ocean, this occurs when there is a linking or yoke between Brahman , or the undifferentiated God-Head, and Atman, or the individual soul.*

And now we move to the text of the Bhagavad Gita...

From Chapter 1. On the Distress of Arjuna:

Dhritirashtra. Ranged thus for battle on the sacred plain—
On Kurukshetra—say, Sanjaya! say
What wrought my people, and the Pandavas?
Sanjaya. When he beheld the host of Pandavas,

[...]

Then, at the signal of the aged king,
With blare to wake the blood, rolling around
Like to a lion's roar, the trumpeter
Blew the great Conch; and, at the noise of it,
Trumpets and drums, cymbals and gongs and horns
Burst into sudden clamour; as the blasts
Of loosened tempest, such the tumult seemed!
Then might be seen, upon their car of gold
Yoked with white steeds, blowing their battle-shells,
Krishna the God, Arjuna at his side:
Krishna, with knotted locks, blew his great conch
Carved of the "Giant's bone;" Arjuna blew
Indra's loud gift

[...]

Weapons unsheathing, bows drawn forth, the war
Instant to break—Arjun, whose ensign-badge
Was Hanuman the monkey, spake this thing
To Krishna the Divine, his charioteer:
"Drive, Dauntless One! to yonder open ground
Betwixt the armies; I would see more nigh
These who will fight with us, those we must slay
To-day, in war's arbitrament; for, sure,
On bloodshed all are bent who throng this plain,
Obeying Dhritirashtra's sinful son."
Thus, by Arjuna prayed, (O Bharata!)

Between the hosts that heavenly Charioteer
Drove the bright car, reining its milk-white steeds
Where Bhishma led, and Drona, and their Lords.
"See!" spake he to Arjuna, "where they stand,
Thy kindred of the Kurus:" and the Prince
Marked on each hand the kinsmen of his house,
Grandsires and sires, uncles and brothers and sons,
Cousins and sons-in-law and nephews, mixed
With friends and honoured elders; some this side,
Some that side ranged: and, seeing those opposed,
Such kith grown enemies—Arjuna's heart
Melted with pity, while he uttered this:
Arjuna. Krishna! as I behold, come here to shed
Their common blood, yon concourse of our kin,
My members fail, my tongue dries in my mouth,
A shudder thrills my body, and my hair
Bristles with horror; from my weak hand slips
Gandiv, the goodly bow; a fever burns
My skin to parching; hardly may I stand;
The life within me seems to swim and faint;

Nothing do I foresee save woe and wail!
It is not good, O Keshav! nought of good
Can spring from mutual slaughter! Lo, I hate
Triumph and domination, wealth and ease,
Thus sadly won! Aho! what victory
Can bring delight, Govinda! what rich spoils
Could profit; what rule recompense; what span
Of life itself seem sweet, bought with such blood?
Seeing that these stand here, ready to die,
For whose sake life was fair, and pleasure pleased,
And power grew precious: grandsires, sires, and sons,
Brothers, and fathers-in-law, and sons-in-law,
Elders and friends! Shall I deal death on these
Even though they seek to slay us? Not one blow,
O Madhusudan! will I strike to gain
The rule of all Three Worlds; then, how much less
To seize an earthly kingdom! Killing these
Must breed but anguish, Krishna! If they be
Guilty, we shall grow guilty by their deaths;
Their sins will light on us, if we shall slay
Those sons of Dhritirashtra, and our kin;

[...]

Better I deem it, if my kinsmen strike,
To face them weaponless, and bare my breast
To shaft and spear, than answer blow with blow.
So speaking, in the face of those two hosts,
Arjuna sank upon his chariot-seat,
And let fall bow and arrows, sick at heart.

From Chapter 2. On Sankhya Yoga or the Book of Doctrines:

Sanjaya. Him, filled with such compassion and such grief,
With eyes tear-dimmed, despondent, in stern words
The Driver, Madhusudan, thus addressed:
Krishna. How hath this weakness taken thee?
Whence springs
The inglorious trouble, shameful to the brave,
Barring the path of virtue? Nay, Arjun!
Forbid thyself to feebleness! it mars
Thy warrior-name! cast off the coward-fit!
Wake! Be thyself! Arise, Scourge of thy Foes!
Arjuna. How can I, in the battle, shoot with shafts
On Bhishma, or on Drona—O thou Chief!—
Both worshipful, both honourable men?
Better to live on beggar's bread
With those we love alive,
Than taste their blood in rich feasts spread,
And guiltily survive!
Ah! were it worse—who knows?—to be
Victor or vanquished here,
When those confront us angrily
Whose death leaves living drear?
In pity lost, by doubtings tossed,
My thoughts—distracted—turn
To Thee, the Guide I reverence most,
That I may counsel learn:
I know not what would heal the grief
Burned into soul and sense,
If I were earth's unchallenged chief—
A god—and these gone thence!
Sanjaya. So spake Arjuna to the Lord of Hearts,

And sighing, "I will not fight!" held silence then.
To whom, with tender smile, (O Bharata!)
While the Prince wept despairing 'twixt those hosts,
Krishna made answer in divinest verse:
Krishna. Thou grievest where no grief should be! thou speak'st
Words lacking wisdom! for the wise in heart
Mourn not for those that live, nor those that die.
Nor I, nor thou, nor any one of these,
Ever was not, nor ever will not be,
For ever and for ever afterwards.
All, that doth live, lives always! To man's frame
As there come infancy and youth and age,
So come there raisings-up and layings-down
Of other and of other life-abodes,
Which the wise know, and fear not. This that irks—
Thy sense-life, thrilling to the elements—
Bringing thee heat and cold, sorrows and joys,
'Tis brief and mutable! Bear with it, Prince!
As the wise bear. The soul which is not moved,
The soul that with a strong and constant calm
Takes sorrow and takes joy indifferently,
Lives in the life undying! That which is
Can never cease to be; that which is not
Will not exist. To see this truth of both
Is theirs who part essence from accident,
Substance from shadow. Indestructible,
Learn thou! the Life is, spreading life through all;
It cannot anywhere, by any means,
Be anywise diminished, stayed, or changed.
But for these fleeting frames which it informs
With spirit deathless, endless, infinite,
They perish. Let them perish, Prince! and fight!
He who shall say, "Lo! I have slain a man!"
He who shall think, "Lo! I am slain!" those both
Know naught! Life cannot slay. Life is not slain!
Never the spirit was born; the spirit shall cease to be never;
Never was time it was not; End and Beginning are dreams!
Birthless and deathless and changeless remaineth the spirit for ever;
Death hath not touched it at all, dead though the house of it seems!
Who knoweth it exhaustless, self-sustained,
Immortal, indestructible, shall such
Say, "I have killed a man, or caused to kill?"

Nay, but as when one layeth
His worn-out robes away,
And, taking new ones, sayeth,
"These will I wear to-day!"
So putteth by the spirit
Lightly its garb of flesh,
And passeth to inherit
A residence afresh.
I say to thee weapons reach not the Life;
Flame burns it not, waters cannot o'erwhelm,
Nor dry winds wither it. Impenetrable,
Unentered, unassailed, unharmed, untouched,
Immortal, all-arriving, stable, sure,
Invisible, ineffable, by word
And thought uncompassed, ever all itself,
Thus is the Soul declared! How wilt thou, then—
Knowing it so,—grieve when thou shouldst not grieve?
How, if thou hearest that the man new-dead
Is, like the man new-born, still living man—
One same, existent Spirit—wilt thou weep?
The end of birth is death; the end of death
Is birth: this is ordained! and mournest thou,
Chief of the stalwart arm! for what befalls
Which could not otherwise befall? The birth
Of living things comes unperceived; the death
Comes unperceived; between them, beings perceive:
What is there sorrowful herein, dear Prince?
Wonderful, wistful, to contemplate!
Difficult, doubtful, to speak upon!
Strange and great for tongue to relate,
Mystical hearing for every one!
Nor wotteth man this, what a marvel it is,
When seeing, and saying, and hearing are done!
This Life within all living things, my Prince!
Hides beyond harm; scorn thou to suffer, then,
For that which cannot suffer. Do thy part!
Be mindful of thy name, and tremble not!
Nought better can betide a martial soul
Than lawful war; happy the warrior
To whom comes joy of battle—comes, as now,
Glorious and fair, unsought; opening for him
A gateway unto Heav'n. But, if thou shunn'st

This honourable field—a Kshattriya—
If, knowing thy duty and thy task, thou bidd'st
Duty and task go by—that shall be sin!
And those to come shall speak thee infamy
From age to age; but infamy is worse
For men of noble blood to bear than death!
The chiefs upon their battle-chariots
Will deem 'twas fear that drove thee from the fray.
Of those who held thee mighty-souled the scorn
Thou must abide, while all thine enemies
Will scatter bitter speech of thee, to mock
The valour which thou hadst; what fate could fall
More grievously than this?

[…]

Therefore, arise, thou Son of Kunti! brace
Thine arm for conflict, nerve thy heart to meet—
As things alike to thee—pleasure or pain,
Profit or ruin, victory or defeat:
So minded, gird thee to the fight, for so
Thou shalt not sin!

From Chapter 3. On Karma Yoga, or the Virtue of Good Works:

Arjuna. Thou whom all mortals praise, Janardana!
If meditation be a nobler thing
Than action, wherefore, then, great Kesava!
Dost thou impel me to this dreadful fight?
Now am I by thy doubtful speech disturbed!
Tell me one thing, and tell me certainly;
By what road shall I find the better end?
Krishna. I told thee, blameless Lord! there be paths
Shown to this world; two schools of wisdom. First
The Sankhya's, which doth save in way of works
Prescribed by reason; next, the Yog, which bids
Attain by meditation, spiritually:
Yet these are one! No man shall 'scape from act
By shunning action; nay, and none shall come
By mere renouncements unto perfectness.
Nay, and no jot of time, at any time,

Rests any actionless; his nature's law
Compels him, even unwilling, into act;
[For thought is act in fancy]. He who sits
Suppressing all the instruments of flesh,
Yet in his idle heart thinking on them,
Plays the inept and guilty hypocrite:
But he who, with strong body serving mind,
Gives up his mortal powers to worthy work,
Not seeking gain, Arjuna! such an one
Is honourable. Do thine allotted task!
Work is more excellent than idleness;
The body's life proceeds not, lacking work.
There is a task of holiness to do,
Unlike world-binding toil, which bindeth not
The faithful soul; such earthly duty do
Free from desire, and thou shalt well perform
Thy heavenly purpose.

[…]

Your 'Cow of Plenty,' giving back her milk
Of all abundance. Worship the gods thereby;
The gods shall yield thee grace. Those meats ye
The gods will grant to Labour, when it pays
Tithes in the altar-flame. But if one eats
Fruits of the earth, rendering to kindly Heaven
No gift of toil, that thief steals from his world.
Who eat of food after their sacrifice
Are quit of fault, but they that spread a feast
All for themselves, eat sin and drink of sin.
By food the living live; food comes of rain,
And rain comes by the pious sacrifice,
And sacrifice is paid with tithes of toil;
Thus action is of Brahma, who is One,
The Only, All-pervading; at all times
Present in sacrifice. He that abstains
To help the rolling wheels of this great world,
Glutting his idle sense, lives a lost life,
Shameful and vain. Existing for himself,
Self-concentrated, serving self alone,
No part hath he in aught; nothing achieved,
Nought wrought or unwrought toucheth him; no hope

Of help for all the living things of earth
Depends from him. Therefore, thy task prescribed
With spirit unattached gladly perform,
Since in performance of plain duty man
Mounts to his highest bliss.

From Chapter 4. On Jnana Yoga, or the Book of Religion and Knowledge:

Krishna. Albeit I be
Unborn, undying, indestructible,
The Lord of all things living; not the less—
By Maya, by my magic which I stamp
On floating Nature-forms, the primal vast—
I come, and go, and come. When Righteousness
Declines, O Bharata! when Wickedness
Is strong, I rise, from age to age, and take
Visible shape, and move a man with men,
Succouring the good, thrusting the evil back,
And setting Virtue on her seat again.
Who knows the truth touching my births on earth
And my divine work, when he quits the flesh
Puts on its load no more, falls no more down
To earthly birth: to Me he comes, dear Prince!
Many there be who come! from fear set free,
From anger, from desire; keeping their hearts
Fixed upon me—my Faithful—purified
By sacred flame of Knowledge. Such as these
Mix with my being. Whoso worship me,
Them I exalt; but all men everywhere
Shall fall into my path; albeit, those souls
Which seek reward for works, make sacrifice
Now, to the lower gods. I say to thee
Here have they their reward. But I am He
Made the Four Castes, and portioned them a place
After their qualities and gifts. Yea, I
Created, the Reposeful; I that live
Immortally, made all those mortal births:
For works soil not my essence, being works
Wrought uninvolved. Who knows me acting thus
Unchained by action, action binds not him;
And, so perceiving, all those saints of old

Worked, seeking for deliverance. Work thou
As, in the days gone by, thy fathers did.
Thou sayst, perplexed, It hath been asked before
By singers and by sages, "What is act,
And what inaction?" I will teach thee this,
And, knowing, thou shalt learn which work doth save
Needs must one rightly meditate those three—
Doing, not doing, and undoing. Here
Thorny and dark the path is! He who sees
How action may be rest, rest action—he
Is wisest 'mid his kind; he hath the truth!
He doeth well, acting or resting. Freed
In all his works from prickings of desire,
Burned clean in act by the white fire of truth,
The wise call that man wise; and such an one,
Renouncing fruit of deeds, always content.
Always self-satisfying, if he works,
Doth nothing that shall stain his separate soul,
Which—quit of fear and hope—subduing self—
Rejecting outward impulse—yielding up
To body's need nothing save body, dwells
Sinless amid all sin, with equal calm
Taking what may befall, by grief unmoved,
Unmoved by joy, unenvyingly; the same
In good and evil fortunes; nowise bound
By bond of deeds. Nay, but of such an one,
Whose crave is gone, whose soul is liberate,
Whose heart is set on truth—of such an one
What work he does is work of sacrifice,
Which passeth purely into ash and smoke
Consumed upon the altar! All's then God!

[...]

Cut then atwain
With sword of wisdom, Son of Bharata!
This doubt that binds thy heart-beats! cleave the bond
Born of thy ignorance! Be bold and wise!
Give thyself to the field with me! Arise!

From Chapter 5. On Karmasanyasa Yoga, or Renouncing the Fruits of Works:

Arjuna. Yet, Krishna at the one time thou dost laud
Surcease of works, and, at another time,
Service through work. Of these twain plainly tell
Which is the better way?
Krishna. To cease from works
Is well, and to do works in holiness
Is well; and both conduct to bliss supreme;
But of these twain the better way is his
Who working piously refraineth not.

[...]

Krishna. The Saint who shuts outside his placid soul
All touch of sense, letting no contact through;
Whose quiet eyes gaze straight from fixed brows,
Whose outward breath and inward breath are drawn
Equal and slow through nostrils still and close;
That one—with organs, heart, and mind constrained,
Bent on deliverance, having put away
Passion, and fear, and rage; hath even now,
Obtained deliverance, ever and ever freed.
Yea! for he knows Me Who am He that heeds
The sacrifice and worship, God revealed;
And He who heeds not, being Lord of Worlds,
Lover of all that lives, God unrevealed,
Wherein who will shall find surety and shield!

From Chapter 11. Viswarupadarsanam, or the Book of Manifesting the One and Manifold:

But, sore amazed,
Thrilled, o'erfilled, dazzled, and dazed,
Arjuna knelt; and bowed his head,
And clasped his palms; and cried, and said:
Arjuna. Yea! I have seen! I see!
Lord! all is wrapped in Thee!
The gods are in Thy glorious frame! the creatures
Of earth, and heaven, and hell
In Thy Divine form dwell,

And in Thy countenance shine all the features
Of Brahma, sitting lone
Upon His lotus-throne;
Of saints and sages, and the serpent races
Ananta, Vasuki;
Yea! mightiest Lord! I see
Thy thousand thousand arms and breasts, and faces,
And eyes, on every side
Perfect, diversified;
And nowhere end of Thee, nowhere beginning,
Nowhere a centre! Shifts—
Wherever soul's gaze lifts—
Thy central Self, all-wielding, and all-winning!
Infinite King! I see
The anadem on Thee,
The club, the shell, the discus; see Thee burning
In beams insufferable,
Lighting earth, heaven, and hell
With brilliance blazing, glowing, flashing; turning
Darkness to dazzling day,
Look I whichever way;
Ah, Lord! I worship Thee, the Undivided,
The Uttermost of thought,
The Treasure-Palace wrought
To hold the wealth of the worlds; the Shield provided
To shelter Virtue's laws;
The Fount whence Life's stream draws
All waters of all rivers of all being:
The One Unborn, Unending:
Unchanging and Unblending!
With might and majesty, past thought, past seeing!
Silver of moon and gold
Of sun are glories rolled
From Thy great eyes; Thy visage, beaming tender
Throughout the stars and skies,
Doth to warm life surprise
Thy Universe. The worlds are filled with wonder
Of Thy perfections! Space
Star-sprinkled, and void place
From pole to pole of the Blue, from bound to bound,
Hath Thee in every spot,
Thee, Thee! Where Thou art not,

O Holy, Marvellous Form! is nowhere found!
O Mystic, Awful One!
At sight of Thee, made known,
The Three Worlds quake; the lower gods draw nigh Thee;
They fold their palms, and bow
Body, and breast, and brow,
And, whispering worship, laud and magnify Thee!
Rishis and Siddhas cry
"Hail! Highest Majesty!
From sage and singer breaks the hymn of glory
In dulcet harmony,
Sounding the praise of Thee;
While countless companies take up the story,
Rudras, who ride the storms,
Th' Adityas' shining forms,
Vasus and Sadhyas, Viswas, Ushmapas;
Maruts, and those great Twins
The heavenly, fair, Aswins,
Gandharvas, Rakshasas, Siddhas, and Asuras,—
These see Thee, and revere
In sudden-stricken fear;
Yea! the Worlds—seeing Thee with form stupendous,
With faces manifold,
With eyes which all behold,
Unnumbered eyes, vast arms, members tremendous,
Flanks, lit with sun and star,
Feet planted near and far,
Tushes of terror, mouths wrathful and tender;—
The Three wide Worlds before Thee
Adore, as I adore Thee,
Quake, as I quake, to witness so much splendour!
I mark Thee strike the skies
With front, in wondrous wise
Huge, rainbow-painted, glittering; and thy mouth
Opened, and orbs which see
All things, whatever be
In all Thy worlds, east, west, and north and south.
O Eyes of God! O Head!
My strength of soul is fled,
Gone is heart's force, rebuked is mind's desire!
When I behold Thee so,
With awful brows a-glow,

With burning glance, and lips lighted by fire
Fierce as those flames which shall
Consume, at close of all,
Earth, Heaven! Ah me! I see no Earth and Heaven!
Thee, Lord of Lords! I see,
Thee only—only Thee!
Now let Thy mercy unto me be given,
Thou Refuge of the World!
Lo! to the cavern hurled
Of Thy wide-opened throat, and lips white-tushed,
I see our noblest ones,
Great Dhritarashtra's sons,
Bhishma, Drona, and Karna, caught and crushed!
The Kings and Chiefs drawn in,
That gaping gorge within;
The best of both these armies torn and riven!
Between Thy jaws they lie
Mangled full bloodily,
Ground into dust and death! Like streams down-driven
With helpless haste, which go
In headlong furious flow
Straight to the gulfing deeps of th' unfilled ocean,
So to that flaming cave
Those heroes great and brave
Pour, in unending streams, with helpless motion!
Like moths which in the night
Flutter towards a light,
Drawn to their fiery doom, flying and dying,
So to their death still throng,
Blind, dazzled, borne along
Ceaselessly, all those multitudes, wild flying!
Thou, that hast fashioned men,
Devourest them again,
One with another, great and small, alike!
The creatures whom Thou mak'st,
With flaming jaws Thou tak'st,
Lapping them up! Lord God! Thy terrors strike
From end to end of earth,
Filling life full, from birth
To death, with deadly, burning, lurid dread!
Ah, Vishnu! make me know
Why is Thy visage so?

[…]

Guru of Gurus; more
To reverence and adore
Than all which is adorable and high!
How, in the wide worlds three
Should any equal be?
Should any other share Thy Majesty?
Therefore, with body bent
And reverent intent,
I praise, and serve, and seek Thee, asking grace.
As father to a son,
As friend to friend, as one
Who loveth to his lover, turn Thy face
In gentleness on me!
Good is it I did see
This unknown marvel of Thy Form! But fear
Mingles with joy! Retake,
Dear Lord! for pity's sake
Thine earthly shape, which earthly eyes may bear!
Be merciful, and show
The visage that I know;
Let me regard Thee, as of yore, arrayed
With disc and forehead-gem,
With mace and anadem,
Thou that sustainest all things! Undismayed
Let me once more behold
The form I loved of old,
Thou of the thousand arms and countless eyes!
This frightened heart is fain
To see restored again
My Charioteer, in Krishna's kind disguise.
Krishna. Yea! thou hast seen, Arjuna! because I loved thee well,
The secret countenance of Me, revealed by mystic spell,
Shining, and wonderful, and majestic, manifold,
Which none save thou in all the years had favour to behold;
For not by Vedas cometh this, nor sacrifice, nor alms,
Nor works well-done, nor penance long, nor prayers, nor chanted psalms,
That mortal eyes should bear to view the Immortal Soul unclad,
Prince of the Kurus! This was kept for thee alone! Be glad!
Let no more trouble shake thy heart, because thine eyes have seen
My terror with My glory. As I before have been

So will I be again for thee; with lightened heart behold!
Once more I am thy Krishna, the form thou knew'st of old!

Sanjaya. These words to Arjuna spake
Vasudev, and straight did take
Back again the semblance dear
Of the well-loved charioteer;
Peace and joy it did restore
When the Prince beheld once more
Mighty BRAHMA'S form and face
Clothed in Krishna's gentle grace.

From Chapter 12. On Bhakti Yoga, or the Book of the Religion of Faith and Devotion:
Arjuna. Lord! of the men who serve Thee—true in heart—
As God revealed; and of the men who serve,
Worshipping Thee Unrevealed, Unbodied, Far,
Which take the better way of faith and life?

Krishna. Whoever serve Me—as I show Myself—
Constantly true, in full devotion fixed,
Those hold I very holy. But who serve—
Worshipping Me The One, The Invisible,
The Unrevealed, Unnamed, Unthinkable,
Uttermost, All-pervading, Highest, Sure—
Who thus adore Me, mastering their sense,
Of one set mind to all, glad in all good,
These blessed souls come unto Me.
Yet, hard
The travail is for such as bend their minds
To reach th' Unmanifest. That viewless path
Shall scarce be trod by man bearing the flesh!
But whereso any doeth all his deeds
Renouncing self for Me, full of Me, fixed
To serve only the Highest, night and day
Musing on Me—him will I swiftly lift
Forth from life's ocean of distress and death,
Whose soul clings fast to Me. Cling thou to Me!
Clasp Me with heart and mind! so shalt thou dwell
Surely with Me on high. But if thy thought
Droops from such height; if thou be'st weak to set
Body and soul upon Me constantly,
Despair not! give Me lower service! I seek

To reach Me, worshipping with steadfast will;
And, if thou canst not worship steadfastly,
Work for Me, toil in works pleasing to Me!
For he that laboureth right for love of Me
Shall finally attain! But, if in this
Thy faint heart fails, bring Me thy failure! find
Refuge in Me! let fruits of labour go,
Renouncing hope for Me, with lowliest heart,
So shalt thou come; for, though to know is more
Than diligence, yet worship better is
Than knowing, and renouncing better still.
Near to renunciation—very near—
Dwelleth Eternal Peace!
Who hateth nought
Of all which lives, living himself benign,
Compassionate, from arrogance exempt,
Exempt from love of self, unchangeable
By good or ill; patient, contented, firm
In faith, mastering himself, true to his word,
Seeking Me, heart and soul; vowed unto Me,—
That man I love! Who troubleth not his kind,
And is not troubled by them; clear of wrath,
Living too high for gladness, grief, or fear,
That man I love! Who, dwelling quiet-eyed,
Stainless, serene, well-balanced, unperplexed,
Working with Me, yet from all works detached,
That man I love! Who, fixed in faith on Me,
Dotes upon none, scorns none; rejoices not,
And grieves not, letting good or evil hap
Light when it will, and when it will depart,
That man I love! Who, unto friend and foe
Keeping an equal heart, with equal mind
Bears shame and glory; with an equal peace
Takes heat and cold, pleasure and pain; abides
Quit of desires, hears praise or calumny
In passionless restraint, unmoved by each;
Linked by no ties to earth, steadfast in Me,
That man I love! But most of all I love
Those happy ones to whom 'tis life to live
In single fervid faith and love unseeing,
Drinking the blessed Amrit of my Being!

From Chapter 14. Gunatrayavibhaga Yoga, or the Book of Religion by Separation from the Qualities :

Krishna. Yet farther will I open unto thee
This wisdom of all wisdoms, uttermost,
The which possessing, all My saints have passed
To perfectness. On such high verities
Reliant, rising into fellowship
With Me, they are not born again at birth
Of Kalpas, nor at Pralyas suffer change!
This Universe the womb is where I plant
Seed of all lives! Thence, Prince of India, comes
Birth to all beings! Whoso, Kunti's Son!
Mothers each mortal form, Brahma conceives,
And I am He that fathers, sending seed!
Sattwan, Raias, and Tamas, so are named
The qualities of Nature, "Soothfastness,"
"Passion," and "Ignorance." These three bind down
The changeless Spirit in the changeful flesh.
Whereof sweet "Soothfastness," by purity
Living unsullied and enlightened, binds
The sinless Soul to happiness and truth;
And Passion, being kin to appetite,
And breeding impulse and propensity,
Binds the embodied Soul, O Kunti's Son!
By tie of works. But Ignorance, begot
Of Darkness, blinding mortal men, binds down
Their souls to stupor, sloth, and drowsiness.
Yea, Prince of India! Soothfastness binds souls
In pleasant wise to flesh; and Passion binds
By toilsome strain; but Ignorance, which blots
The beams of wisdom, binds the soul to sloth.
Passion and Ignorance, once overcome,
Leave Soothfastness, O Bharata! Where this
With Ignorance are absent, Passion rules;
And Ignorance in hearts not good nor quick.
When at all gateways of the Body shines
The Lamp of Knowledge, then may one see well
Soothfastness settled in that city reigns;
Where longing is, and ardour, and unrest,
Impulse to strive and gain, and avarice,
Those spring from Passion—Prince!—engrained; and where

Darkness and dulness, sloth and stupor are,
'Tis Ignorance hath caused them, Kuru Chief!
Moreover, when a soul departeth, fixed
In Soothfastness, it goeth to the place—
Perfect and pure—of those that know all Truth.
If it departeth in set habitude
Of Impulse, it shall pass into the world
Of spirits tied to works; and, if it dies
In hardened Ignorance, that blinded soul
Is born anew in some unlighted womb.
The fruit of Soothfastness is true and sweet;
The fruit of lusts is pain and toil; the fruit
Of Ignorance is deeper darkness. Yea!
For Light brings light, and Passion ache to have;
And gloom, bewilderments, and ignorance
Grow forth from Ignorance. Those of the first
Rise ever higher; those of the second mode
Take a mid place; the darkened souls sink back
To lower deeps, loaded with witlessness!
When, watching life, the living man perceives
The only actors are the Qualities,
And knows what rules beyond the Qualities,
Then is he come nigh unto Me!
The Soul,
Thus passing forth from the Three Qualities—
Whereby arise all bodies—overcomes
Birth, Death, Sorrow, and Age; and drinketh deep
The undying wine of Amrit.
Arjuna. Oh, my Lord!
Which be the signs to know him that hath gone
Past the Three Modes? How liveth he? What way
Leadeth him safe beyond the threefold Modes?
Krishna. He who with equanimity surveys
Lustre of goodness, strife of passion, sloth
Of ignorance, not angry if they are,
Not wishful when they are not: he who sits
A sojourner and stranger in their midst
Unruffled, standing off, saying—serene—
When troubles break, "These be the Qualities!
He unto whom—self-centred—grief and joy
Sound as one word; to whose deep-seeing eyes
The clod, the marble, and the gold are one;

Whose equal heart holds the same gentleness
For lovely and unlovely things, firm-set,
Well-pleased in praise and dispraise; satisfied
With honour or dishonour; unto friends
And unto foes alike in tolerance;
Detached from undertakings, he is named
Surmounter of the Qualities!

And such—
With single, fervent faith adoring Me,
Passing beyond the Qualities, conforms
To Brahma, and attains Me!

For I am
That whereof Brahma is the likeness! Mine
The Amrit is; and Immortality
Is mine; and mine perfect Felicity!

Chapter 16. Daivasarasaupadwibhaga Yoga, or the Book of the Separateness of the Divine and Undivine:

Krishna. Fearlessness, singleness of soul, the will
Always to strive for wisdom; opened hand
And governed appetites; and piety,
And love of lonely study; humbleness,
Uprightness, heed to injure nought which lives,
Truthfulness, slowness unto wrath, a mind
That lightly letteth go what others prize;
And equanimity, and charity
Which spieth no man's faults; and tenderness
Towards all that suffer; a contented heart,
Fluttered by no desires; a bearing mild,
Modest, and grave, with manhood nobly mixed,
With patience, fortitude, and purity;
An unrevengeful spirit, never given
To rate itself too high; such be the signs,
O Indian Prince! of him whose feet are set
On that fair path which leads to heavenly birth!

Deceitfulness, and arrogance, and pride,
Quickness to anger, harsh and evil speech,

And ignorance, to its own darkness blind,—
These be the signs, My Prince! of him whose birth
Is fated for the regions of the vile.

The Heavenly Birth brings to deliverance,
So should'st thou know! The birth with Asuras
Brings into bondage. Be thou joyous, Prince!
Whose lot is set apart for heavenly Birth.

Two stamps there are marked on all living men,
Divine and Undivine; I spake to thee
By what marks thou shouldst know the Heavenly Man,
Hear from me now of the Unheavenly!

They comprehend not, the Unheavenly,
How Souls go forth from Me; nor how they come
Back unto Me: nor is there Truth in these,
Nor purity, nor rule of Life. "This world
Hath not a Law, nor Order, nor a Lord,"
So say they: "nor hath risen up by Cause
Following on Cause, in perfect purposing,
But is none other than a House of Lust."
And, this thing thinking, all those ruined ones—
Of little wit, dark-minded—give themselves
To evil deeds, the curses of their kind.
Surrendered to desires insatiable,
Full of deceitfulness, folly, and pride,
In blindness cleaving to their errors, caught
Into the sinful course, they trust this lie
As it were true—this lie which leads to death—
Finding in Pleasure all the good which is,
And crying "Here it finisheth!"

[…]

The Doors of Hell
Are threefold, whereby men to ruin pass,—
The door of Lust, the door of Wrath, the door
Of Avarice. Let a man shun those three!
He who shall turn aside from entering
All those three gates of Narak, wendeth straight
To find his peace, and comes to Swarga's gate.

From Chapter 18. Mokshasanyasa Yoga, or the Book of Religion by Deliverance and Renunciation:

Arjuna. Fain would I better know, Thou Glorious One!
The very truth—Heart's Lord!—of Sannyas,
Abstention; and Renunciation, Lord!
Tyaga; and what separates these twain!
Krishna. The poets rightly teach that Sannyas
Is the foregoing of all acts which spring
Out of desire; and their wisest say
Tyaga is renouncing fruit of acts.

[…]

He who acts
Free from self-seeking, humble, resolute,
Steadfast, in good or evil hap the same,
Content to do aright—he "truly" acts.
There is th' "impassioned" doer. He that works
From impulse, seeking profit, rude and bold
To overcome, unchastened; slave by turns
Of sorrow and of joy: of Rajas he!
And there be evil doers; loose of heart,
Low-minded, stubborn, fraudulent, remiss,
Dull, slow, despondent—children of the "dark."

[…]

For nothing lives on earth, nor 'midst the gods
In utmost heaven, but hath its being bound
With these three Qualities, by Nature framed.
The work of Brahmans, Kshattriyas, Vaisyas,
And Sudras, O thou Slayer of thy Foes!
Is fixed by reason of the Qualities
Planted in each:
A Brahman's virtues, Prince
Born of his nature, are serenity,
Self-mastery, religion, purity,
Patience, uprightness, learning, and to know
The truth of things which be. A Kshattriya's pride,
Born of his nature, lives in valour, fire,
Constancy, skilfulness, spirit in fight,

And open-handedness and noble mien,
As of a lord of men. A Vaisya's task,
Born with his nature, is to till the ground,
Tend cattle, venture trade. A Sudra's state,
Suiting his nature, is to minister.
Whoso performeth—diligent, content—
The work allotted him, whate'er it be,
Lays hold of perfectness! Hear how a man
Findeth perfection, being so content:
He findeth it through worship—wrought by work—
Of HIM that is the Source of all which lives,
Of HIM by Whom the universe was stretched.
Better thine own work is, though done with fault,
Than doing others' work, ev'n excellently.

[...]

Sanjaya. Thus gathered I the gracious speech of Krishna, O my King!
Thus have I told, with heart a-thrill, this wise and wondrous thing
By great Vyasa's learning writ, how Krishna's self made known
The Yoga, being Yoga's Lord. So is the high truth shown!
And aye, when I remember, O Lord my King, again
Arjuna and the God in talk, and all this holy strain,
Great is my gladness: when I muse that splendour, passing speech,
Of Hari, visible and plain, there is no tongue to reach
My marvel and my love and bliss. O Archer-Prince! all hail!
O Krishna, Lord of Yoga! surely there shall not fail
Blessing, and victory, and power, for Thy most mighty sake,
Where this song comes of Arjun, and how with God he spake.

HERE ENDS, WITH CHAPTER XVIII,
Entitled "Mokshasanyasayog,"
Or "The Book of Religion by Deliverance and Renunciation,"
THE BHAGAVAD-GITA.
THE END

Chapter 2
Buddhism

The Four Noble Truths and the Eightfold Path

In this passage, we encounter the words of the Buddha himself, talking about the central ideas of Buddhism. Herein, he reveals the Four Noble Truths, and the Eightfold Path to Enlightenment.

The Four Noble Truths hold that: 1) life involves suffering; 2) suffering arises from attachments; 3) suffering can be eliminated; and 4) there is a path that can be followed to reach an end of suffering and to obtain enlightenment. A first blush, these are deceptively simple, yet each comes with its own complexities. This reading delves into many of these.

Contained in the fourth noble truth are specifics about what to do, focusing around bolstering wisdom, morality and concentration. This brings the seeker to the Eightfold Path: 1) Right Understanding (sometimes referred to as Right Knowledge); 2) Right Mindfulness (or Right Aspiration); 3) Right Speech; 4) Right Action (or Right Behavior); 5) Right Living (or Right Livelihood); 6) Right Effort; 7) Right Attentiveness (or Right Mindfulness); and 8) Right Concentration (Right Absorption).

The first two of the Eightfold Path orient the seeker toward Wisdom. Right Understanding involves first and foremost understanding the Four Noble Truths. It also involves avoiding the "3 poisons" of anger, greed and delusion. In a related vein, Right Mindfulness helps keep a person free from lust, cruelty and ill-will toward others. In a word, it keeps us focused on compassion.

The next three of the Eightfold Path orient the seeker toward Morality. Right Speech counsels against lying, but also against idle chatter and gossip. Right Action (or Right Behavior) involves following ethical precepts, such as those contained in the ethical part of the Ten Commandments, and means avoiding killing, illicit sex and stealing. Right Living (or Right Livelihood) directs followers to make a living in something that allows for compassion and does not interfere with another's ability to follow the Dharmic path themselves; slave trading and selling liquor or illicit drugs, for example, would violate the precepts of Right Living.

The final three of the eightfold path orient the seeker toward Concentration. Right Effort means to turn one's efforts in the direction of enlightenment and away from delusion. There is counsel to avoid that which is base, overcome one's desires for attachments, develop righteous patterns of living, and maintain them once established. Right Attentiveness (or Right Mindfulness) involves managing one's attention properly. By tuning into the body, feelings, the mind and the objects in the mind, a person may gradually develop the ability to manage the attention. Finally, Right Concentration (or Right Absorption) comes as one develops a "one-pointedness" of attention to things such as the breath and the fruits of Right Attentiveness.

The aspects of the Eightfold Path are not mutually exclusive. Rather, they reinforce each other. It is said that each of the eight contain all of the eight. Another useful metaphor is that of a wheel. Rather than a path, which is linear, it is sometimes useful to think of these as spokes on a wheel. In fact, a common symbol for Buddhism is an eight-spoked wheel, with each of the spokes corresponding to one leg of the eightfold path.

Buddhism has two major areas of focus that ultimately become one: achieving enlightenment and being compassionate. Working toward one necessarily involves the other. Following the path may lead the seeker to the true goal of "unshakeable deliverance of the heart," or becoming one with Nirvana.

Let us now consider the wisdom of the Buddha...

Buddha, in His Own Words

(The Four Noble Truths and the Eightfold Path)

The Four Noble Truths

Thus has it been said by the Buddha, the Enlightened One: It is through not understanding, not realizing four things, that I, Disciples, as well as you, had to wander so long through this round of rebirths. And what are these four things? They are the Noble Truth of Suffering, the Noble Truth of the Origin of Suffering, the Noble Truth of the Extinction of Suffering, the Noble Truth of the Path that leads to the Extinction of Suffering.

As long as the absolutely true knowledge and insight as regards these Four Noble Truths was not quite clear in me, so long was I not sure, whether I had won that supreme Enlightenment which is unsurpassed in all the world with its heavenly beings, evil spirits and gods, amongst all the hosts of ascetics and priests, heavenly beings and men. But as soon as the absolutely true knowledge and insight as regards these Four

Noble Truths had become perfectly clear in me, there arose in me the assurance that I had won that supreme Enlightenment unsurpassed.

And I discovered that profound truth, so difficult to perceive, difficult to understand, tranquilizing and sublime, which is not to be gained by mere reasoning, and is visible only to the wise. The world, however, is given to pleasure, delighted with pleasure, enchanted with pleasure. Verily, such beings will hardly understand the law of conditionality, the Dependent Origination of every thing; incomprehensible to them will also be the end of all formations, the forsaking of every substratum of rebirth, the fading away of craving; detachment, extinction, Nirvana.

Yet there are beings whose eyes are only a little covered with dust: they will understand the truth.

First Truth

The Noble Truth of Suffering

What, now, is the Noble Truth of Suffering?

Birth is suffering; Decay is suffering; Death is suffering; Sorrow, Lamentation, Pain, Grief, and Despair, are suffering; not to get what one desires, is suffering; in short: the Five Groups of Existence are suffering.

What, now, is Birth? The birth of beings belonging to this or that order of beings, their being born, their conception and springing into existence, the manifestation of the groups of existence, the arising of sense activity—this is called Birth.

And what is Decay? The decay of beings belonging to this or that order of beings; their getting aged, frail, grey, and wrinkled; the failing of their vital force, the wearing out of the senses—this is called Decay.

And what is Death? The parting and vanishing of beings out of this or that order of beings, their destruction, disappearance, death, the completion of their life-period, dissolution of the groups of existence, the discarding of the body—this is called Death.

And what is Sorrow? The sorrow arising through this or that loss or misfortune which one encounters, the worrying oneself, the state of being alarmed, inward sorrow, inward woe—this is called Sorrow.

And what is Lamentation? Whatsoever, through this or that loss or misfortune which befalls one, is wail and lament, wailing and lamenting, the state of woe and lamentation this is called Lamentation.

And what is Pain? The bodily pain and unpleasantness, the painful and unpleasant feeling produced by bodily contact—this is called Pain.

And what is Grief? The mental pain and unpleasantness, the painful and unpleasant feeling produced by mental contact—this is called Grief.

And what is Despair? Distress and despair arising through this or that loss or misfortune which one encounters, distressfulness, and desperation—this is called Despair.

And what is the "suffering of not getting what one desires?" To beings subject to birth there comes the desire: "O that we were not subject to birth! O that no new birth was before us!" Subject to decay, disease, death, sorrow, lamentation, pain, grief, and despair, the desire comes to them: "O that we were not subject to these things! O that these things were not before us!" But this cannot be got by mere desiring; and not to get what one desires, is suffering.

[...]

Dependent Origination of Consciousness

Now, though one's eye be intact, yet if the external forms do not fall within the field of vision, and no corresponding conjunction takes place, in that case there occurs no formation of the corresponding aspect of consciousness. Or, though one eye be intact, and the external forms fall within the field of vision, yet if no corresponding conjunction takes place, in that case also there occurs no formation of the corresponding aspect of consciousness.

If, however, one's eye is intact, and the external forms fall within the field of vision, and the corresponding conjunction takes place, in that case there arises the corresponding aspect of consciousness.

Hence, I say: the arising of consciousness is dependent upon conditions; and without these conditions, no consciousness arises. And upon whatsoever conditions the arising of consciousness is dependent, after these it is called.

Consciousness whose arising depends on the eye and forms, is called "eye-consciousness."

Consciousness whose arising depends on the ear and sound, is called "ear-consciousness."

Consciousness whose arising depends on the olfactory organ and odors, is called "nose-consciousness."

Consciousness whose arising depends on the tongue and taste, is called "tongue-consciousness."

Consciousness whose arising depends on the body and bodily contacts, is called "body-consciousness."

Consciousness whose arising depends on the mind and ideas, is called "mind-consciousness."

Whatsoever there is of "corporeality" in the consciousness thus arisen, that belongs to the Group of Corporeality. There is of "feeling"—bodily ease, pain, joy, sadness, or indifferent feeling—belongs to the Group of Feeling. Whatsoever there is of "perception"—visual objects, sounds, odors, tastes, bodily impressions, or mind objects—belongs to the Group of Perception.

Whatsoever there are of mental "formations"—impression, volition, etc.—belong to the Group of mental Formations. Whatsoever there is of "consciousness" therein, belongs to the Group of Consciousness.

And it is impossible that any one can explain the passing out of one existence, and the entering into a new existence, or the growth, increase, and development of consciousness, independent of corporeality, feeling, perception, and mental formations.

[...]

Samsara, the Wheel of Existence

Inconceivable is the beginning of this Samsara; not to be discovered is any first beginning of beings, who, obstructed by ignorance, and ensnared by craving, are hurrying and hastening through this round of rebirths.

[Samsara—the Wheel of Existence, lit., the "Perpetual Wandering"—is the name by which is designated the sea of life ever restlessly heaving up and down, the symbol of this continuous process of ever again and again being born, growing old, suffering, and dying. More precisely put: Samsara is the unbroken chain of the fivefold Khandha-combinations, which, constantly changing from moment to moment, follow continuously one upon the other through inconceivable periods of time. Of this Samsara, a single lifetime constitutes only a vanishingly tiny fraction; hence, to be able to comprehend the first noble truth, one must let one's gaze rest upon the Samsara, upon this frightful chain of rebirths, and not merely upon one single lifetime, which, of course, may be sometimes not very painful.]

Which do you think is the more: the flood of tears, which weeping and wailing you have shed upon this long way—hurrying and hastening through this round of rebirths, united with the undesired, separated from the desired this, or the waters of the four oceans?

Long time have you suffered the death of father and mother, of sons, daughters, brothers, and sisters. And whilst you were thus suffering, you have, verily, shed more tears upon this long way than there is water in the four oceans.

Which do you think is the more: the streams of blood that, through your being beheaded, have flowed upon this long way, or the waters in the four oceans?

Long time have you been caught as dacoits, or highwaymen, or adulterers; and, through your being beheaded, verily, more blood has flowed upon this long way than there is water in the four oceans.

But how is this possible?

Inconceivable is the beginning of this Samsara; not to be discovered is any first beginning of beings, who, obstructed by ignorance, and ensnared by craving, are hurrying and hastening through this round of rebirths.

And thus have you long time undergone suffering, undergone torment, undergone misfortune, and filled the graveyards full; verily, long enough to be dissatisfied with all the forms of existence, long enough to turn away, and free yourselves from them all.

The Noble Truth of the Origin of Suffering

What, now, is the Noble Truth of the Origin of Suffering? It is that craving which gives rise to fresh rebirth, and, bound up with pleasure and lust, now here, now there, finds ever fresh delight.

[In the absolute sense, it is no real being, no self-determined, unchangeable, Ego-entity that is reborn. Moreover, there is nothing that remains the same even for two consecutive moments; for the Five Khandhas, or Groups of Existence, are in a state of perpetual change, of continual dissolution and renewal. They die every moment, and every moment new ones are born. Hence it follows that there is no such thing as a real existence, or "being" (Latin esse), but only as it were an endless process, a continuous change, a "becoming," consisting in a "producing," and in a "being produced"; in a "process of action," and in a "process of reaction," or "rebirth."

This process of perpetual "producing" and "being produced" may best be compared with an ocean wave. In the case of a wave, there is not the slightest quantity of water traveling over the surface of the sea. But the wave structure, that hastens over the surface of the water, creating the appearance of one and the same mass of water, is, in reality, nothing but the continuous rising and falling of continuous, but quite different, masses of water, produced by the transmission of force generated by the wind. Even so, the Buddha did not teach that Ego-entities hasten through the ocean of rebirth, but merely life-waves, which, according to their nature and activities (good, or evil), manifest themselves here as men, there as animals, and elsewhere as invisible beings.]

The Threefold Craving

There is the "Sensual Craving," the "Craving for Eternal-Annihilation." "Existence," the "Craving for Self-Annihilation."

[The "Craving for Eternal Existence," according to the Visuddhi-Magga, is intimately connected with the so-called Eternity-Belief, i.e., the belief in an absolute, eternal, Ego-entity persisting independently of our body.

The Craving for Self-Annihilation is the outcome of the so-called Annihilation-Belief, the delusive materialistic notion of an Ego which is annihilated at death, and which does not stand in any causal relation with the time before birth or after death.]

But, where does this craving arise and take root? Wherever in the world there are delightful and pleasurable things, there this craving arises and takes root. Eye, ear, nose, tongue, body, and mind, are delightful and pleasurable: there this craving arises and takes root.

Visual objects, sounds, smells, tastes, bodily impressions, and mind-objects, are delightful and pleasurable: there this craving arises and takes root.

Consciousness, sense impression, feeling born of sense impression, perception, will, craving, thinking, and reflecting, are delightful and pleasurable: there this craving arises and takes root.

If, namely, when perceiving a visual object, a sound, odor, taste, bodily impression, or a mind object, the object is pleasant, one is attracted; and if unpleasant, one is repelled.

Thus, whatever kind of "Feeling" one experiences—pleasant, unpleasant, or indifferent—one approves of, and cherishes the feeling, and clings to it; and while doing so, lust springs up; but lust for feelings, means Clinging; and on Clinging, depends the "Process of Becoming"; on the Process of Becoming (Karma-process), depends (future) "Birth"; and dependent on Birth, are Decay and Death, Sorrow, Lamentation, Pain, Grief, and Despair. Thus arises this whole mass of suffering.

This is called the Noble Truth of the Origin of Suffering.

Heaping Up of Present Suffering

Verily, due to sensuous craving, conditioned through sensuous craving, impelled by sensuous craving, entirely moved by sensuous craving, kings fight with kings, princes with princes, priests with priests, citizens with citizens; the mother quarrels with the son, the son with the mother, the father with the son, the son with the father; brother quarrels with brother, brother with sister, sister with brother, friend with friend. Thus, given to dissension, quarreling and fighting, they fall upon one another with fists, sticks, or weapons.

And thereby they suffer death or deadly pain.

And further, due to sensuous craving, conditioned through sensuous craving, impelled by sensuous craving, entirely moved by sensuous craving, people break into houses, rob, plunder, pillage whole houses, commit highway robbery, seduce the wives of others. Then, the rulers have such people caught, and inflict on them various forms of punishment. And thereby they incur death or deadly pain. Now, this is the misery of sensuous craving, the heaping up of suffering in this present life, due to sensuous craving, conditioned through sensuous craving, caused by sensuous craving, entirely dependent on sensuous craving.

Heaping Up of Future Suffering

And further, people take the evil way in deeds, the evil way in words, the evil way in thoughts; and by taking the evil way in deeds, words, and thoughts, at the dissolution of the body, after death, they fall into a downward state of existence, a state of suffering, into perdition, and the abyss of hell. But, this is the misery of sensuous craving, the heaping up of suffering in the future life, due to sensuous craving, conditioned through sensuous craving, caused by sensuous craving, entirely dependent on sensuous craving.

Not in the air, nor ocean-midst,

Nor hidden in the mountain clefts,
Nowhere is found a place on earth,
Where man is freed from evil deeds.

Inheritance of Deeds (KARMA)

For, owners of their deeds (karma) are the beings, heirs of their deeds; their deeds are the womb from which they sprang; with their deeds they are bound up; their deeds are their refuge.

Whatever deeds they do—good or evil—of such they will be the heirs.

And wherever the beings spring into existence, there their deeds will ripen; and wherever their deeds ripen, there they will earn the fruits of those deeds, be it in this life, or be it in the next life, or be it in any other future life.

There will come a time, when the mighty ocean will dry up, vanish, and be no more. There will come a time, when the mighty earth will be devoured by fire, perish, and be no more. But, yet there will be no end to the suffering of beings, who, obstructed by ignorance, and ensnared by craving, are hurrying and hastening through this round of rebirths.

Third Truth

The Noble Truth of the Extinction of Suffering

What, now, is the Noble Truth of the Extinction of Suffering? It is the complete fading away and extinction of this craving, its forsaking and giving up, the liberation and detachment from it.

But where may this craving vanish, where may it be extinguished?

Wherever in the world there are delightful and pleasurable things, there this craving may vanish, there it may be extinguished.

Be it in the past, present, or future, whosoever of the monks or priests regards the delightful and pleasurable things in the world as "impermanent," "miserable," and "without an Ego," as a disease and cancer; it is he who overcomes the craving.

And released from Sensual Craving, released from the Craving for Existence, he does not return, does not enter again into existence.

Dependent Extinction of All Phenomena

For, through the total fading away and extinction of Craving, Clinging is extinguished; through the extinction of clinging, the Process of Becoming is extinguished; through the extinction of the (karmic) process of becoming, Rebirth is extinguished; and through the extinction of rebirth, Decay and Death, Sorrow, Lamentation, Suffering,

Grief, and Despair, are extinguished. Thus comes about the extinction of this whole mass of suffering.

Hence, the annihilation, cessation, and overcoming of corporeality, feeling, perception, mental formations, and consciousness, this is the extinction of suffering, the end of disease, the overcoming of old age and death.

[The undulatory motion, which we call wave—which in the spectator creates the illusion of a single mass of water moving over the surface of the lake—is produced and fed by the wind, and maintained by the stored-up energies. After the wind has ceased, and no fresh wind again whips up the water, the stored-up energies will gradually be consumed, and the whole undulatory motion come to an end. Similarly, if fire does not get new fuel, it will become extinct. Just so, this Five-Khandha-process, which, in the ignorant worldling, creates the illusion of an Ego-entity—is produced and fed by the life-affirming craving, and maintained for some time by means of the stored-up life-energies. Now, after the fuel, i.e., the craving and clinging to life, has ceased, and no new craving impels again this Five-Khandha-process, life will continue as long as there are still life-energies stored up, but at their destruction at death, the Five-Khandha-process will reach final extinction.

Thus, nirvana or "Extinction" (Sanskrit: to cease blowing, to become extinct), may be considered under two aspects:

1. "Extinction of Impurities," reached at the attainment of Arahatship, or Holiness, which takes place during the life-time.
2. "Extinction of the Five-Khandha-process," which takes place at the death of the Arahat.]

Nirvana

This, truly, is the Peace, this is the Highest, namely the end of all formations, the forsaking of every substratum of rebirth, the fading away of craving: detachment, extinction—Nirvana.

Enraptured with lust, enraged with anger, blinded by delusion, overwhelmed, with mind ensnared, man aims at his own ruin, at others' ruin, at the ruin of both parties, and he experiences mental pain and grief. But, if lust, anger, and delusion are given up, man aims neither at his own ruin, nor at others' ruin, nor at the ruin of both parties, and he experiences no mental pain and grief. Thus is Nirvana immediate, visible in this life, inviting, attractive, and comprehensible to the wise.

The extinction of greed, the extinction of anger, the extinction of delusion: this, indeed, is called Nirvana.

The Arahat, or Holy One

And for a disciple thus freed, in whose heart dwells peace, there is nothing to be added to what has been done, and naught more remains for him to do. Just as a rock of one solid mass remains unshaken by the wind, even so, neither forms, nor sounds, nor odors, nor tastes, nor contacts of any kind, neither the desired, nor the undesired, can cause such an one to waver. Steadfast is his mind, gained is deliverance.

And he who has considered all the contrasts on this earth, and is no more disturbed by anything whatever in the world, the Peaceful One, freed from rage, from sorrow, and from longing, he has passed beyond birth and decay.

The Immutable

There is a realm, where there is neither the solid, nor the fluid, neither heat, nor motion, neither this world, nor any other world, neither sun, nor moon. This I call neither arising, nor passing away, neither standing still nor being born, nor dying. There is neither foothold, nor development, nor any basis. This is the end of suffering.

There is an Unborn, Unoriginated, Uncreated, Unformed. If there were not this Unborn, this Unoriginated, this Uncreated, this Unformed, escape from the world of the born, the originated, the created, the formed, would not be possible.

But since there is an Unborn, Unoriginated, Uncreated, Unformed, therefore is escape possible from the world of the born, the originated, the created, the formed.

Fourth Truth

The Noble Truth of the Path that Leads to the Extinction of Suffering

The Two Extremes and the Middle Path

To give oneself up to indulgence in sensual pleasure, the base, common, vulgar, unholy, unprofitable; and also to give oneself up to self-mortification, the painful, unholy, unprofitable: both these two extremes the Perfect One has avoided, and found out the Middle Path, which makes one both to see and to know, which leads to peace, to discernment, to enlightenment, to Nirvana.

The Eightfold Path

It is the Noble Eightfold Path, the way that leads to the extinction of suffering, namely:

1. Right Understanding,
2. Right Mindedness, which together are Wisdom.
3. Right Speech,
4. Right Action,
5. Right Living, which together are Morality.

6. Right Effort,

7. Right Attentiveness,

8. Right Concentration, which together are Concentration.

This is the Middle Path which the Perfect One has found out, which makes one both to see and to know, which leads to peace, to discernment, to enlightenment, to Nirvana.

Free from pain and torture is this path, free from groaning and suffering; it is the perfect path.

Truly, like this path there is no other path to the purity of insight. If you follow this path, you will put an end to suffering.

But each one has to struggle for himself, the Perfect Ones have only pointed out the way.

Give ear then, for the Immortal is found. I reveal, I set forth the Truth. As I reveal it to you, so act! And that supreme goal of the holy life, for the sake of which, sons of good families rightly go forth from home to the homeless state: this you will, in no long time, in this very life, make known to yourself, realize, and make your own.

The Eightfold Path

First Step

Right Understanding

What, now, is Right Understanding? It is understanding the Four Truths. To understand suffering; to understand the origin of suffering; to understand the extinction of suffering; to understand the path that leads to the extinction of suffering: This is called Right Understanding.

Or, when the noble disciple understands what is karmically wholesome, and the root of wholesome karma; what is karmically unwholesome, and the root of unwholesome karma, then he has Right Understanding.

["Karmically unwholesome" is every volitional act of body, speech, or mind which is rooted in greed, hatred, or delusion, and produces evil and painful results in this or any future form of existence.]

What, now, is "karmically unwholesome?"

In Bodily Action it is destruction of living beings; stealing; and unlawful sexual intercourse. In Verbal Action it is lying; tale-bearing; harsh language; and frivolous talk. In Mental Action it is covetousness; ill-will; and wrong views.

And what is the root of unwholesome karma? Greed is a root of unwholesome karma; Anger is a root of unwholesome karma; Delusion is a root of unwholesome karma.

[The state of greed, as well as that of anger, is always accompanied by delusion; and delusion, ignorance, is the primary root of all evil.]

Therefore, I say, these demeritorious actions are of three kinds: due to greed, due to anger, or due to delusion.

What, now, is "karmically wholesome?"

In Bodily Action it is to abstain from killing; to abstain from stealing; and to abstain from unlawful sexual intercourse.

In Verbal Action it is to abstain from lying; to abstain from tale-bearing; to abstain from harsh language; and to abstain from frivolous talk.

In Mental Action it is absence of covetousness; absence of ill-will; and right understanding.

And what is the root of wholesome karma? Absence of greed (unselfishness) is a root of wholesome karma; absence of anger (benevolence) is a root of wholesome karma; absence of delusion (wisdom) is a root of wholesome karma.

Or, when one understands that corporeality, feeling, perception, mental formation, and consciousness, are transient [subject to suffering, and without an Ego], also in that case one possesses Right Understanding.

Unprofitable Questions

Should anyone say that he does not wish to lead the holy life under the Blessed One, unless the Blessed One first tells him, whether the world is eternal or temporal, finite or infinite; whether the life principle is identical with the body, or something different; whether the Perfect One continues after death, and so on such a man would die, ere the Perfect One could tell him all this.

It is as if a man were pierced by a poisoned arrow, and his friends, companions, or near relations, should send for a surgeon; but that man should say: "I will not have this arrow pulled out, until I know who the man is that has wounded me: whether he is a noble, a priest, a citizen, or a servant"; or: "what his name is, and to what family he belongs"; or: "whether he is tall, or short, or of medium height."

Verily, such a man would die, ere he could adequately learn all this.

Therefore, the man who seeks his own welfare, should pull out this arrow—this arrow of lamentation, pain, and sorrow.

[…]

The Two Understandings

Therefore, I say, Right Understanding is of two kinds:

1. The view that alms and offerings are not useless; that there is fruit and result, both of good and bad actions; that there are such things as this life, and the next life; that

father and mother as spontaneously born beings (in the heavenly worlds) are no mere words; that there are monks and priests who are spotless and perfect, who can explain this life and the next life, which they themselves have understood: this is called the "Mundane Right Understanding," which yields worldly fruits, and brings good results.

2. But whatsoever there is of wisdom, of penetration, of right understanding, conjoined with the Path—the mind being turned away from the world, and conjoined with the path, the holy path being turned away from the world, and conjoined with the path, the holy path being pursued—this is called the "Ultramundane Right Understanding," which is not of the world, but is ultramundane, and conjoined with the Path.

[Thus, there are two kinds of the Eightfold Path: the "mundane," practiced by the "worldling"; and the "ultra-mundane," practiced by the "Noble Ones."]

Now, in understanding wrong understanding as wrong, and right understanding as right, one practices Right Understanding [1st step]; and in making efforts to overcome wrong understanding, and to arouse right understanding, one practices. Right Effort [6th step]; and in overcoming wrong understanding with attentive mind, and dwelling with attentive mind in the possession of right understanding, one practices Right-Attentiveness [7th step]. Hence, there are three things that accompany and follow upon right understanding, namely: right understanding, right effort, and right attentiveness.

[…]

Past, Present, and Future

If, now, any one should ask—"Have you been in the past, and is it untrue that you have not been? Will you be in the future, and is it untrue that you will not be? Are you, and is it untrue that you are not?"—you may say that you have been in the past, and it is untrue that you have not been; that you will be in the future, and it is untrue that you will not be; that you are, and it is untrue that you are not.

In the past only the past existence was real, but unreal the future and present existence. In the future only the future existence will be real, but unreal the past and present existence. Now only the present existence is real, but unreal the past and future existence.

Verily, he who perceives the Dependent Origination, perceives the truth and he who perceives the truth, perceives the dependent origination. For, just as from the cow comes milk, from milk curds, from curds butter, from butter ghee, from ghee the scum of ghee; and when it is milk, it is not counted as curds, or butter, or ghee, or scum of ghee, but only as milk; and when it is curds, it is only counted as curds—just so was my past existence at that time real, but unreal the future and present existence; and my future existence will be at one time real, but unreal the past and present existence; and my present existence is now real, but unreal the past and future existence. All these are merely popular designations and expressions, mere conventional terms of speaking, mere popular notions. The Perfect One, indeed, makes use of these, without, however, clinging to them.

Thus, he who does not understand corporeality, feeling, perception, mental formations and consciousness according to reality [i.e., as void of a personality, or Ego], and not their arising, their extinction, and the way to their extinction, he is liable to believe, either that the Perfect One continues after death, or that he does not continue after death, and so forth.

Verily, if one holds the view that the vital principle [Ego] is identical with this body, in that case a holy life is not possible; or, if one holds the view that the vital principle is something quite different from the body, in that case also a holy life is not possible. Both these two Extremes the Perfect One has avoided, and shown the Middle Doctrine, saying:

Dependent Origination

On Delusion depend the Karma-Formations. On the karma-formations depends Consciousness [starting with rebirth-consciousness in the womb of the mother]. On consciousness depends the Mental and Physical Existence. On the mental and physical existence depend the Six Sense-Organs. On the six sense-organs depends the Sensory Impression. On the sensory impression depends Feeling. On feeling depends Craving. On craving depends Clinging. On clinging depends the Process of Becoming. On the process of becoming [here: karma process] depends Rebirth. On rebirth depend Decay and Death, sorrow, lamentation, pain, grief and despair. Thus arises this whole mass of suffering. This is called the noble truth of the origin of suffering.

In whom, however, Delusion has disappeared and wisdom arisen, such a disciple heaps up neither meritorious, nor demeritorious, nor imperturbable Karma-formations.

Thus, through the entire fading away and extinction of this Delusion, the Karma-Formations are extinguished. Through the extinction of the Karma-formations, Consciousness [rebirth] is extinguished. Through the extinction of consciousness, the Mental and Physical Existence is extinguished. Through the extinction of the mental and physical existence, the six Sense-Organs are extinguished. Through the extinction of the six sense-organs, the Sensory Impression is extinguished. Through the extinction of the sensory impression, Feeling is extinguished. Through the extinction of feeling, Craving is extinguished. Through the extinction of craving, Clinging is extinguished. Through the extinction of clinging, the Process of Becoming is extinguished. Through the extinction of the process of becoming, Rebirth is extinguished. Through the extinction of rebirth, Decay and Death, sorrow, lamentation, pain, grief and despair are extinguished. Thus takes place the extinction of this whole mass of suffering. This is called the Noble Truth of the Extinction of Suffering.

Karma: Rebirth—Producing and Barren

Verily, because beings, obstructed by Delusion, and ensnared by Craving, now here now there seek ever fresh delight, therefore such action comes to ever fresh Rebirth.

And the action that is done out of greed, anger and delusion, that springs from them, has its source and origin there: this action ripens wherever one is reborn; and wherever this action ripens, there one experiences the fruits of this action, be it in this life, or the next life, or in some future life.

However, through the fading away of delusion through the arising of wisdom, through the extinction of craving, no future rebirth takes place again.

For the actions, which are not done out of greed, anger and delusion, which have not sprung from them, which have not their source and origin there—such actions are, through the absence of greed, anger and delusion, abandoned, rooted out, like a palm-tree torn out of the soil, destroyed, and not liable to spring up again.

In this respect one may rightly say of me: that I teach annihilation, that I propound my doctrine for the purpose of annihilation, and that I herein train my disciples; for, certainly, I do teach annihilation—the annihilation, namely, of greed, anger and delusion, as well as of the manifold evil and unwholesome things.

["Dependent Origination" is the teaching of the strict conformity to law of everything that happens, whether in the realm of the physical, or the psychical. It shows how the totality of phenomena, physical and mental, the entire phenomenal world that depends wholly upon the six senses, together with all its suffering—and this is the vital point of the teaching—is not the mere play of blind chance, but has an existence that is dependent upon conditions; and that, precisely with the removal of these conditions, those things that have arisen in dependence upon them—thus also all suffering—must perforce disappear and cease to be.]

Second Step

Right-Mindedness

What, now, is Right-Mindedness? It is thoughts free from lust; thoughts free from ill-will; thoughts free from cruelty. This is called right-mindedness.

Now, Right-Mindedness, let me tell you, is of two kinds:

1. Thoughts free from lust, from ill-will, and from cruelty—this is called the "Mundane Right-Mindedness," which yields worldly fruits and brings good results.
2. But, whatsoever there is of thinking, considering, reasoning, thought, ratiocination, application—the mind being holy, being turned away from the world, and conjoined with the path, the holy path being pursued—these "Verbal Operations" of the mind are called the "Ultramundane Right-Mindedness" which is not of the world, but is ultra mundane, and conjoined with the paths.

Now, in understanding wrong-mindedness as wrong, and right-mindedness as right, one practices Right Understanding [1st step]; and in making efforts to overcome evil-mindedness, and to arouse right-mindedness, one practices Right Effort [6th step]; and in overcoming evil-mindedness with attentive mind, and dwelling with attentive mind in possession of right-mindedness, one practices Right Attentiveness [7th step]. Hence, there are three things that accompany and follow upon right-mindedness, namely: right understanding, right effort, and right attentiveness.

Third Step

Right Speech

What, now, is Right Speech? It is abstaining from lying; abstaining from tale-bearing; abstaining from harsh language; abstaining from vain talk.

There, someone avoids lying, and abstains from it. He speaks the truth, is devoted to the truth, reliable, worthy of confidence, is not a deceiver of men. Being at a meeting, or amongst people, or in the midst of his relatives, or in a society, or in the king's court, and called upon and asked as witness, to tell what he knows, he answers, if he knows nothing: "I know nothing"; and if he knows, he answers: "I know"; if he has seen nothing, he answers: "I have seen nothing," and if he has seen, he answers: "I have seen." Thus, he never knowingly speaks a lie, neither for the sake of his own advantage, nor for the sake of another person's advantage, nor for the sake of any advantage whatsoever.

He avoids tale-bearing, and abstains from it. What he has heard here, he does not repeat there, so as to cause dissension there; and what he heard there, he does not repeat here, so as to cause dissension here. Thus he unites those that are divided; and those that are united, he encourages. Concord gladdens him, he delights and rejoices in concord, and it is concord that he spreads by his words.

He avoids harsh language, and abstains from it. He speaks such words as are gentle, soothing to the ear, loving, going to the heart, courteous and dear, and agreeable to many.

[In Majjhima-Nikaya, No. 21, the Buddha says: "Even, O monks, should robbers and murderers saw through your limbs and joints, whoso gave way to anger thereat, would not be following my advice. For thus ought you to train yourselves:

"Undisturbed shall our mind remain, no evil words shall escape our lips; friendly and full of sympathy shall we remain, with heart full of love, and free from any hidden malice; and that person shall we penetrate with loving thoughts, wide, deep, boundless, freed from anger and hatred."]

He avoids vain talk, and abstains from it. He speaks at the right time, in accordance with facts, speaks what is useful, speaks about the law and the discipline; his speech is like a treasure, at the right moment accompanied by arguments, moderate and full of sense.

This is called right speech.

Now, right speech, let me tell you, is of two kinds:

1. Abstaining from lying, from tale-bearing, from harsh language, and from vain talk—this is called the "Mundane Right Speech," which yields worldly fruits and brings good results.
2. But the abhorrence of the practice of this four-fold wrong speech, the abstaining, withholding, refraining therefrom—the mind being holy, being turned away from the world, and conjoined with the path, the holy path being pursued—this is called the "Ultramundane Right Speech, which is not of the world, but is ultramundane, and conjoined with the paths.

Now, in understanding wrong speech as wrong, and right speech as right, one practices Right Understanding [1st step); and in making efforts to overcome evil speech and to arouse right speech, one practices Right Effort [6th step]; and in overcoming wrong speech with attentive mind, and dwelling with attentive mind in possession of right speech, one practices Right Attentiveness [7th step]. Hence, there are three things that accompany and follow upon right attentiveness.

Fourth Step

Right Action

What, now, is Right Action? It is abstaining from killing; abstaining from stealing; abstaining from unlawful sexual intercourse.

There, someone avoids the killing of living beings, and abstains from it. Without stick or sword, conscientious, full of sympathy, he is anxious for the welfare of all living beings.

He avoids stealing, and abstains from it; what another person possesses of goods and chattels in the village or in the wood, that he does not take away with thievish intent.

He avoids unlawful sexual intercourse, and abstains from it. He has no intercourse with such persons as are still under the protection of father, mother, brother, sister or relatives, nor with married women, nor female convicts, nor, lastly, with betrothed girls.

This is called Right Action.

Now, Right Action, let me tell you, is of two kinds:

1. Abstaining from killing, from stealing, and from unlawful sexual intercourse—this is called the "Mundane Right Action," which yields worldly fruits and brings good results. But the abhorrence of the practice of this three-fold wrong action, the abstaining, withholding, refraining therefrom—the mind being holy, being turned away from the world, and conjoined with the path, the holy path being pursued:

this is called the "Ultramundane Right Action," which is not of the world, but is ultramundane, and conjoined with the paths.

Now, in understanding wrong action as wrong, and right action as right, one practices Right Understanding [1st step]; and in making efforts to overcome wrong action, and to arouse right action, one practices Right Effort [6th step]; and in overcoming wrong action with attentive mind, and dwelling with attentive mind in possession of right action, one practices Right Attentiveness [7th step]. Hence, there are three things that accompany and follow upon right action, namely: right understanding, right effort, and right attentiveness.

Fifth Step

Right Living

What, now, is Right Living? When the noble disciple, avoiding a wrong way of living, gets his livelihood by a right way of living, this is called Right Living.
    Now, right living, let me tell you, is of two kinds:

1. When the noble disciple, avoiding wrong living, gets his livelihood by a right way of living—this is called the "Mundane Right Living," which yields worldly fruits and brings good results.
2. But the abhorrence of wrong living, the abstaining, withholding, refraining therefrom—the mind being holy, being turned away from the world, and conjoined with the path, the holy path being pursued—this is called the "Ultramundane Right Living," which is not of the world, but is ultramundane, and conjoined with the paths.

Now, in understanding wrong living as wrong, and right living as right, one practices Right Understanding [1st step]; and in making efforts to overcome wrong living, to arouse right living, one practices Right Effort [6th step]; and in overcoming wrong living with attentive mind, and dwelling with attentive mind in possession of right living, one practices Right Attentiveness [7th step]. Hence, there are three things that accompany and follow upon right living, namely: right understanding, right effort, and right attentiveness.

Sixth Step

Right Effort

What, now, is Right Effort? There are Four Great Efforts: the effort to avoid, the effort to overcome, the effort to develop, and the effort to maintain.

What, now, is the effort to avoid? There, the disciple incites his mind to avoid the arising of evil, demeritorious things that have not yet arisen; and he strives, puts forth his energy, strains his mind and struggles.

Thus, when he perceives a form with the eye, a sound with the ear, an odor with the nose, a taste with the tongue, a contact with the body, or an object with the mind, he neither adheres to the whole, nor to its parts. And he strives to ward off that through which evil and demeritorious things, greed and sorrow, would arise, if he remained with unguarded senses; and he watches over his senses, restrains his senses.

Possessed of this noble "Control over the Senses," he experiences inwardly a feeling of joy, into which no evil thing can enter. This is called the effort to avoid.

What, now, is the effort to Overcome? There, the disciple incites his mind to overcome the evil, demeritorious things that have already arisen; and he strives, puts forth his energy, strains his mind and struggles.

He does not retain any thought of sensual lust, ill-will, or grief, or any other evil and demeritorious states that may have arisen; he abandons them, dispels them, destroys them, causes them to disappear.

Five Methods of Expelling Evil Thoughts

If, whilst regarding a certain object, there arise in the disciple, on account of it, evil and demeritorious thoughts connected with greed, anger and delusion, then the disciple should, by means of this object, gain another and wholesome object. Or, he should reflect on the misery of these thoughts: "Unwholesome, truly, are these thoughts! Blameable are these thoughts! Of painful result are these thoughts!" Or, he should pay no attention to these thoughts. Or, he should consider the compound nature of these thoughts. Or, with teeth clenched and tongue pressed against the gums, he should, with his mind, restrain, suppress and root out these thoughts; and in doing so, these evil and demeritorious thoughts of greed, anger and delusion will dissolve and disappear; and the mind will inwardly become settled and calm, composed and concentrated.

This is called the effort to overcome.

What, now, is the effort to Develop? There the disciple incites his will to arouse meritorious conditions that have not yet arisen; and he strives, puts forth his energy, strains his mind and struggles.

Thus he develops the "Elements of Enlightenment," bent on solitude, on detachment, on extinction, and ending in deliverance, namely: Attentiveness, Investigation of the Law, Energy, Rapture, Tranquility, Concentration, and Equanimity. This is called the effort to develop.

What, now, is the effort to Maintain? There, the disciple incites his will to maintain the meritorious conditions that have already arisen, and not to let them disappear, but to bring them to growth, to maturity and to the full perfection of development; and he strives, puts forth his energy, strains his mind and struggles.

Thus, for example, he keeps firmly in his mind a favorable object of concentration that has arisen, as the mental image of a skeleton, of a corpse infested by worms, of a corpse blue-black in color, of a festering corpse, of a corpse riddled with holes, of a corpse swollen up.

This is called the effort to maintain.

Truly, the disciple who is possessed of faith and has penetrated the Teaching of the Master, he is filled with the thought: "May rather skin, sinews and bones wither away, may the flesh and blood of my body dry up: I shall not give up my efforts so long as I have not attained whatever is attainable by manly perseverance, energy and endeavor!"

This is called right effort.

The effort of Avoiding, Overcoming,
Of Developing and Maintaining:
These four great efforts have been shown
By him, the scion of the sun.
And he who firmly clings to them,
May put an end to all the pain.

Seventh Step

Right Attentiveness

What, now, is Right Attentiveness? The only way that leads to the attainment of purity, to the overcoming of sorrow and lamentation, to the end of pain and grief, to the entering upon the right path and the realization of Nirvana, is the "Four Fundamentals of Attentiveness." And which are these four? In them, the disciple dwells in contemplation of the Body, in contemplation of Feeling, in contemplation of the Mind, in contemplation of the Mind-objects, ardent, clearly conscious and attentive, after putting away worldly greed and grief.

Contemplation of the Body

But, how does the disciple dwell in contemplation of the body?

There, the disciple retires to the forest, to the foot of a tree, or to a solitary place, sits himself down, with legs crossed, body erect, and with attentiveness fixed before him.

With attentive mind he breathes in, with attentive mind he breathes out. When making a long inhalation, he knows: "I make a long inhalation"; when making a long exhalation, he knows: "I make a long exhalation"; when making a short inhalation, he knows: "I make a short inhalation"; when making a short exhalation, he knows: "I make a short exhalation." "Clearly perceiving the entire [breath]-body, I will breathe in": thus he trains himself; "clearly perceiving the entire [breath]-body, I will breathe out": thus he trains himself.

"Calming this bodily function, I will breathe in": thus he trains himself; "calming this bodily function, I will breathe out": thus he trains himself.

Thus he dwells in contemplation of the body, either with regard to his own person, or to other persons, or to both. He beholds how the body arises; beholds how it passes away; beholds the arising and passing away of the body. "A body is there-

A body is there, but no living being, no individual, no woman,
no man, no self, and nothing that belongs to a self; neither a
person, nor anything belonging to a person

this clear consciousness is present in him, because of his knowledge and mindfulness, and he lives independent, unattached to anything in the world. Thus does the disciple dwell in contemplation of the body.

And further, whilst going, standing, sitting, or lying down, the disciple understands the expressions: "I go"; "I stand"; "I sit"; "I lie down"; he understands any position of the body.

[The disciple understands that it is not a being, a real Ego, that goes, stands, etc., but that it is by a mere figure of speech that one says: "I go," "I stand," and so forth.]

And further, the disciple is clearly conscious in his going and coming; clearly conscious in looking forward and backward; clearly conscious in bending and stretching; clearly conscious in eating, drinking, chewing, and tasting; clearly conscious in discharging excrement and urine; clearly conscious in walking, standing, sitting, falling asleep and awakening; clearly conscious in speaking and in keeping silent.

"In all the disciple is doing, he is clearly conscious: of his intention, of his advantage, of his duty, of the reality."

[…]

"A body is there" this clear consciousness is present in him, because of his knowledge and mindfulness; and he lives independent, unattached to anything in the world. Thus does the disciple dwell in contemplation of the body.

The Ten Blessings

Once the contemplation of the body is practiced, developed, often repeated, has become one's habit, one's foundation, is firmly established, strengthened and well perfected, one may expect ten blessings:

Over Delight and Discontent one has mastery; one does not allow himself to be overcome by discontent; one subdues it, as soon as it arises. One conquers Fear and Anxiety; one does not allow himself to be overcome by fear and anxiety; one subdues them, as soon as they arise. One endures cold and heat, hunger and thirst, wind and sun, attacks by gadflies, mosquitoes and reptiles; patiently one endures wicked and malicious speech, as well as bodily pains, that befall one, though they be piercing, sharp, bitter, unpleasant, disagreeable and dangerous to life. The four "Trances," the mind bestowing happiness even here: these one may enjoy at will, without difficulty, without effort.

One may enjoy the different "Magical Powers." With the "Heavenly Ear," the purified, the super-human, one may hear both kinds of sounds, the heavenly and the earthly, the distant and the near. With the mind one may obtain "Insight into the Hearts of Other Beings of other persons. One may obtain "Remembrance of many Previous Births."

With the "Heavenly Eye," the purified, the super-human, one may see beings vanish and reappear, the base and the noble, the beautiful and the ugly, the happy and the unfortunate; one may perceive how beings are reborn according to their deeds.

One may, through the "Cessation of Passions," come to know for oneself, even in this life, the stainless deliverance of mind, the deliverance through wisdom.

Contemplation of the Feelings

But how does the disciple dwell in contemplation of the feelings?

In experiencing feelings, the disciple knows: "I have an indifferent agreeable feeling," or "I have a disagreeable feeling," or "I have an indifferent feeling," or "I have a worldly agreeable feeling," or "I have an unworldly agreeable feeling," or "I have a worldly disagreeable feeling," or "I have an unworldly disagreeable feeling," or "I have a worldly indifferent feeling," or "I have an unworldly indifferent feeling."

Thus he dwells in contemplation of the feelings, either with regard to his own person, or to other persons, or to both. He beholds how the feelings arise; beholds how they pass away; beholds the arising and passing away of the feelings. "Feelings are there": this clear consciousness is present in him, because of his knowledge and mindfulness; and he lives independent, unattached to anything in the world. Thus does the disciple dwell in contemplation of the feelings.

[The disciple understands that the expression "I feel" has no validity except as an expression of common speech; he understands that, in the absolute sense, there are only feelings, and that there is no Ego, no person, no experience of the feelings.]

Contemplation of the Mind

But how does the disciple dwell in contemplation of the mind? The disciple knows the greedy mind as greedy, and the not greedy mind as not greedy; knows the angry mind as angry, and the not angry mind as not angry; knows the deluded mind as deluded, and the undeluded mind as undeluded. He knows the cramped mind as cramped, and the scattered mind as scattered; knows the developed mind as developed, and the undeveloped mind as undeveloped; knows the surpassable mind as surpassable, and the unsurpassable mind as unsurpassable; knows the concentrated mind as concentrated, and the unconcentrated mind as unconcentrated; knows the freed mind as freed, and the unfreed mind as unfreed.

["Mind" is here used as a collective for the moments of consciousness. Being identical with consciousness, it should not be translated by "thought." "Thought" and "thinking" correspond rather to the "verbal operations of the mind"; they are not, like consciousness, of primary, but of secondary nature, and are entirely absent in all sensuous consciousness, as well as in the second, third and fourth Trances. (See eighth step).]

Thus he dwells in contemplation of the mind, either with regard to his own person, or to other persons, or to both. He beholds how consciousness arises; beholds how it passes away; beholds the arising and passing away of consciousness. "Mind is there"— this clear consciousness is present in him, because of his knowledge and mindfulness; and he lives independent, unattached to anything in the world. Thus does the disciple dwell in contemplation of the mind.

Contemplation of Phenomena (Mind-Objects)

But how does the disciple dwell in contemplation of the phenomena?

First, the disciple dwells in contemplation of the phenomena, of the "Five Hindrances."

He knows when there is "Lust" in him: "In me is lust"; knows when there is "Anger" in him: "In me is anger"; knows when there is "Torpor and Drowsiness" in him: "In me is torpor and drowsiness"; knows when there is "Restlessness and Mental Worry" in him: "In me is restlessness and mental worry"; knows when there are "Doubts" in him: "In me are doubts." He knows when these hindrances are not in him: "In me these hindrances are not." He knows how they come to arise; knows how, once arisen, they are overcome; knows how, once overcome, they do not rise again in the future.

[For example, Lust arises through unwise thinking on the agreeable and delightful. it may be suppressed by the following six methods: fixing the mind upon an idea that arouses disgust; contemplation of the loathsomeness of the body; controlling one's six senses; moderation in eating; friendship with wise and good men; right instruction. Lust is forever extinguished upon entrance into Anagamiship; Restlessness is extinguished by reaching Arahatship; Mental Worry, by reaching Sotapanship.]

And further: the disciple dwells in contemplation of the phenomena, of the five Groups of Existence. He knows what Corporeality is, how it arises, how it passes away; knows what Feeling is, how it arises, how it away; knows what Perception is, how it arises, how it passes away; knows what the Mental Formations are, how they arise, how they pass away; knows what Consciousness is, how it arises, how it passes away.

And further: the disciple dwells in contemplation of the phenomena of the six Subjective-Objective Sense-Bases. He knows eye and visual objects, ear and sounds, nose and odors, tongue and tastes, body and touches, mind and mind objects; and the fetter that arises in dependence on them, he also knows. He knows how the fetter comes to arise, knows how the fetter is overcome, and how the abandoned fetter does not rise again in future.

And further: the disciple dwells in contemplation of the phenomena of the seven Elements of Enlightenment. The disciple knows when there is Attentiveness in him; when there is Investigation of the Law in him; when there is Energy in him; when there is Enthusiasm in him; when there is Tranquility in him; when there is Concentration in him; when there is Equanimity in him. He knows when it is not in him, knows how it comes to arise, and how it is fully developed.

And further: the disciple dwells in contemplation of the phenomena of the Four Noble Truths. He knows, according to reality, what Suffering is; knows according to reality, what the Origin of Suffering is; knows according to reality, what the Extinction of Suffering is; knows according to reality, what the Path is that leads to the Extinction of Suffering.

Thus he dwells in contemplation of the phenomena, either with regard to his own person, or to other persons, or to both. He beholds how the phenomena arise; beholds how they pass away; beholds the arising and passing away of the phenomena. "Phenomena are there, this consciousness is present in him, because of his knowledge and mindfulness; and he lives independent, unattached to anything in the world. Thus does the disciple dwell in contemplation of the phenomena.

The only way that leads to the attainment of purity, to the overcoming of sorrow and lamentation, to the end of pain and grief, to the entering upon the right path, and the realization of Nirvana, is these four fundamentals of attentiveness.

Nirvana Through Watching Over Breathing

"Watching over In- and Out-breathing" practiced and developed, brings the four Fundamentals of Attentiveness to perfection; the four fundamentals of attentiveness, practiced and developed bring the seven Elements of Enlightenment to perfection; the seven elements of enlightenment, practiced and developed, bring Wisdom and Deliverance to perfection.

But how does Watching over In- and Out-breathing, practiced and developed, bring the four Fundamentals of Attentiveness to perfection?

I. Whenever the disciple is conscious in making a long inhalation or exhalation, or in making a short inhalation or exhalation, or is training himself to inhale or exhale whilst feeling the whole [breath]-body, or whilst calming down this bodily function—at such a time the disciple is dwelling in "contemplation of the body," of energy, clearly conscious, attentive, after subduing worldly greed and grief. For, inhalation and exhalation I call one amongst the corporeal phenomena.

II. Whenever the disciple is training himself to inhale or exhale whilst feeling rapture, or joy, or the mental functions, or whilst calming down the mental functions—at such a time he is dwelling in "contemplation of the feelings," full of energy, clearly conscious, attentive, after subduing worldly greed and grief. For, the full awareness of in-and out-breathing I call one amongst the feelings.

III. Whenever the disciple is training himself to inhale or exhale whilst feeling the mind, or whilst gladdening the mind or whilst concentrating the mind, or whilst setting the mind free—at such a time he is dwelling in "contemplation of the mind," full of energy, clearly conscious, attentive, after subduing worldly greed and grief. For, without attentiveness and clear consciousness, I say, there is no Watching over In-and Out-breathing.

IV. Whenever the disciple is training himself to inhale or exhale whilst contemplating impermanence, or the fading away of passion, or extinction, or detachment at such a time he is dwelling in "contemplation of the phenomena," full of energy, clearly conscious, attentive, after subduing worldly greed and grief.

Watching over In-and Out-breathing, thus practiced and developed, brings the four Fundamentals of Attentiveness to perfection.

But how do the four Fundamentals of Attentiveness, practiced and developed, bring the seven Elements of Enlightenment to full perfection?

Whenever the disciple is dwelling in contemplation of body, feeling, mind and phenomena, strenuous, clearly conscious, attentive, after subduing worldly greed and grief—at such a time his attentiveness is undisturbed; and whenever his attentiveness is present and undisturbed, at such a time he has gained and is developing the Element of Enlightenment "Attentiveness"; and thus this element of enlightenment reaches fullest perfection.

And whenever, whilst dwelling with attentive mind, he wisely investigates, examines and thinks over the Law—at such a time he has gained and is developing the Element of Enlightenment "Investigation of the Law"; and thus this element of enlightenment reaches fullest perfection.

And whenever, whilst wisely investigating, examining and thinking over the law, his energy is firm and unshaken—at such a time he has gained and is developing the Element of Enlightenment "Energy"; and thus this element of enlightenment reaches fullest perfection.

And whenever in him, whilst firm in energy, arises supersensuous rapture—at such a time he has gained and is developing the Element of Enlightenment "Rapture"; and thus this element of enlightenment reaches fullest perfection.

And whenever, whilst enraptured in mind, his spiritual frame and his mind become tranquil—at such a time he has gained and is developing the Element of Enlightenment "Tranquility"; and thus this element of enlightenment reaches fullest perfection.

And whenever, whilst being tranquilized in his spiritual frame and happy, his mind becomes concentrated—at such a time he has gained and is developing the Element of

Enlightenment "Concentration; and thus this element of enlightenment reaches fullest perfection.

And whenever he thoroughly looks with indifference on his mind thus concentrated—at such a time he has gained and is developing the Element of Enlightenment "Equanimity."

The four fundamentals of attentiveness, thus practiced and developed, bring the seven elements of enlightenment to full perfection.

But how do the seven elements of enlightenment, practiced and developed, bring Wisdom and Deliverance to full perfection?

There, the disciple is developing the elements of enlightenment: Attentiveness, Investigation of the Law, Energy, Rapture, Tranquility.

Concentration and Equanimity, bent on detachment, on absence of desire, on extinction and renunciation.

Thus practiced and developed, do the seven elements of enlightenment bring wisdom and deliverance to full perfection.

Just as the elephant hunter drives a huge stake into the ground and chains the wild elephant to it by the neck, in order to drive out of him his wonted forest ways and wishes, his forest unruliness, obstinacy and violence, and to accustom him to the environment of the village, and to teach him such good behavior as is required amongst men: in like manner also has the noble disciple to fix his mind firmly to these four fundamentals of attentiveness, so that he may drive out of himself his wonted worldly ways and wishes, his wonted worldly unruliness, obstinacy and violence, and win to the True, and realize Nirvana.

Eighth Step

Right Concentration

What, now, is Right Concentration? Fixing the mind to a single object ("One-pointedness of mind"): this is concentration.

The four Fundamentals of Attentiveness (seventh step): these are the objects of concentration.

The four Great Efforts (sixth step): these are the requisites for concentration.

The practicing, developing and cultivating of these things: this is the "Development" of concentration.

[Right Concentration has two degrees of development:

1. "Neighborhood-Concentration," which approaches the first trance, without however attaining it;
2. "Attainment-Concentration," which is the concentration present in the four trances. The attainment of the trances, however, is not a requisite for the realization of the Four Ultramundane Paths of Holiness; and neither Neighborhood-Concentration

nor Attainment-Concentration, as such, in any way possesses the power of conferring entry into the Four Ultramundane Paths; hence, in them is really no power to free oneself permanently from evil things. The realization of the Four Ultramundane Paths is possible only at the moment of insight into the impermanency, miserable nature, and impersonality of phenomenal process of existence. This insight is attainable only during Neighborhood-Concentration, not during Attainment-Concentration.

He who has realized one or other of the Four Ultramundane Paths without ever having attained the Trances, is called a "Dry-visioned One," or one whose passions are "dried up by Insight." He, however, who after cultivating the Trances has reached one of the Ultramundane Paths, is called "one who has taken tranquility as his vehicle."]

[…]

Attentiveness and Clear Consciousness

Clearly conscious is he in his going and coming; clearly conscious in looking forward and backward; clearly conscious in bending and stretching his body; clearly conscious in eating, drinking, chewing and tasting; dearly conscious in discharging excrement and urine; clearly conscious in walking, standing, sitting, falling asleep and awakening; clearly conscious in speaking and keeping silent.

Now, being equipped with this lofty Morality, equipped with this noble Control of the Senses, and filled with this noble "Attentiveness and Clear Consciousness, he chooses a secluded dwelling in the forest, at the foot of a tree, on a mountain, in a cleft, in a rock cave, on a burial ground, on a woody table-land, in the open air, or on a heap of straw. Having returned from his alms-round, after the meal, he sits himself down with legs crossed, body erect, with attentiveness fixed before him.

Absence of the Five Hindrances

He has cast away Lust; he dwells with a heart free from lust; from lust he cleanses his heart.

He has cast away Ill-will; he dwells with a heart free from ill-will; cherishing love and compassion toward all living beings, he cleanses his heart from ill-will.

He has cast away Torpor and Dullness; he dwells free from torpor and dullness; loving the light, with watchful mind, with clear consciousness, he cleanses his mind from torpor and dullness.

He has cast away Restlessness and Mental Worry; dwelling with mind undisturbed, with heart full of peace, he cleanses his mind from restlessness and mental worry.

He has cast away Doubt; dwelling free from doubt, full of confidence in the good, he cleanses his heart from doubt.

[…]

Insight

But whatsoever there is of feeling, perception, mental formation, or consciousness—all these phenomena he regards as "impermanent," "subject to pain," as infirm, as an ulcer, a thorn, a misery, a burden, an enemy, a disturbance, as empty and "void of an Ego"; and turning away from these things, he directs his mind towards the abiding, thus: "This, verily, is the Peace, this is the Highest, namely the end of all formations, the forsaking of every substratum of rebirth, the fading away of craving; detachment, extinction: Nirvana."

And in this state he reaches the "Cessation of Passions."

Nirvana

And his heart becomes free from sensual passion, free from the passion for existence, free from the passion of ignorance. "Freed am I!": this knowledge arises in the liberated one; and he knows: "Exhausted is rebirth, fulfilled the Holy Life; what was to be done, has been done; naught remains more for this world to do."

Forever am I liberated,
This is the last time that I'm born,
No new existence waits for me.

This, verily, is the highest, holiest wisdom: to know that all suffering has passed away.
This, verily, is the highest, holiest peace: appeasement of greed, hatred and delusion.

The Silent Thinker

"I am" is a vain thought; "I am not" a vain thought; "I shall be" is a vain thought; "I shall not be" is a vain thought. Vain thoughts are a sickness, an ulcer, a thorn. But after overcoming all vain thoughts, one is called "silent thinker." And the thinker, the Silent One, does no more arise, no more pass away, no more tremble, no more desire. For there is nothing in him that he should arise again. And as he arises no more, how should he grow old again? And as he grows no more old, how should he die again? And as he dies no more, how should he tremble? And as he trembles no more, how should he have desire?

The True Goal

Hence, the purpose of the Holy Life does not consist in acquiring alms, honor, or fame, nor in gaining morality, concentration, or the eye of knowledge. That unshakable deliverance of the heart: that, verily, is the object of the Holy Life, that is its essence, that is its goal.

And those, who formerly, in the past, were Holy and Enlightened Ones, those Blessed Ones also have pointed out to their disciples this self-same goal, as has been pointed out by me to my disciples. And those, who afterwards, in the future, will be Holy and Enlightened Ones, those Blessed Ones also will point out to their disciples this self-same goal, as has been pointed out by me to my disciples.

However, Disciples, it may be that (after my passing away) you might think: "Gone is the doctrine of our Master. We have no Master more." But you should not think; for the Law and the Discipline, which I have taught you, Will, after my death, be your master.

The Law be your light,

The Law be your refuge!

Do not look for any other refuge!

Disciples, the doctrines, which I advised you to penetrate, you should well preserve, well guard, so that this Holy Life may take its course and continue for ages, for the weal and welfare of the many, as a consolation to the world, for the happiness, weal and welfare of heavenly beings and men.

THE END

Chapter 3
Confucianism

The Analects of Confucius

Confucius (or K'ung Fu Tzu, who lived in China from 551–479 B.C.E.) was one of the most prominent thinkers in history, and was particularly influential in Asian culture. Living during what has been characterized by historians as the Axial Age, he was a contemporary of Lao Tzu (whom he met), and perhaps with the historical Buddha as well (although there is no evidence he met the Buddha).

Confucius is credited with articulating a thoroughgoing ethical philosophy. His Analects that we consider here were compiled by students and followers in the decades after Confucius's death. Addressing a wide array of topics, the common form is one of conversation, where one of his disciples asks a question, and Confucius (or "The Master") answers. In this regard, they are to the Western reader somewhat reminiscent of Plato's dialogic accounts of the teachings of Socrates.

Confucian ethics center around an interrelated set of norms and ways of seeing the world. The idea of ren (or jen) is one of the earliest articulations of the golden rule—in this instance, do not do to others what you would not want to happen to you. More broadly, there is a good will that guides all the Confucian virtues. Chun tzu involves treating others with kindness and hospitality. It is the opposite of pettiness and involves acting in ways that are guided by ren.

The virtue of li, has several aspects, centered around acting rightly in relation to the roles a person fills. If a person is a parent, he or she should be the best parent they can be. Likewise, for a child, one should be the best son or daughter possible; this is sometimes referred to as filial piety. In fact, Confucius saw five "constant" relationships, in which the very most important roles were lived out: parent–child; husband–wife; older sibling–younger sibling; mentor–protégé; and ruler–subject. Here it bears noting that Confucianism places

a huge emphasis on family, both immediate and extended. Ritual ancestor worship flour-
ished in Confucian culture.

The idea of acting rightly, or with propriety, also involves a related Confucian value
that is reminiscent of Aristotle's idea of the golden mean. A person or collective acting
righteously should avoid extremes—should practice centeredness, or centricity in all
things. While Confucianism and Taoism differ in many key respects, they are similar in
many important ways as well. This idea of avoiding extremes and living a life of balance
is important in both.

Another Confucian virtue that is also central to Taoist philosophy is that of te (so cen-
tral in fact, that it shows up in the title of the Tao Te Ching). By itself, te means power—but
it is power used well, tempered by the other virtues, particularly ren. While each of the five
constant relationships involves power differences, the person wielding the greater power
also has the obligation to use it in a way that is uplifting. A parent may at times be called
by duty to discipline a child, for example; but that should never be done out of anger or
pettiness—rather, it should proceed from a basis of good will.

Confucian ethics also emphasize arts and culture. Following this idea (wen), each
person in a society should have some art they develop. It serves then as a meditative and
humanizing influence throughout the society. The particulars of which art can someone
practice can vary (flower arranging, martial arts, or calligraphy, for example), but every-
one in the society should have some art.

Stemming from these ideals are important Confucian ethical principles. Whenever pos-
sible, differences should be settled informally. People should not have emotional displays,
particularly anger. More generally, if there is a confrontation, particularly one in which
people "lose" their center, it reflects poorly on everyone involved. In a related vein, there
was a value on settling differences through negotiation or diplomacy.

In sum then, the Confucian ethic is complex and multi-faceted. It puts an emphasis on
good will, righteous action, respect for others and for oneself, and moderation in all things.

We now consider the Analects of Confucius…

Confucian Analects

Confucius

translated by James Legge [1893]

1

The Master "Is it not pleasant to learn with a constant perseverance and application?"

"Is it not delightful to have friends coming from distant quarters?"

"Is he not a man of complete virtue, who feels no discomposure though men may take no note of him?"

The philosopher Yu said, "They are few who, being filial and fraternal, are fond of offending against their superiors. There have been none, who, not liking to offend against their superiors, have been fond of stirring up confusion.

"The superior man bends his attention to what is radical. That being established, all practical courses naturally grow up. Filial piety and fraternal submission—are they not the root of all benevolent actions?"

The Master said, "Fine words and an insinuating appearance are seldom associated with true virtue."

The philosopher Tsang said, "I daily examine myself on three points: whether, in transacting business for others, I may have been not faithful; whether, in intercourse with friends, I may have been not sincere; whether I may have not mastered and practiced the instructions of my teacher."

The Master said, "To rule a country of a thousand chariots, there must be reverent attention to business, and sincerity; economy in expenditure, and love for men; and the employment of the people at the proper seasons."

The Master said, "A youth, when at home, should be filial, and, abroad, respectful to his elders. He should be earnest and truthful.

He should overflow in love to all, and cultivate the friendship of the good. When he has time and opportunity, after the performance of these things, he should employ them in polite studies."

Tsze-hsia said, "If a man withdraws his mind from the love of beauty, and applies it as sincerely to the love of the virtuous; if, in serving his parents, he can exert his utmost strength; if, in serving his prince, he can devote his life; if, in his intercourse with his friends, his words are sincere: although men say that he has not learned, I will certainly say that he has."

The Master said, "If the scholar be not grave, he will not call forth any veneration, and his learning will not be solid."

"Hold faithfulness and sincerity as first principles."

"Have no friends not equal to yourself."

"When you have faults, do not fear to abandon them."

The philosopher Tsang said, "Let there be a careful attention to perform the funeral rites to parents, and let them be followed when long gone with the ceremonies of sacrifice; then the virtue of the people will resume its proper excellence."

Tsze-ch'in asked Tsze-kung saying, "When our master comes to any country, he does not fail to learn all about its government. Does he ask his information? or is it given to him?"

Tsze-kung said, "Our master is benign, upright, courteous, temperate, and complaisant and thus he gets his information. The master's mode of asking information, is it not different from that of other men?"

The Master said, "While a man's father is alive, look at the bent of his will; when his father is dead, look at his conduct. If for three years he does not alter from the way of his father, he may be called filial."

The philosopher Yu said, "In practicing the rules of propriety, a natural ease is to be prized. In the ways prescribed by the ancient kings, this is the excellent quality, and in things small and great we follow them."

"Yet it is not to be observed in all cases. If one, knowing how such ease should be prized, manifests it, without regulating it by the rules of propriety, this likewise is not to be done."

The philosopher Yu said, "When agreements are made according to what is right, what is spoken can be made good. When respect is shown according to what is proper, one keeps far from shame and disgrace. When the parties upon whom a man leans are proper persons to be intimate with, he can make them his guides and masters."

The Master said, "He who aims to be a man of complete virtue in his food does not seek to gratify his appetite, nor in his dwelling place does he seek the appliances of ease; he is earnest in what he is doing, and careful in his speech; he frequents the company of men of principle that he may be rectified: such a person may be said indeed to love to learn."

Tsze-kung said, "What do you pronounce concerning the poor man who yet does not flatter, and the rich man who is not proud?" The Master replied, "They will do; but they are not equal to him, who, though poor, is yet cheerful, and to him, who, though rich, loves the rules of propriety."

Tsze-kung replied, "It is said in the Book of Poetry, 'As you cut and then file, as you carve and then polish.' The meaning is the same, I apprehend, as that which you have just expressed."

The Master said, "With one like Ts'ze, I can begin to talk about the odes. I told him one point, and he knew its proper sequence."

The Master said, "I will not be afflicted at men's not knowing me; I will be afflicted that I do not know men."

2

The Master said, "He who exercises government by means of his virtue may be compared to the north polar star, which keeps its place and all the stars turn towards it."

The Master said, "In the Book of Poetry are three hundred pieces, but the design of them all may be embraced in one sentence—Having no depraved thoughts.'"

The Master said, "If the people be led by laws, and uniformity sought to be given them by punishments, they will try to avoid the punishment, but have no sense of shame.

"If they be led by virtue, and uniformity sought to be given them by the rules of propriety, they will have the sense of shame, and moreover will become good."

The Master said, "At fifteen, I had my mind bent on learning."

"At thirty, I stood firm."

"At forty, I had no doubts."

"At fifty, I knew the decrees of Heaven."

"At sixty, my ear was an obedient organ for the reception of truth."

"At seventy, I could follow what my heart desired, without transgressing what was right."

Mang I asked what filial piety was. The Master said, "It is not being disobedient."

Soon after, as Fan Ch'ih was driving him, the Master told him, saying, "Mang-sun asked me what filial piety was, and I answered him, 'not being disobedient.'"

Fan Ch'ih said, "What did you mean?" The Master replied, "That parents, when alive, be served according to propriety; that, when dead, they should be buried according to propriety; and that they should be sacrificed to according to propriety."

Mang Wu asked what filial piety was. The Master said, "Parents are anxious lest their children should be sick."

Tsze-yu asked what filial piety was. The Master said, "The filial piety nowadays means the support of one's parents. But dogs and horses likewise are able to do something in the way of support; without reverence, what is there to distinguish the one support given from the other?"

Tsze-hsia asked what filial piety was. The Master said, "The difficulty is with the countenance. If, when their elders have any troublesome affairs, the young take the toil of them, and if, when the young have wine and food, they set them before their elders, is THIS to be considered filial piety?"

The Master said, "I have talked with Hui for a whole day, and he has not made any objection to anything I said; as if he were stupid. He has retired, and I have examined his conduct when away from me, and found him able to illustrate my teachings. Hui! He is not stupid."

The Master said, "See what a man does."

"Mark his motives.

"Examine in what things he rests."

"How can a man conceal his character?"

The Master said, "If a man keeps cherishing his old knowledge, so as continually to be acquiring new, he may be a teacher of others."

The Master said, "The accomplished scholar is not a utensil."

Tsze-kung asked what constituted the superior man. The Master said, "He acts before he speaks, and afterwards speaks according to his actions."

The Master said, "The superior man is catholic and not partisan. The mean man is partisan and not catholic."

The Master said, "Learning without thought is labor lost; thought without learning is perilous."

The Master said, "The study of strange doctrines is injurious indeed!"

The Master said, "Yu, shall I teach you what knowledge is? When you know a thing, to hold that you know it; and when you do not know a thing, to allow that you do not know it—this is knowledge."

Tsze-chang was learning with a view to official emolument.

The Master said, "Hear much and put aside the points of which you stand in doubt, while you speak cautiously at the same time of the others: then you will afford few occasions for blame. See much and put aside the things which seem perilous, while you are cautious at the same time in carrying the others into practice: then you will have few occasions for repentance. When one gives few occasions for blame in his words, and few occasions for repentance in his conduct, he is in the way to get emolument."

The Duke Ai asked, saying, "What should be done in order to secure the submission of the people?" Confucius replied, "Advance the upright and set aside the crooked, then the people will submit. Advance the crooked and set aside the upright, then the people will not submit."

Chi K'ang asked how to cause the people to reverence their ruler, to be faithful to him, and to go on to nerve themselves to virtue. The Master said, "Let him preside over them with gravity; then they will reverence him. Let him be final and kind to all; then they will be faithful to him. Let him advance the good and teach the incompetent; then they will eagerly seek to be virtuous."

Someone addressed Confucius, saying, "Sir, why are you not engaged in the government?"

The Master said, "What does the Shu-ching say of filial piety? 'You are final, you discharge your brotherly duties. These qualities are displayed in government.' This then also constitutes the exercise of government. Why must there be THAT making one be in the government?"

The Master said, "I do not know how a man without truthfulness is to get on. How can a large carriage be made to go without the crossbar for yoking the oxen to, or a small carriage without the arrangement for yoking the horses?"

Tsze-chang asked whether the affairs of ten ages after could be known.

Confucius said, "The Yin dynasty followed the regulations of the Hsia: wherein it took from or added to them may be known. The Chau dynasty has followed the regulations of Yin: wherein it took from or added to them may be known. Some other may follow the Chau, but though it should be at the distance of a hundred ages, its affairs may be known."

The Master said, "For a man to sacrifice to a spirit which does not belong to him is flattery."

"To see what is right and not to do it is want of courage."

[...]

The Master said, "It is virtuous manners which constitute the excellence of a neighborhood. If a man in selecting a residence do not fix on one where such prevail, how can he be wise?"

The Master said, "Those who are without virtue cannot abide long either in a condition of poverty and hardship, or in a condition of enjoyment. The virtuous rest in virtue; the wise desire virtue."

The Master said, "It is only the truly virtuous man, who can love, or who can hate, others."

The Master said, "If the will be set on virtue, there will be no practice of wickedness."

The Master said, "Riches and honors are what men desire. If they cannot be obtained in the proper way, they should not be held. Poverty and meanness are what men dislike. If they cannot be avoided in the proper way, they should not be avoided."

"If a superior man abandon virtue, how can he fulfill the requirements of that name?"

"The superior man does not, even for the space of a single meal, act contrary to virtue. In moments of haste, he cleaves to it. In seasons of danger, he cleaves to it."

The Master said, "I have not seen a person who loved virtue, or one who hated what was not virtuous. He who loved virtue, would esteem nothing above it. He who hated what is not virtuous, would practice virtue in such a way that he would not allow anything that is not virtuous to approach his person."

"Is any one able for one day to apply his strength to virtue? I have not seen the case in which his strength would be insufficient."

"Should there possibly be any such case, I have not seen it." The Master said, "The faults of men are characteristic of the class to which they belong. By observing a man's faults, it may be known that he is virtuous."

The Master said, "If a man in the morning hear the right way, he may die in the evening hear regret."

The Master said, "A scholar, whose mind is set on truth, and who is ashamed of bad clothes and bad food, is not fit to be discoursed with."

The Master said, "The superior man, in the world, does not set his mind either for anything, or against anything; what is right he will follow."

The Master said, "The superior man thinks of virtue; the small man thinks of comfort. The superior man thinks of the sanctions of law; the small man thinks of favors which he may receive."

The Master said: "He who acts with a constant view to his own advantage will be much murmured against."

The Master said, "If a prince is able to govern his kingdom with the complaisance proper to the rules of propriety, what difficulty will he have? If he cannot govern it with that complaisance, what has he to do with the rules of propriety?"

The Master said, "A man should say, I am not concerned that I have no place, I am concerned how I may fit myself for one. I am not concerned that I am not known, I seek to be worthy to be known."

The Master said, "Shan, my doctrine is that of an all-pervading unity." The disciple Tsang replied, "Yes."

The Master went out, and the other disciples asked, saying, "What do his words mean?" Tsang said, "The doctrine of our master is to be true to the principles—of our nature and the benevolent exercise of them to others—this and nothing more."

The Master said, "The mind of the superior man is conversant with righteousness; the mind of the mean man is conversant with gain."

The Master said, "When we see men of worth, we should think of equaling them; when we see men of a contrary character, we should turn inwards and examine ourselves."

The Master said, "In serving his parents, a son may remonstrate with them, but gently; when he sees that they do not incline to follow his advice, he shows an increased degree of reverence, but does not abandon his purpose; and should they punish him, he does not allow himself to murmur."

The Master said, "While his parents are alive, the son may not go abroad to a distance. If he does go abroad, he must have a fixed place to which he goes."

The Master said, "If the son for three years does not alter from the way of his father, he may be called filial."

The Master said, "The years of parents may by no means not be kept in the memory, as an occasion at once for joy and for fear."

The Master said, "The reason why the ancients did not readily give utterance to their words, was that they feared lest their actions should not come up to them."

The Master said, "The cautious seldom err."

The Master said, "The superior man wishes to be slow in his speech and earnest in his conduct."

The Master said, "Virtue is not left to stand alone. He who practices it will have neighbors."

Tsze-yu said, "In serving a prince, frequent remonstrances lead to disgrace. Between friends, frequent reproofs make the friendship distant."

[…]

6

[…]

The Master said, "Who can go out but by the door? How is it that men will not walk according to these ways?"

The Master said, "Where the solid qualities are in excess of accomplishments, we have rusticity; where the accomplishments are in excess of the solid qualities, we have the manners of a clerk. When the accomplishments and solid qualities are equally blended, we then have the man of virtue."

The Master said, "Man is born for uprightness. If a man lose his uprightness, and yet live, his escape from death is the effect of mere good fortune."

The Master said, "They who know the truth are not equal to those who love it, and they who love it are not equal to those who delight in it."

The Master said, "To those whose talents are above mediocrity, the highest subjects may be announced. To those who are below mediocrity, the highest subjects may not be announced."

Fan Ch'ih asked what constituted wisdom. The Master said, "To give one's self earnestly to the duties due to men, and, while respecting spiritual beings, to keep aloof from them, may be called wisdom." He asked about perfect virtue. The Master said, "The man of virtue makes the difficulty to be overcome his first business, and success only a subsequent consideration—this may be called perfect virtue."

The Master said, "The wise find pleasure in water; the virtuous find pleasure in hills. The wise are active; the virtuous are tranquil. The wise are joyful; the virtuous are long-lived."

[…]

"Now the man of perfect virtue, wishing to be established himself, seeks also to establish others; wishing to be enlarged himself, he seeks also to enlarge others."

"To be able to judge of others by what is nigh in ourselves—this may be called the art of virtue."

[…]

7

The Master said, "A transmitter and not a maker, believing in and loving the ancients, I venture to compare myself with our old P'ang."

The Master said, "The silent treasuring up of knowledge; learning without satiety; and instructing others without being wearied: which one of these things belongs to me?"

The Master said, "The leaving virtue without proper cultivation; the not thoroughly discussing what is learned; not being able to move towards righteousness of which a knowledge is gained; and not being able to change what is not good: these are the things which occasion me solicitude."

When the Master was unoccupied with business, his manner was easy, and he looked pleased.

The Master said, "Extreme is my decay. For a long time, I have not dreamed, as I was wont to do, that I saw the duke of Chau."

The Master said, "Let the will be set on the path of duty."

"Let every attainment in what is good be firmly grasped."

"Let perfect virtue be accorded with."

"Let relaxation and enjoyment be found in the polite arts."

The Master said, "From the man bringing his bundle of dried flesh for my teaching upwards, I have never refused instruction to any one."

The Master said, "I do not open up the truth to one who is not eager to get knowledge, nor help out any one who is not anxious to explain himself. When I have presented one corner of a subject to any one, and he cannot from it learn the other three, I do not repeat my lesson."

When the Master was eating by the side of a mourner, he never ate to the full.

He did not sing on the same day in which he had been weeping.

The Master said to Yen Yuan, "When called to office, to undertake its duties; when not so called, to he retired; it is only I and you who have attained to this."

Tsze-lu said, "If you had the conduct of the armies of a great state, whom would you have to act with you?"

The Master said, "I would not have him to act with me, who will unarmed attack a tiger, or cross a river without a boat, dying without any regret. My associate must be the man who proceeds to action full of solicitude, who is fond of adjusting his plans, and then carries them into execution."

The Master said, "If the search for riches is sure to be successful, though I should become a groom with whip in hand to get them, I will do so. As the search may not be successful, I will follow after that which I love."

The things in reference to which the Master exercised the greatest caution were fasting, war, and sickness.

[…]

The Master said, "I am not one who was born in the possession of knowledge; I am one who is fond of antiquity, and earnest in seeking it there."

The subjects on which the Master did not talk, were extraordinary things, feats of strength, disorder, and spiritual beings.

The Master said, "When I walk along with two others, they may serve me as my teachers. I will select their good qualities and follow them, their bad qualities and avoid them."

The Master said, "Heaven produced the virtue that is in me. Hwan T'ui—what can he do to me?"

The Master said, "Do you think, my disciples, that I have any concealments? I conceal nothing from you. There is nothing which I do that is not shown to you, my disciples; that is my way."

There were four things which the Master taught: letters, ethics, devotion of soul, and truthfulness.

The Master said, "A sage it is not mine to see; could I see a man of real talent and virtue, that would satisfy me."

The Master said, "A good man it is not mine to see; could I see a man possessed of constancy, that would satisfy me.

"Having not and yet affecting to have, empty and yet affecting to be full, straitened and yet affecting to be at ease: it is difficult with such characteristics to have constancy."

The Master angled, but did not use a net. He shot, but not at birds perching.

The Master said, "There may be those who act without knowing why.

I do not do so. Hearing much and selecting what is good and following it; seeing much and keeping it in memory: this is the second style of knowledge."

It was difficult to talk profitably and reputably with the people of Hu-hsiang, and a lad of that place having had an interview with the Master, the disciples doubted.

The Master said, "I admit people's approach to me without committing myself as to what they may do when they have retired. Why must one be so severe? If a man purify himself to wait upon me, I receive him so purified, without guaranteeing his past conduct."

The Master said, "Is virtue a thing remote? I wish to be virtuous, and lo! virtue is at hand."

[…]

The Master said, "Extravagance leads to insubordination, and parsimony to meanness. It is better to be mean than to be insubordinate."

The Master said, "The superior man is satisfied and composed; the mean man is always full of distress."

The Master was mild, and yet dignified; majestic, and yet not fierce; respectful, and yet easy.

8

The Master said, "T'ai-po may be said to have reached the highest point of virtuous action. Thrice he declined the kingdom, and the people in ignorance of his motives could not express their approbation of his conduct."

The Master said, "Respectfulness, without the rules of propriety, becomes laborious bustle; carefulness, without the rules of propriety, becomes timidity; boldness, without the rules of propriety, becomes insubordination; straightforwardness, without the rules of propriety, becomes rudeness."

"When those who are in high stations perform well all their duties to their relations, the people are aroused to virtue. When old friends are not neglected by them, the people are preserved from meanness."

[…]

The Master said, "It is not easy to find a man who has learned for three years without coming to be good."

The Master said, "With sincere faith he unites the love of learning; holding firm to death, he is perfecting the excellence of his course."

"Such an one will not enter a tottering state, nor dwell in a disorganized one. When right principles of government prevail in the kingdom, he will show himself; when they are prostrated, he will keep concealed."

"When a country is well governed, poverty and a mean condition are things to be ashamed of. When a country is ill governed, riches and honor are things to be ashamed of."

The Master said, "He who is not in any particular office has nothing to do with plans for the administration of its duties."

The Master said, "When the music master Chih first entered on his office, the finish of the Kwan Tsu was magnificent; how it filled the ears!"

The Master said, "Ardent and yet not upright, stupid and yet not attentive; simple and yet not sincere: such persons I do not understand."

The Master said, "Learn as if you could not reach your object, and were always fearing also lest you should lose it."

[...]

9

[...]

There were four things from which the Master was entirely free. He had no foregone conclusions, no arbitrary predeterminations, no obstinacy, and no egoism.

[...]

The Master said, "Abroad, to serve the high ministers and nobles; at home, to serve one's father and elder brothers; in all duties to the dead, not to dare not to exert one's self; and not to be overcome of wine: which one of these things do I attain to?"

The Master standing by a stream, said, "It passes on just like this, not ceasing day or night!"

The Master said, "I have not seen one who loves virtue as he loves beauty."

The Master said, "The prosecution of learning may be compared to what may happen in raising a mound. If there want but one basket of earth to complete the work, and I stop, the stopping is my own work.

It may be compared to throwing down the earth on the level ground.

Though but one basketful is thrown at a time, the advancing with it my own going forward."

The Master said, "Never flagging when I set forth anything to him; ah! that is Hui."
The Master said of Yen Yuan, "Alas! I saw his constant advance. I never saw him stop in his progress."

The Master said, "There are cases in which the blade springs, but the plant does not go on to flower! There are cases where it flowers but fruit is not subsequently produced!"

The Master said, "A youth is to be regarded with respect. How do we know that his future will not be equal to our present? If he reach the age of forty or fifty, and has not made himself heard of, then indeed he will not be worth being regarded with respect."

The Master said, "Can men refuse to assent to the words of strict admonition? But it is reforming the conduct because of them which is valuable. Can men refuse to be pleased with words of gentle advice?

But it is unfolding their aim which is valuable. If a man be pleased with these words, but does not unfold their aim, and assents to those, but does not reform his conduct, I can really do nothing with him."

The Master said, "Hold faithfulness and sincerity as first principles. Have no friends not equal to yourself. When you have faults, do not fear to abandon them."

The Master said, "The commander of the forces of a large state may be carried off, but the will of even a common man cannot be taken from him."

The Master said, "Dressed himself in a tattered robe quilted with hemp, yet standing by the side of men dressed in furs, and not ashamed; ah! it is Yu who is equal to this!"

"He dislikes none, he covets nothing; what can he do but what is good!"

Tsze-lu kept continually repeating these words of the ode, when the Master said, "Those things are by no means sufficient to constitute perfect excellence."

The Master said, "When the year becomes cold, then we know how the pine and the cypress are the last to lose their leaves."

The Master said, "The wise are free from perplexities; the virtuous from anxiety; and the bold from fear."

The Master said, "There are some with whom we may study in common, but we shall find them unable to go along with us to principles.

Perhaps we may go on with them to principles, but we shall find them unable to get established in those along with us. Or if we may get so established along with them, we shall find them unable to weigh occurring events along with us."

"How the flowers of the aspen-plum flutter and turn! Do I not think of you? But your house is distant."

The Master said, "It is the want of thought about it. How is it distant?"

10

Confucius, in his village, looked simple and sincere, and as if he were not able to speak.

When he was in the prince's ancestral temple, or in the court, he spoke minutely on every point, but cautiously.

When he was waiting at court, in speaking with the great officers of the lower grade, he spoke freely, but in a straightforward manner; in speaking with those of the higher grade, he did so blandly, but precisely.

When the ruler was present, his manner displayed respectful uneasiness; it was grave, but self-possessed.

When the prince called him to employ him in the reception of a visitor, his countenance appeared to change, and his legs to move forward with difficulty.

He inclined himself to the other officers among whom he stood, moving his left or right arm, as their position required, but keeping the skirts of his robe before and behind evenly adjusted.

He hastened forward, with his arms like the wings of a bird.

When the guest had retired, he would report to the prince, "The visitor is not turning round any more."

When he entered the palace gate, he seemed to bend his body, as if it were not sufficient to admit him.

When he was standing, he did not occupy the middle of the gateway; when he passed in or out, he did not tread upon the threshold.

When he was passing the vacant place of the prince, his countenance appeared to change, and his legs to bend under him, and his words came as if he hardly had breath to utter them.

He ascended the reception hall, holding up his robe with both his hands, and his body bent; holding in his breath also, as if he dared not breathe.

When he came out from the audience, as soon as he had descended one step, he began to relax his countenance, and had a satisfied look.

When he had got the bottom of the steps, he advanced rapidly to his place, with his arms like wings, and on occupying it, his manner still showed respectful uneasiness.

When he was carrying the scepter of his ruler, he seemed to bend his body, as if he were not able to bear its weight. He did not hold it higher than the position of the hands in making a bow, nor lower than their position in giving anything to another. His countenance seemed to change, and look apprehensive, and he dragged his feet along as if they were held by something to the ground.

In presenting the presents with which he was charged, he wore a placid appearance.

At his private audience, he looked highly pleased.

The superior man did not use a deep purple, or a puce color, in the ornaments of his dress.

Even in his undress, he did not wear anything of a red or reddish color.

In warm weather, he had a single garment either of coarse or fine texture, but he wore it displayed over an inner garment.

Over lamb's fur he wore a garment of black; over fawn's fur one of white; and over fox's fur one of yellow.

The fur robe of his undress was long, with the right sleeve short.

He required his sleeping dress to be half as long again as his body.

When staying at home, he used thick furs of the fox or the badger.

When he put off mourning, he wore all the appendages of the girdle.

His undergarment, except when it was required to be of the curtain shape, was made of silk cut narrow above and wide below.

He did not wear lamb's fur or a black cap on a visit of condolence.

On the first day of the month he put on his court robes, and presented himself at court.

When fasting, he thought it necessary to have his clothes brightly clean and made of linen cloth.

When fasting, he thought it necessary to change his food, and also to change the place where he commonly sat in the apartment.

He did not dislike to have his rice finely cleaned, nor to have his mince meat cut quite small.

He did not eat rice which had been injured by heat or damp and turned sour, nor fish or flesh which was gone. He did not eat what was discolored, or what was of a bad flavor, nor anything which was ill-cooked, or was not in season.

He did not eat meat which was not cut properly, nor what was served without its proper sauce.

Though there might be a large quantity of meat, he would not allow what he took to exceed the due proportion for the rice. It was only in wine that he laid down no limit for himself, but he did not allow himself to be confused by it.

He did not partake of wine and dried meat bought in the market.

He was never without ginger when he ate. He did not eat much.

When he had been assisting at the prince's sacrifice, he did not keep the flesh which he received overnight. The flesh of his family sacrifice he did not keep over three days. If kept over three days, people could not eat it.

When eating, he did not converse. When in bed, he did not speak.

Although his food might be coarse rice and vegetable soup, he would offer a little of it in sacrifice with a grave, respectful air.

If his mat was not straight, he did not sit on it.

[…]

12

[…]

"If doing what is to be done be made the first business, and success a secondary consideration: is not this the way to exalt virtue? To assail one's own wickedness and not assail that of others; is not this the way to correct cherished evil? For a morning's anger to disregard one's own life, and involve that of his parents; is not this a case of delusion?"

Fan Ch'ih asked about benevolence. The Master said, "It is to love all men." He asked about knowledge. The Master said, "It is to know all men."

[...]

13

[...]

"If names be not correct, language is not in accordance with the truth of things. If language be not in accordance with the truth of things, affairs cannot be carried on to success."

"When affairs cannot be carried on to success, proprieties and music do not flourish. When proprieties and music do not flourish, punishments will not be properly awarded. When punishments are not properly awarded, the people do not know how to move hand or foot."

"Therefore a superior man considers it necessary that the names he uses may be spoken appropriately, and also that what he speaks may be carried out appropriately. What the superior man requires is just that in his words there may be nothing incorrect."

Fan Ch'ih requested to be taught husbandry. The Master said, "I am not so good for that as an old husbandman." He requested also to be taught gardening, and was answered, "I am not so good for that as an old gardener."

Fan Ch'ih having gone out, the Master said, "A small man, indeed, is Fan Hsu! If a superior man love propriety, the people will not dare not to be reverent. If he love righteousness, the people will not dare not to submit to his example. If he love good faith, the people will not dare not to be sincere. Now, when these things obtain, the people from all quarters will come to him, bearing their children on their backs; what need has he of a knowledge of husbandry?"

The Master said, "Though a man may be able to recite the three hundred odes, yet if, when intrusted with a governmental charge, he knows not how to act, or if, when sent to any quarter on a mission, he cannot give his replies unassisted, notwithstanding the extent of his learning, of what practical use is it?"

The Master said, "When a prince's personal conduct is correct, his government is effective without the issuing of orders. If his personal conduct is not correct, he may issue orders, but they will not be followed."

[...]

The Master said, "The superior man is easy to serve and difficult to please. If you try to please him in any way which is not accordant with right, he will not be pleased. But in his employment of men, he uses them according to their capacity. The mean man is difficult to serve, and easy to please. If you try to please him, though it be in a way which is not accordant with right, he may be pleased. But in his employment of men, he wishes them to be equal to everything."

The Master said, "The superior man has a dignified ease without pride. The mean man has pride without a dignified ease."

The Master said, "The firm, the enduring, the simple, and the modest are near to virtue."

Tsze-lu asked, saying, "What qualities must a man possess to entitle him to be called a scholar?" The Master said, "He must be thus: earnest, urgent, and bland; among his friends, earnest and urgent; among his brethren, bland."

The Master said, "Let a good man teach the people seven years, and they may then likewise be employed in war."

The Master said, "To lead an uninstructed people to war, is to throw them away."

14

Hsien asked what was shameful. The Master said, "When good government prevails in a state, to be thinking only of salary; and, when bad government prevails, to be thinking, in the same way, only of salary—this is shameful."

"When the love of superiority, boasting, resentments, and covetousness are repressed, this may be deemed perfect virtue."

The Master said, "This may be regarded as the achievement of what is difficult. But I do not know that it is to be deemed perfect virtue."

The Master said, "The scholar who cherishes the love of comfort is not fit to be deemed a scholar."

The Master said, "When good government prevails in a state, language may be lofty and bold, and actions the same. When bad government prevails, the actions may be lofty and bold, but the language may be with some reserve."

The Master said, "The virtuous will be sure to speak correctly, but those whose speech is good may not always be virtuous. Men of principle are sure to be bold, but those who are bold may not always be men of principle."

[…]

The Master said, "When rulers love to observe the rules of propriety, the people respond readily to the calls on them for service."

Tsze-lu asked what constituted the superior man. The Master said, "The cultivation of himself in reverential carefulness." "And is his all?" said Tsze-lu. "He cultivates himself so as to give rest to others," was the reply. "And is this all?" again asked Tsze-lu. The Master said, "He cultivates himself so as to give rest to all the people. He cultivates himself so as to give rest to all the people…"

[…]

[...]

The Master said, "If a man take no thought about what is distant, he will find sorrow near at hand."

The Master said, "It is all over! I have not seen one who loves virtue as he loves beauty."

The Master said, "Was not Tsang Wan like one who had stolen his situation? He knew the virtue and the talents of Hui of Liu-hsia, and yet did not procure that he should stand with him in court."

The Master said, "He who requires much from himself and little from others, will keep himself from being the object of resentment."

The Master said, "When a man is not in the habit of saying, 'What shall I think of this? What shall I think of this?' I can indeed do nothing with him!"

The Master said, "When a number of people are together, for a whole day, without their conversation turning on righteousness, and when they are fond of carrying out the suggestions of a small shrewdness; theirs is indeed a hard case."

The Master said, "The superior man in everything considers righteousness to be essential. He performs it according to the rules of propriety. He brings it forth in humility. He completes it with sincerity. This is indeed a superior man."

The Master said, "The superior man is distressed by his want of ability. He is not distressed by men's not knowing him."

The Master said, "The superior man dislikes the thought of his name not being mentioned after his death."

The Master said, "What the superior man seeks, is in himself. What the mean man seeks, is in others."

The Master said, "The superior man is dignified, but does not wrangle. He is sociable, but not a partisan."

[...]

[...]

"I have heard that rulers of states and chiefs of families are not troubled lest their people should be few, but are troubled lest they should not keep their several places; that they are not troubled with fears of poverty, but are troubled with fears of a want of contented repose among the people in their several places. For when the people keep their several places, there will be no poverty; when harmony prevails, there will be no scarcity of people; and when there is such a contented repose, there will be no rebellious upsettings."

"So it is. Therefore, if remoter people are not submissive, all the influences of civil culture and virtue are to be cultivated to attract them to be so; and when they have been so attracted, they must be made contented and tranquil."

[...]

Confucius said, "When good government prevails in the empire, ceremonies, music, and punitive military expeditions proceed from the son of Heaven. When bad government prevails in the empire, ceremonies, music, and punitive military expeditions proceed from the princes. When these things proceed from the princes, as a rule, the cases will be few in which they do not lose their power in ten generations. When they proceed from the great officers of the princes, as a rule, the case will be few in which they do not lose their power in five generations. When the subsidiary ministers of the great officers hold in their grasp the orders of the state, as a rule the cases will be few in which they do not lose their power in three generations."

"When right principles prevail in the kingdom, government will not be in the hands of the great officers."

"When right principles prevail in the kingdom, there will be no discussions among the common people."

Confucius said, "The revenue of the state has left the ducal house now for five generations. The government has been in the hands of the great officers for four generations. On this account, the descendants of the three Hwan are much reduced."

Confucius said, "There are three friendships which are advantageous, and three which are injurious. Friendship with the uplight; friendship with the sincere; and friendship with the man of much observation—these are advantageous. Friendship with the man of specious airs; friendship with the insinuatingly soft; and friendship with the glib-tongued—these are injurious."

Confucius said, "There are three things men find enjoyment in which are advantageous, and three things they find enjoyment in which are injurious. To find enjoyment in the discriminating study of ceremonies and music; to find enjoyment in speaking of the goodness of others; to find enjoyment in having many worthy friends: these are advantageous. To find enjoyment in extravagant pleasures; to find enjoyment in idleness and sauntering; to find enjoyment in the pleasures of feasting—these are injurious."

Confucius said, "There are three errors to which they who stand in the presence of a man of virtue and station are liable. They may speak when it does not come to them to speak—this is called rashness."

"They may not speak when it comes to them to speak—this is called concealment. They may speak without looking at the countenance of their superior—this is called blindness."

Confucius said, "There are three things which the superior man guards against. In youth, when the physical powers are not yet settled, he guards against lust. When he is strong and the physical powers are full of vigor, he guards against quarrelsomeness. When he is old, and the animal powers are decayed, he guards against covetousness."

Confucius said, "There are three things of which the superior man stands in awe. He stands in awe of the ordinances of Heaven. He stands in awe of great men. He stands in awe of the words of sages."

"The mean man does not know the ordinances of Heaven, and consequently does not stand in awe of them. He is disrespectful to great men. He makes sport of the words of sages."

Confucius said, "Those who are born with the possession of knowledge are the highest class of men. Those who learn, and so readily get possession of knowledge, are the next. Those who are dull and stupid, and yet compass the learning, are another class next to these."

"As to those who are dull and stupid and yet do not learn; they are the lowest of the people."

Confucius said, "The superior man has nine things which are subjects with him of thoughtful consideration. In regard to the use of his eyes, he is anxious to see clearly. In regard to the use of his ears, he is anxious to hear distinctly. In regard to his countenance, he is anxious that it should be benign. In regard to his demeanor, he is anxious that it should be respectful. In regard to his speech, he is anxious that it should be sincere. In regard to his doing of business, he is anxious that it should be reverently careful. In regard to what he doubts about, he is anxious to question others. When he is angry, he thinks of the difficulties his anger may involve him in. When he sees gain to be got, he thinks of righteousness."

Confucius said, "Contemplating good, and pursuing it, as if they could not reach it; contemplating evil! and shrinking from it, as they would from thrusting the hand into boiling water: I have seen such men, as I have heard such words."

"Living in retirement to study their aims, and practicing righteousness to carry out their principles: I have heard these words, but I have not seen such men."

[…]

17

<..>

Tsze-chang asked Confucius about perfect virtue. Confucius said, "To be able to practice five things everywhere under heaven constitutes perfect virtue." He begged to ask what they were, and was told, "Gravity, generosity of soul, sincerity, earnestness, and kindness. If you are grave, you will not be treated with disrespect. If you are generous, you will win all. If you are sincere, people will repose trust in you. If you are earnest, you will accomplish much. If you are kind, this will enable you to employ the services of others."

[…]

20

[…]

Tsze-chang asked Confucius, saying, "In what way should a person in authority act in order that he may conduct government properly?" The Master replied, "Let him honor the five excellent, and banish away the four bad, things; then may he conduct government properly." Tsze-chang said, "What are meant by the five excellent things?" The Master said, "When the person in authority is beneficent without great expenditure; when he lays tasks on the people without their repining; when he pursues what he desires without being covetous; when he maintains a dignified ease without being proud; when he is majestic without being fierce."

Tsze-chang said, "What is meant by being beneficent without great expenditure?" The Master replied, "When the person in authority makes more beneficial to the people the things from which they naturally derive benefit; is not this being beneficent without great expenditure? When he chooses the labors which are proper, and makes them labor on them, who will repine? When his desires are set on benevolent government, and he secures it, who will accuse him of covetousness? Whether he has to do with many people or few, or with things great or small, he does not dare to indicate any disrespect; is not this to maintain a dignified ease without any pride? He adjusts his clothes and cap, and throws a dignity into his looks, so that, thus dignified, he is looked at with awe; is not this to be majestic without being fierce?"

Tsze-chang then asked, "What are meant by the four bad things?"

The Master said, "To put the people to death without having instructed them—this is called cruelty. To require from them, suddenly, the full tale of work, without having given them warning—this is called oppression. To issue orders as if without urgency, at first, and, when the time comes, to insist on them with severity—this is called injury. And, generally, in the giving pay or rewards to men, to do it in a stingy way—this is called acting the part of a mere official."

The Master said, "Without recognizing the ordinances of Heaven, it is impossible to be a superior man."

"Without an acquaintance with the rules of Propriety, it is impossible for the character to be established."

"Without knowing the force of words, it is impossible to know men."

THE END

Chapter 4
Taoism

The Tao Te Ching

By Lao-tzu

The orientation of the Tao finds lessons in all things, particularly nature. There is a wisdom in nature that tends to get lost as people remove themselves from it. To follow the way of the Tao necessarily involves a profound sense of connectedness with the natural environment, and to live a life guided by an ecological consciousness.

The Tao Te Ching is ascribed to the sage, Lao Tzu (Laozi). The legend has it that Lao Tzu was leaving civilization to live as a hermit in the wilds. He was recognized by a border guard who refused to let him go until he agreed to write down what he knew. Like Socrates in the West, Lao Tzu doubted he actually knew anything. At the insistence of the guard, however, Lao Tzu did write the Tao Te Ching. By some counts, this is second only to the Bible as having the most copies printed throughout history.

The Tao Te Ching is organized in 81 short chapters. In much of it, the paradoxes of life are highlighted, because everything (the tao) is composed of complementarities, or yin/yang pairs. As one can see from a close look at the symbol of the Tao, in the heart of yang is yin, and in the heart of yin is yang. Opposites are becoming one another as part of the grand scheme of life itself.

There is a fractal quality of the Tao, such that its principles are found on all levels, from the tiny atom, with its complementary proton/electron pairs, to the largest systems, and everything in between. The human body's autonomic nervous system, for example, is organized into what Western medicine characterizes as a sympathetic (aiding in fight or flight) system, and a parasympathetic (aiding in digestion, for example). Both are necessary for the healthy operation of the body. When they get out of balance, problems ensue. Much of Taoist philosophy can be seen in such terms. The important thing is balance and centeredness. On this the Taoist and the Confucian ethic are quite close. In everything, it is important to live a life of centeredness, balance and moderation.

Whatever rises must fall. There is a sense of humility in Taoism, born of the sense that triumph and disaster are two sides of the same coin. The word humility comes from the same root as humus, or the decomposing remains of once mighty life such as a tall tree, that is part of the cycle of nature that will become a part of the earth before it is used once again as part of a living, growing entity. The small becomes great and the great becomes small, and it is all part of the unity and complementarity of the tao.

A Taoist principle is that of wu-wei, literally meaning something like doing by not doing. The point of wu-wei is to find the natural flow and timing of life, and to enter into it without fighting it. Think, for example, of a surfer riding a wave. The wave will not be tamed or dominated. At best, the surfer is able to find balance and harmonize with the energy of the wave, thereby riding it rather than being crushed by its energy.

Taoist healing arts, such as qi gong, are based in this principle of balance, and of eliminating blockages of life energy, or ch'i. The Taoist art of feng shui is based on harmonizing living spaces with the universal ch'i energy. Martial arts such as tai ch'i chuan are based on these principles as well. In a related vein, the principle of te, or the judicious use of power in harmony with the universe, is important in Taoism, as it is in Confucianism.

But whereas the focus in Confucianism is more on propriety in social settings, Taoism's focus is more on harmonizing with natural energy. While the two then are quite close in some ways, they are quite different in many regards. Whereas the Confucian seeks to find wisdom through study and learning the classics, performing ritual and obeying society's rules, the Taoist seeks wisdom through harmonizing with nature, practicing tai ch'i and eschewing ritual.

The Taoist seeks to discover and harmonize with the laws of nature, much more so than the humanly created ones. By pushing too hard, one invites the universe to push back, and the results may not be to one's liking, but this too is integral to the tao.

The only thing permanent for the Taoist is change. Ultimately, there is a unity in all things. The idea of wu-ming—literally the "no name" means the return to the original primal force of the Tao.

Let us now consider the Tao Te Ching...

J. Legge, Translator
(Sacred Books of the East, Vol 39) [1891]

1

The Tao that can be trodden is not the enduring and unchanging Tao. The name that can be named is not the enduring and unchanging name.

(Conceived of as) having no name, it is the Originator of heaven and earth; (conceived of as) having a name, it is the Mother of all things.

Always without desire we must be found,
If its deep mystery we would sound;
But if desire always within us be,

Its outer fringe is all that we shall see.

Under these two aspects, it is really the same; but as development takes place, it receives the different names. Together we call them the Mystery. Where the Mystery is the deepest is the gate of all that is subtle and wonderful.

2

All in the world know the beauty of the beautiful, and in doing this they have (the idea of) what ugliness is; they all know the skill of the skilful, and in doing this they have (the idea of) what the want of skill is.

So it is that existence and non-existence give birth the one to (the idea of) the other; that difficulty and ease produce the one (the idea of) the other; that length and shortness fashion out the one the figure of the other; that (the ideas of) height and lowness arise from the contrast of the one with the other; that the musical notes and tones become harmonious through the relation of one with another; and that being before and behind give the idea of one following another.

Therefore the sage manages affairs without doing anything, and conveys his instructions without the use of speech.

All things spring up, and there is not one which declines to show itself; they grow, and there is no claim made for their ownership; they go through their processes, and there is no expectation (of a reward for the results). The work is accomplished, and there is no resting in it (as an achievement).

The work is done, but how no one can see; 'Tis this that makes the power not cease to be.

3

Not to value and employ men of superior ability is the way to keep the people from rivalry among themselves; not to prize articles which are difficult to procure is the way to keep them from becoming thieves; not to show them what is likely to excite their desires is the way to keep their minds from disorder.

Therefore the sage, in the exercise of his government, empties their minds, fills their bellies, weakens their wills, and strengthens their bones.

He constantly (tries to) keep them without knowledge and without desire, and where there are those who have knowledge, to keep them from presuming to act (on it). When there is this abstinence from action, good order is universal.

4

The Tao is (like) the emptiness of a vessel; and in our employment of it we must be on our guard against all fullness. How deep and unfathomable it is, as if it were the Honoured Ancestor of all things!

We should blunt our sharp points, and unravel the complications of things; we should attemper our brightness, and bring ourselves into agreement with the obscurity of others. How pure and still the Tao is, as if it would ever so continue!

I do not know whose son it is. It might appear to have been before God.

5

Heaven and earth do not act from (the impulse of) any wish to be benevolent; they deal with all things as the dogs of grass are dealt with. The sages do not act from (any wish to be) benevolent; they deal with the people as the dogs of grass are dealt with.

May not the space between heaven and earth be compared to a bellows?

'Tis emptied, yet it loses not its power;
'Tis moved again, and sends forth air the more.
Much speech to swift exhaustion lead we see;
Your inner being guard, and keep it free.

6

The valley spirit dies not, aye the same;
The female mystery thus do we name.
Its gate, from which at first they issued forth,
Is called the root from which grew heaven and earth.
Long and unbroken does its power remain,
Used gently, and without the touch of pain.

7

Heaven is long-enduring and earth continues long. The reason why heaven and earth are able to endure and continue thus long is because they do not live of, or for, themselves. This is how they are able to continue and endure.

Therefore the sage puts his own person last, and yet it is found in the foremost place; he treats his person as if it were foreign to him, and yet that person is preserved. Is it not because he has no personal and private ends, that therefore such ends are realised?

8

The highest excellence is like (that of) water. The excellence of water appears in its benefiting all things, and in its occupying, without striving (to the contrary), the low place which all men dislike. Hence (its way) is near to (that of) the Tao.

The excellence of a residence is in (the suitability of) the place; that of the mind is in abysmal stillness; that of associations is in their being with the virtuous; that of government is in its securing good order; that of (the conduct of) affairs is in its ability; and that of (the initiation of) any movement is in its timeliness.

And when (one with the highest excellence) does not wrangle (about his low position), no one finds fault with him.

9

It is better to leave a vessel unfilled, than to attempt to carry it when it is full. If you keep feeling a point that has been sharpened, the point cannot long preserve its sharpness.

When gold and jade fill the hall, their possessor cannot keep them safe. When wealth and honours lead to arrogancy, this brings its evil on itself. When the work is done, and one's name is becoming distinguished, to withdraw into obscurity is the way of Heaven.

10

When the intelligent and animal souls are held together in one embrace, they can be kept from separating. When one gives undivided attention to the (vital) breath, and brings it to the utmost degree of pliancy, he can become as a (tender) babe. When he has cleansed away the most mysterious sights (of his imagination), he can become without a flaw.

In loving the people and ruling the state, cannot he proceed without any (purpose of) action? In the opening and shutting of his gates of heaven, cannot he do so as a female bird? While his intelligence reaches in every direction, cannot he (appear to) be without knowledge?

(The Tao) produces (all things) and nourishes them; it produces them and does not claim them as its own; it does all, and yet does not boast of it; it presides over all, and yet does not control them. This is what is called 'The mysterious Quality' (of the Tao).

11

The thirty spokes unite in the one nave; but it is on the empty space (for the axle), that the use of the wheel depends. Clay is fashioned into vessels; but it is on their empty hollowness, that their use depends. The door and windows are cut out (from the walls) to form an apartment; but it is on the empty space (within), that its use depends. Therefore, what has a (positive) existence serves for profitable adaptation, and what has not that for (actual) usefulness.

12

Colour's five hues from th' eyes their sight will take; Music's five notes the ears as deaf can make; The flavours five deprive the mouth of taste; The chariot course, and the wild hunting waste Make mad the mind; and objects rare and strange, Sought for, men's conduct will to evil change.

Therefore the sage seeks to satisfy (the craving of) the belly, and not the (insatiable longing of the) eyes. He puts from him the latter, and prefers to seek the former.

13

Favour and disgrace would seem equally to be feared; honour and great calamity, to be regarded as personal conditions (of the same kind).

[…]

Therefore he who would administer the kingdom, honouring it as he honours his own person, may be employed to govern it, and he who would administer it with the love which he bears to his own person may be entrusted with it.

14

We look at it, and we do not see it, and we name it 'the Equable.' We listen to it, and we do not hear it, and we name it 'the Inaudible.' We try to grasp it, and do not get hold of it, and we name it 'the Subtle.' With these three qualities, it cannot be made the subject of description; and hence we blend them together and obtain The One.

Its upper part is not bright, and its lower part is not obscure. Ceaseless in its action, it yet cannot be named, and then it again returns and becomes nothing. This is called the Form of the Formless, and the Semblance of the Invisible—this is called the Fleeting and Indeterminable.

We meet it and do not see its Front; we follow it, and do not see its Back. When we can lay hold of the Tao of old to direct the things of the present day, and are able to know it as it was of old in the beginning, this is called (unwinding) the clue of Tao.

15

[…]

Who can (make) the muddy water (clear)? Let it be still, and it will gradually become clear. Who can secure the condition of rest? Let movement go on, and the condition of rest will gradually arise.

They who preserve this method of the Tao do not wish to be full (of themselves). It is through their not being full of themselves that they can afford to seem worn and not appear new and complete.

16

The (state of) vacancy should be brought to the utmost degree, and that of stillness guarded with unwearying vigour.

[…]

This returning to their root is what we call the state of stillness; and that stillness may be called a reporting that they have fulfilled their appointed end.

[…]

Possessed of the Tao, he endures long; and to the end of his bodily life, is exempt from all danger of decay.

17

In the highest antiquity, (the people) did not know that there were (their rulers). In the next age they loved them and praised them. In the next they feared them; in the next they despised them.

Thus it was that when faith (in the Tao) was deficient (in the rulers) a want of faith in them ensued (in the people).

How irresolute did those (earliest rulers) appear, showing (by their reticence) the importance which they set upon their words!

Their work was done and their undertakings were successful, while the people all said, 'We are as we are, of ourselves!'

18

When the Great Tao (Way or Method) ceased to be observed, benevolence and righteousness came into vogue. (Then) appeared wisdom and shrewdness, and there ensued great hypocrisy.

When harmony no longer prevailed throughout the six kinships, filial sons found their manifestation; when the states and clans fell into disorder, loyal ministers appeared.

19

If we could renounce our sageness and discard our wisdom, it would be better for the people a hundredfold. If we could renounce our benevolence and discard our righteousness, the people would again become filial and kindly. If we could renounce our artful contrivances and discard our (scheming for) gain, there would be no thieves nor robbers.

Those three methods (of government)
Thought olden ways in elegance did fail
And made these names their want of worth to veil;
But simple views, and courses plain and true
Would selfish ends and many lusts eschew.

[...]

21

The grandest forms of active force
From Tao come, their only source.
Who can of Tao the nature tell?
Our sight it flies, our touch as well.
Eluding sight, eluding touch,
The forms of things all in it crouch;
Eluding touch, eluding sight,
There are their semblances, all right.
Profound it is, dark and obscure;
Things' essences all there endure.
Those essences the truth enfold
Of what, when seen, shall then be told.
Now it is so; 'twas so of old.
Its name—what passes not away;
So, in their beautiful array,
Things form and never know decay.

How know I that it is so with all the beauties of existing things? By this (nature of
the Tao).

22

The partial becomes complete; the crooked, straight; the empty, full; the worn
out, new. He whose (desires) are few gets them; he whose (desires) are many goes
astray.

Therefore the sage holds in his embrace the one thing (of humility), and manifests
it to all the world. He is free from self-display, and therefore he shines; from self-
assertion, and therefore he is distinguished; from self-boasting, and therefore his merit
is acknowledged; from self-complacency, and therefore he acquires superiority. It is
because he is thus free from striving that therefore no one in the world is able to strive
with him.

That saying of the ancients that 'the partial becomes complete' was not vainly spoken:—all real completion is comprehended under it.

23

Abstaining from speech marks him who is obeying the spontaneity of his nature. A violent wind does not last for a whole morning; a sudden rain does not last for the whole day. To whom is it that these (two) things are owing? To Heaven and Earth. If Heaven and Earth cannot make such (spasmodic) actings last long, how much less can man!

[…]

24

He who stands on his tiptoes does not stand firm; he who stretches his legs does not walk (easily). (So), he who displays himself does not shine; he who asserts his own views is not distinguished; he who vaunts himself does not find his merit acknowledged; he who is self-conceited has no superiority allowed to him. Such conditions, viewed from the standpoint of the Tao, are like remnants of food, or a tumour on the body, which all dislike. Hence those who pursue (the course) of the Tao do not adopt and allow them.

25

There was something undefined and complete, coming into existence before Heaven and Earth. How still it was and formless, standing alone, and undergoing no change, reaching everywhere and in no danger (of being exhausted)! It may be regarded as the Mother of all things.

I do not know its name, and I give it the designation of the Tao (the Way or Course). Making an effort (further) to give it a name I call it The Great.

Great, it passes on (in constant flow). Passing on, it becomes remote. Having become remote, it returns. Therefore the Tao is great; Heaven is great; Earth is great; and the (sage) king is also great. In the universe there are four that are great, and the (sage) king is one of them.

Man takes his law from the Earth; the Earth takes its law from Heaven; Heaven takes its law from the Tao. The law of the Tao is its being what it is.

26

Gravity is the root of lightness; stillness, the ruler of movement.

Therefore a wise prince, marching the whole day, does not go far from his baggage waggons. Although he may have brilliant prospects to look at, he quietly remains (in his proper place), indifferent to them. How should the lord of a myriad chariots carry himself lightly before the kingdom? If he do act lightly, he has lost his root (of gravity); if he proceed to active movement, he will lose his throne.

27

The skilful traveller leaves no traces of his wheels or footsteps; the skilful speaker says nothing that can be found fault with or blamed; the skilful reckoner uses no tallies; the skilful closer needs no bolts or bars, while to open what he has shut will be impossible; the skilful binder uses no strings or knots, while to unloose what he has bound will be impossible. In the same way the sage is always skilful at saving men, and so he does not cast away any man; he is always skilful at saving things, and so he does not cast away anything. This is called 'Hiding the light of his procedure.'

[…]

28

Who knows his manhood's strength,
Yet still his female feebleness maintains;
As to one channel flow the many drains,
All come to him, yea, all beneath the sky.
Thus he the constant excellence retains;
The simple child again, free from all stains.

[…]

Who knows how glory shines,
Yet loves disgrace, nor e'er for it is pale;
Behold his presence in a spacious vale,
To which men come from all beneath the sky.
The unchanging excellence completes its tale;
The simple infant man in him we hail.

The unwrought material, when divided and distributed, forms vessels. The sage, when employed, becomes the Head of all the Officers (of government); and in his greatest regulations he employs no violent measures.

29

If any one should wish to get the kingdom for himself, and to effect this by what he does, I see that he will not succeed. The kingdom is a spirit-like thing, and cannot be got by active doing. He who would so win it destroys it; he who would hold it in his grasp loses it.

The course and nature of things is such that
What was in front is now behind;
What warmed anon we freezing find.
Strength is of weakness oft the spoil;
The store in ruins mocks our toil.

Hence the sage puts away excessive effort, extravagance, and easy indulgence.

30

He who would assist a lord of men in harmony with the Tao will not assert his mastery in the kingdom by force of arms. Such a course is sure to meet with its proper return.

Wherever a host is stationed, briars and thorns spring up. In the sequence of great armies there are sure to be bad years.

A skilful (commander) strikes a decisive blow, and stops. He does not dare (by continuing his operations) to assert and complete his mastery. He will strike the blow, but will be on his guard against being vain or boastful or arrogant in consequence of it. He strikes it as a matter of necessity; he strikes it, but not from a wish for mastery.

When things have attained their strong maturity they become old.

This may be said to be not in accordance with the Tao: and what is not in accordance with it soon comes to an end.

31

Now arms, however beautiful, are instruments of evil omen, hateful, it may be said, to all creatures. Therefore they who have the Tao do not like to employ them.

[…]

He who has killed multitudes of men should weep for them with the bitterest grief; and the victor in battle has his place (rightly) according to those rites.

32

The Tao, considered as unchanging, has no name.

Though in its primordial simplicity it may be small, the whole world dares not deal with (one embodying) it as a minister. If a feudal prince or the king could guard and hold it, all would spontaneously submit themselves to him.

Heaven and Earth (under its guidance) unite together and send down the sweet dew, which, without the directions of men, reaches equally everywhere as of its own accord.

As soon as it proceeds to action, it has a name. When it once has that name, (men) can know to rest in it. When they know to rest in it, they can be free from all risk of failure and error.

The relation of the Tao to all the world is like that of the great rivers and seas to the streams from the valleys.

33

He who knows other men is discerning; he who knows himself is intelligent. He who overcomes others is strong; he who overcomes himself is mighty. He who is satisfied with his lot is rich; he who goes on acting with energy has a (firm) will.

He who does not fail in the requirements of his position, continues long; he who dies and yet does not perish, has longevity.

34

All-pervading is the Great Tao! It may be found on the left hand and on the right.

All things depend on it for their production, which it gives to them, not one refusing obedience to it. When its work is accomplished, it does not claim the name of having done it. It clothes all things as with a garment, and makes no assumption of being their lord;—it may be named in the smallest things. All things return (to their root and disappear), and do not know that it is it which presides over their doing so;—it may be named in the greatest things.

Hence the sage is able (in the same way) to accomplish his great achievements. It is through his not making himself great that he can accomplish them.

[...]

36

When one is about to take an inspiration, he is sure to make a (previous) expiration; when he is going to weaken another, he will first strengthen him; when he is going to overthrow another, he will first have raised him up; when he is going to despoil another, he will first have made gifts to him:—this is called 'Hiding the light (of his procedure).'

The soft overcomes the hard; and the weak the strong.

Fishes should not be taken from the deep; instruments for the profit of a state should not be shown to the people.

37

The Tao in its regular course does nothing (for the sake of doing it), and so there is nothing which it does not do.

If princes and kings were able to maintain it, all things would of themselves be transformed by them.

If this transformation became to me an object of desire, I would express the desire by the nameless simplicity.

Simplicity without a name
Is free from all external aim.
With no desire, at rest and still,
All things go right as of their will.

38

(Those who) possessed in highest degree the attributes (of the Tao) did not (seek) to show them, and therefore they possessed them (in fullest measure). (Those who) possessed in a lower degree those attributes (sought how) not to lose them, and therefore they did not possess them (in fullest measure).

[...]

Thus it was that when the Tao was lost, its attributes appeared; when its attributes were lost, benevolence appeared; when benevolence was lost, righteousness appeared; and when righteousness was lost, the proprieties appeared.

[...]

39

The things which from of old have got the One (the Tao) are—

Heaven which by it is bright and pure;
Earth rendered thereby firm and sure;
Spirits with powers by it supplied;
Valleys kept full throughout their void
All creatures which through it do live
Princes and kings who from it get

The model which to all they give.

All these are the results of the One (Tao).

[...]

40

The movement of the Tao
By contraries proceeds;
And weakness marks the course
Of Tao's mighty deeds.
All things under heaven sprang from
It as existing (and named); that existence sprang from
It as non-existent (and not named).

41

Scholars of the highest class, when they hear about the Tao, earnestly carry it into practice. Scholars of the middle class, when they have heard about it, seem now to keep it and now to lose it.

Scholars of the lowest class, when they have heard about it, laugh greatly at it. If it were not (thus) laughed at, it would not be fit to be the Tao.

Therefore the sentence-makers have thus expressed themselves:—

'The Tao, when brightest seen, seems light to lack;
Who progress in it makes, seems drawing back;
Its even way is like a rugged track.
Its highest virtue from the vale doth rise;
Its greatest beauty seems to offend the eyes;
And he has most whose lot the least supplies.
Its firmest virtue seems but poor and low;
Its solid truth seems change to undergo;
Its largest square doth yet no corner show
A vessel great, it is the slowest made;
Loud is its sound, but never word it said;
A semblance great, the shadow of a shade.'

The Tao is hidden, and has no name; but it is the Tao which is skilful at imparting (to all things what they need) and making them complete.

42

The Tao produced One; One produced Two; Two produced Three; Three produced All things. All things leave behind them the Obscurity (out of which they have come), and go forward to embrace the Brightness (into which they have emerged), while they are harmonised by the Breath of Vacancy.

[…]

43

The softest thing in the world dashes against and overcomes the hardest; that which has no (substantial) existence enters where there is no crevice. I know hereby what advantage belongs to doing nothing (with a purpose).

There are few in the world who attain to the teaching without words, and the advantage arising from non-action.

44

Or fame or life,
Which do you hold more dear?
Or life or wealth,
To which would you adhere?
Keep life and lose those other things;
Keep them and lose your life:—which brings
Sorrow and pain more near?

Thus we may see,
Who cleaves to fame
Rejects what is more great;
Who loves large stores
Gives up the richer state.

Who is content
Needs fear no shame.
Who knows to stop
Incurs no blame.
From danger free
Long live shall he.

45

Who thinks his great achievements poor

Shall find his vigour long endure.
Of greatest fullness, deemed a void,
Exhaustion ne'er shall stem the tide.
Do thou what's straight still crooked deem;
Thy greatest art still stupid seem,
And eloquence a stammering scream.

Constant action overcomes cold; being still overcomes heat. Purity and stillness give the correct law to all under heaven.

46

When the Tao prevails in the world, they send back their swift horses to (draw) the dung-carts. When the Tao is disregarded in the world, the war-horses breed in the border lands.

There is no guilt greater than to sanction ambition; no calamity greater than to be discontented with one's lot; no fault greater than the wish to be getting. Therefore the sufficiency of contentment is an enduring and unchanging sufficiency.

47

Without going outside his door, one understands (all that takes place) under the sky; without looking out from his window, one sees the Tao of Heaven. The farther that one goes out (from himself), the less he knows.

Therefore the sages got their knowledge without travelling; gave their (right) names to things without seeing them; and accomplished their ends without any purpose of doing so.

48

He who devotes himself to learning (seeks) from day to day to increase (his knowledge); he who devotes himself to the Tao (seeks) from day to day to diminish (his doing).

He diminishes it and again diminishes it, till he arrives at doing nothing (on purpose). Having arrived at this point of non-action, there is nothing which he does not do.

He who gets as his own all under heaven does so by giving himself no trouble (with that end). If one take trouble (with that end), he is not equal to getting as his own all under heaven.

49

The sage has no invariable mind of his own; he makes the mind of the people his mind.

To those who are good (to me), I am good; and to those who are not good (to me), I am also good;—and thus (all) get to be good. To those who are sincere (with me), I am sincere; and to those who are not sincere (with me), I am also sincere;—and thus (all) get to be sincere.

The sage has in the world an appearance of indecision, and keeps his mind in a state of indifference to all. The people all keep their eyes and ears directed to him, and he deals with them all as his children.

50

Men come forth and live; they enter (again) and die.

Of every ten three are ministers of life (to themselves); and three are ministers of death.

There are also three in every ten whose aim is to live, but whose movements tend to the land (or place) of death. And for what reason?

Because of their excessive endeavours to perpetuate life.

[...]

51

All things are produced by the Tao, and nourished by its outflowing operation. They receive their forms according to the nature of each, and are completed according to the circumstances of their condition. Therefore all things without exception honour the Tao, and exalt its outflowing operation.

This honouring of the Tao and exalting of its operation is not the result of any ordination, but always a spontaneous tribute.

Thus it is that the Tao produces (all things), nourishes them, brings them to their full growth, nurses them, completes them, matures them, maintains them, and overspreads them.

It produces them and makes no claim to the possession of them; it carries them through their processes and does not vaunt its ability in doing so; it brings them to maturity and exercises no control over them;—this is called its mysterious operation.

52

(The Tao) which originated all under the sky is to be considered as the mother of them all.

When the mother is found, we know what her children should be.

When one knows that he is his mother's child, and proceeds to guard (the qualities of) the mother that belong to him, to the end of his life he will be free from all peril.

Let him keep his mouth closed, and shut up the portals (of his nostrils), and all his life he will be exempt from laborious exertion.

Let him keep his mouth open, and (spend his breath) in the promotion of his affairs, and all his life there will be no safety for him.

The perception of what is small is (the secret of clear-sightedness; the guarding of what is soft and tender is (the secret of) strength.

Who uses well his light,
Reverting to its (source so) bright,
Will from his body ward all blight,
And hides the unchanging from men's sight.

53

If I were suddenly to become known, and (put into a position to) conduct (a government) according to the Great Tao, what I should be most afraid of would be a boastful display.

[...]

54

What (Tao's) skilful planter plants
Can never be uptorn;
What his skilful arms enfold,
From him can ne'er be borne.
Sons shall bring in lengthening line,
Sacrifices to his shrine.

Tao when nursed within one's self,
His vigour will make true;
And where the family it rules
What riches will accrue!
The neighbourhood where it prevails
In thriving will abound;
And when 'tis seen throughout the state,
Good fortune will be found.
Employ it the kingdom o'er,
And men thrive all around.

[...]

He who has in himself abundantly the attributes (of the Tao) is like an infant. Poisonous insects will not sting him; fierce beasts will not seize him; birds of prey will not strike him.

(The infant's) bones are weak and its sinews soft, but yet its grasp is firm. It knows not yet the union of male and female, and yet its virile member may be excited;—showing the perfection of its physical essence. All day long it will cry without its throat becoming hoarse;—showing the harmony (in its constitution).

> To him by whom this harmony is known,
> (The secret of) the unchanging (Tao) is shown,
> And in the knowledge wisdom finds its throne.
> All life-increasing arts to evil turn;
> Where the mind makes the vital breath to burn,
> (False) is the strength, (and o'er it we should mourn.)

When things have become strong, they (then) become old, which may be said to be contrary to the Tao. Whatever is contrary to the Tao soon ends.

He who knows (the Tao) does not (care to) speak (about it); he who is (ever ready to) speak about it does not know it.

[…]
(Such an one) cannot be treated familiarly or distantly; he is beyond all consideration of profit or injury; of nobility or meanness:—he is the noblest man under heaven.

A state may be ruled by (measures of) correction; weapons of war may be used with crafty dexterity; (but) the kingdom is made one's own (only) by freedom from action and purpose.

How do I know that it is so? By these facts:—In the kingdom the multiplication of prohibitive enactments increases the poverty of the people; the more implements to add to their profit that the people have, the greater disorder is there in the state and clan; the more acts of crafty dexterity that men possess, the more do strange contrivances appear; the more display there is of legislation, the more thieves and robbers there are.

[…]

58

The government that seems the most unwise,
Oft goodness to the people best supplies;
That which is meddling, touching everything,
Will work but ill, and disappointment bring.

[...]

59

For regulating the human (in our constitution) and rendering the (proper) service to the heavenly, there is nothing like moderation.

It is only by this moderation that there is effected an early return (to man's normal state). That early return is what I call the repeated accumulation of the attributes (of the Tao).

[...]

60

Governing a great state is like cooking small fish.

Let the kingdom be governed according to the Tao, and the manes of the departed will not manifest their spiritual energy. It is not that those manes have not that spiritual energy, but it will not be employed to hurt men. It is not that it could not hurt men, but neither does the ruling sage hurt them.

When these two do not injuriously affect each other, their good influences converge in the virtue (of the Tao).

61

What makes a great state is its being (like) a low-lying, down-flowing (stream);—it becomes the centre to which tend (all the small states) under heaven.

(To illustrate from) the case of all females:—the female always overcomes the male by her stillness. Stillness may be considered (a sort of) abasement.

Thus it is that a great state, by condescending to small states, gains them for itself; and that small states, by abasing themselves to a great state, win it over to them. In the one case the abasement leads to gaining adherents, in the other case to procuring favour.

The great state only wishes to unite men together and nourish them; a small state only wishes to be received by, and to serve, the other. Each gets what it desires, but the great state must learn to abase itself.

62

Tao has of all things the most honoured place.
No treasures give good men so rich a grace;
Bad men it guards, and doth their ill efface.

(Its) admirable words can purchase honour; (its) admirable deeds can raise their performer above others. Even men who are not good are not abandoned by it.

[…]

63

(It is the way of the Tao) to act without (thinking of) acting; to conduct affairs without (feeling the) trouble of them; to taste without discerning any flavour; to consider what is small as great, and a few as many; and to recompense injury with kindness.

(The master of it) anticipates things that are difficult while they are easy, and does things that would become great while they are small. All difficult things in the world are sure to arise from a previous state in which they were easy, and all great things from one in which they were small. Therefore the sage, while he never does what is great, is able on that account to accomplish the greatest things.

He who lightly promises is sure to keep but little faith; he who is continually thinking things easy is sure to find them difficult. Therefore the sage sees difficulty even in what seems easy, and so never has any difficulties.

64

That which is at rest is easily kept hold of; before a thing has given indications of its presence, it is easy to take measures against it; that which is brittle is easily broken; that which is very small is easily dispersed. Action should be taken before a thing has made its appearance; order should be secured before disorder has begun.

The tree which fills the arms grew from the tiniest sprout; the tower of nine storeys rose from a (small) heap of earth; the journey of a thousand li commenced with a single step.

He who acts (with an ulterior purpose) does harm; he who takes hold of a thing (in the same way) loses his hold. The sage does not act (so), and therefore does no harm; he does not lay hold (so), and therefore does not lose his hold. (But) people in their conduct of affairs are constantly ruining them when they are on the eve of success. If they were careful at the end, as (they should be) at the beginning, they would not so ruin them.

Therefore the sage desires what (other men) do not desire, and does not prize things difficult to get; he learns what (other men) do not learn, and turns back to what the multitude of men have passed by. Thus he helps the natural development of all things, and does not dare to act (with an ulterior purpose of his own).

65

The ancients who showed their skill in practising the Tao did so, not to enlighten the people, but rather to make them simple and ignorant.

The difficulty in governing the people arises from their having much knowledge. He who (tries to) govern a state by his wisdom is a scourge to it; while he who does not (try to) do so is a blessing.

He who knows these two things finds in them also his model and rule. Ability to know this model and rule constitutes what we call the mysterious excellence (of a governor). Deep and far-reaching is such mysterious excellence, showing indeed its possessor as opposite to others, but leading them to a great conformity to him.

66

That whereby the rivers and seas are able to receive the homage and tribute of all the valley streams, is their skill in being lower than they;—it is thus that they are the kings of them all. So it is that the sage (ruler), wishing to be above men, puts himself by his words below them, and, wishing to be before them, places his person behind them.

In this way though he has his place above them, men do not feel his weight, nor though he has his place before them, do they feel it an injury to them.

Therefore all in the world delight to exalt him and do not weary of him. Because he does not strive, no one finds it possible to strive with him.

67

All the world says that, while my Tao is great, it yet appears to be inferior (to other systems of teaching). Now it is just its greatness that makes it seem to be inferior. If it were like any other (system), for long would its smallness have been known!

But I have three precious things which I prize and hold fast. The first is gentleness; the second is economy; and the third is shrinking from taking precedence of others.

With that gentleness I can be bold; with that economy I can be liberal; shrinking from taking precedence of others, I can become a vessel of the highest honour. Now-a-days they give up gentleness and are all for being bold; economy, and are all for being liberal; the hindmost place, and seek only to be foremost;—(of all which the end is) death.

Gentleness is sure to be victorious even in battle, and firmly to maintain its ground. Heaven will save its possessor, by his (very) gentleness protecting him.

He who in (Tao's) wars has skill
Assumes no martial port;
He who fights with most good will
To rage makes no resort.
He who vanquishes yet still
Keeps from his foes apart;
He whose hests men most fulfil
Yet humbly plies his art.

Thus we say, 'He ne'er contends,
And therein is his might.'
Thus we say, 'Men's wills he bends,
That they with him unite.'
Thus we say, 'Like Heaven's his ends,
No sage of old more bright.'

A master of the art of war has said, 'I do not dare to be the host (to commence the war); I prefer to be the guest (to act on the defensive). I do not dare to advance an inch; I prefer to retire a foot.' This is called marshalling the ranks where there are no ranks; baring the arms (to fight) where there are no arms to bare; grasping the weapon where there is no weapon to grasp; advancing against the enemy where there is no enemy.

There is no calamity greater than lightly engaging in war. To do that is near losing (the gentleness) which is so precious. Thus it is that when opposing weapons are (actually) crossed, he who deplores (the situation) conquers.

My words are very easy to know, and very easy to practise; but there is no one in the world who is able to know and able to practise them.

There is an originating and all-comprehending (principle) in my words, and an authoritative law for the things (which I enforce). It is because they do not know these, that men do not know me.

They who know me are few, and I am on that account (the more) to be prized. It is thus that the sage wears (a poor garb of) hair cloth, while he carries his (signet of) jade in his bosom.

71

To know and yet (think) we do not know is the highest (attainment); not to know (and yet think) we do know is a disease.

It is simply by being pained at (the thought of) having this disease that we are preserved from it. The sage has not the disease.

He knows the pain that would be inseparable from it, and therefore he does not have it.

72

When the people do not fear what they ought to fear, that which is their great dread will come on them.

Let them not thoughtlessly indulge themselves in their ordinary life; let them not act as if weary of what that life depends on.

It is by avoiding such indulgence that such weariness does not arise.

Therefore the sage knows (these things) of himself, but does not parade (his knowledge); loves, but does not (appear to set a) value on, himself. And thus he puts the latter alternative away and makes choice of the former.

73

He whose boldness appears in his daring (to do wrong, in defiance of the laws) is put to death; he whose boldness appears in his not daring (to do so) lives on. Of these two cases the one appears to be advantageous, and the other to be injurious. But

When Heaven's anger smites a man,
Who the cause shall truly scan?

On this account the sage feels a difficulty (as to what to do in the former case).

It is the way of Heaven not to strive, and yet it skillfully overcomes; not to speak, and yet it is skilful in (obtaining a reply; does not call, and yet men come to it of themselves. Its demonstrations are quiet, and yet its plans are skilful and effective. The meshes of the net of Heaven are large; far apart, but letting nothing escape.

74

The people do not fear death; to what purpose is it to (try to) frighten them with death? If the people were always in awe of death, and I could always seize those who do wrong, and put them to death, who would dare to do wrong?

There is always One who presides over the infliction death. He who would inflict death in the room of him who so presides over it may be described as hewing wood instead of a great carpenter. Seldom is it that he who undertakes the hewing, instead of the great carpenter, does not cut his own hands!

75

The people suffer from famine because of the multitude of taxes consumed by their superiors. It is through this that they suffer famine.

The people are difficult to govern because of the (excessive) agency of their superiors (in governing them). It is through this that they are difficult to govern.

The people make light of dying because of the greatness of their labours in seeking for the means of living. It is this which makes them think light of dying. Thus it is that to leave the subject of living altogether out of view is better than to set a high value on it.

76

Man at his birth is supple and weak; at his death, firm and strong. (So it is with) all things. Trees and plants, in their early growth, are soft and brittle; at their death, dry and withered.

Thus it is that firmness and strength are the concomitants of death; softness and weakness, the concomitants of life.

Hence he who (relies on) the strength of his forces does not conquer; and a tree which is strong will fill the out-stretched arms, (and thereby invites the feller.)

Therefore the place of what is firm and strong is below, and that of what is soft and weak is above.

77

May not the Way (or Tao) of Heaven be compared to the (method of) bending a bow? The (part of the bow) which was high is brought low, and what was low is raised up. (So Heaven) diminishes where there is superabundance, and supplements where there is deficiency.

It is the Way of Heaven to diminish superabundance, and to supplement deficiency. It is not so with the way of man. He takes away from those who have not enough to add to his own superabundance.

Who can take his own superabundance and therewith serve all under heaven? Only he who is in possession of the Tao!

Therefore the (ruling) sage acts without claiming the results as his; he achieves his merit and does not rest (arrogantly) in it:—he does not wish to display his superiority.

There is nothing in the world more soft and weak than water, and yet for attacking things that are firm and strong there is nothing that can take precedence of it;—for there is nothing (so effectual) for which it can be changed.

Every one in the world knows that the soft overcomes the hard, and the weak the strong, but no one is able to carry it out in practice.

Therefore a sage has said,
'He who accepts his state's reproach,
Is hailed therefore its altars' lord;
To him who bears men's direful woes
They all the name of King accord.'

Words that are strictly true seem to be paradoxical.

When a reconciliation is effected (between two parties) after a great animosity, there is sure to be a grudge remaining (in the mind of the one who was wrong). And how can this be beneficial (to the other)?

Therefore (to guard against this), the sage keeps the left-hand portion of the record of the engagement, and does not insist on the (speedy) fulfilment of it by the other party. (So), he who has the attributes (of the Tao) regards (only) the conditions of the engagement, while he who has not those attributes regards only the conditions favourable to himself.

In the Way of Heaven, there is no partiality of love; it is always on the side of the good man.

In a little state with a small population, I would so order it, that, though there were individuals with the abilities of ten or a hundred men, there should be no employment of them; I would make the people, while looking on death as a grievous thing, yet not remove elsewhere (to avoid it).

Though they had boats and carriages, they should have no occasion to ride in them; though they had buff coats and sharp weapons, they should have no occasion to don or use them.

I would make the people return to the use of knotted cords (instead of the written characters).

They should think their (coarse) food sweet; their (plain) clothes beautiful; their (poor) dwellings places of rest; and their common (simple) ways sources of enjoyment.

There should be a neighbouring state within sight, and the voices of the fowls and dogs should be heard all the way from it to us, but I would make the people to old age, even to death, not have any intercourse with it.

Sincere words are not fine; fine words are not sincere. Those who are skilled (in the Tao) do not dispute (about it); the disputatious are not skilled in it. Those who know (the Tao) are not extensively learned; the extensively learned do not know it.

The sage does not accumulate (for himself). The more that he expends for others, the more does he possess of his own; the more that he gives to others, the more does he have himself.

With all the sharpness of the Way of Heaven, it injures not; with all the doing in the way of the sage he does not strive.

Chapter 5
Judaism

The Tanakh—The Jewish Bible

The Tanakh or Jewish Bible is structured in three major parts: the Torah, or the Mosaic Books of Genesis, Exodus, Leviticus, Numbers, and Deuteronomy; the Nevi'im, or the Books of the Prophets and Kings; and the Ketuvim, composed of other writings such as the Psalms and Proverbs. These are the books of the Old Testament of the Christian Bible, albeit in a somewhat different order.

The Torah is considered as the most sacred of texts, and it is the Torah that receives the most of our attention here. We have selections from Genesis, Exodus, and Deuteronomy. The passages from Genesis speak to Jewish ideas about the creation of the earth and of humankind, in the persons of Adam and Eve. Later, it tells the story of God's covenant with Abraham, in which the Jewish people become God's chosen people.

Christianity and Islam also hearken back to God's covenant with Abraham. While the number of Jewish people in contemporary times is relatively small (estimates converge at about 14 million worldwide), these other two "Abrahamic" religions taken together now comprise a bit over half of the world's population.

The Book of Exodus picks up where the Book of Genesis leaves off. Exodus tells the story of key parts of Jewish history, including the life of Moses as the leader of the Jewish people, and their 40 years of wandering in the desert wilderness.

The Book of Exodus is loaded with key events in Jewish history. It chronicles the original Passover, which is still commemorated every year in the Spring, as an integral part of the Jewish calendar.

Exodus tells of the Jewish people leaving Egypt and the parting of the Red Sea so that they can escape just before the army of the Egyptian Pharoah. While in the desert, the people are spared of starvation by being given manna from Heaven. Moses receives the Law from God in the form of the Ten Commandments.

The story of the Jewish people is continued. We pick it up again at the end of the Book of Deuteronomy. Moses, now old and failing, dies in Moab, after viewing the Promised Land from atop Mount Nebo. The Jewish people do eventually enter the Promised Land. Ironically though, Moses, their great leader, dies just before he himself could enter the Promised Land. Upon the death of Moses, Joshua becomes the leader.

From the Nevi'im, we have selections from the Major Prophet, Jeremiah. In these passages, Jeremiah castigates the Jewish people for worshipping false idols. Although God led the people of Israel out of slavery in Egypt and into the Promised Land, the people have not been sufficiently grateful. Rather, they have paid homage to false gods and, in so doing, have violated the Law given from God to Moses that we encounter in Exodus. Jeremiah prophesies that because they have incurred the wrath of God, the nation will suffer crushing defeat and captivity in Babylon. As we see in the last chapter of Jeremiah, the fall of Jerusalem to the Babylonians does indeed come to pass.

From the Ketuvim, we have the Psalms. This is, incidentally, the longest of the books of the Tanakh. Many of them take the form of poetry or song. A large number of them were written by David. One of the most well known and often recited is the 23rd Psalm, sometimes referred to as a "Psalm of David." We also consider the 137th Psalm, from the time of the Babylonian captivity. The haunting refrain of the first line of this Psalm ("By the rivers of Babylon...") has made it into modern folk songs, sometimes sung in Taize fashion.

The choice from the Book of Proverbs, chapter 8, is a meditation on wisdom. The ultimate source of wisdom is God. Wisdom, it goes on to say, is more precious than earthly possessions such as gold or the finest jewels.

Let us now turn to the Tanakh...

Genesis Chapter 1

In the beginning God created the heaven and the earth. And the earth was without form, and void; and darkness was upon the face of the deep. And the Spirit of God moved upon the face of the waters. And God said, Let there be light: and there was light. And God saw the light, that it was good: and God divided the light from the darkness. And God called the light Day, and the darkness he called Night. And the evening and the morning were the first day. And God said, Let there be a firmament in the midst of the waters, and let it divide the waters from the waters. And God made the firmament, and divided the waters which were under the firmament from the waters which were above the firmament: and it was so. And God called the firmament Heaven. And the evening and the morning were the second day. And God said, Let the waters under the heaven be gathered together unto one place, and let the dry land appear: and it was so. And God called the dry land Earth; and the gathering together of the waters called he Seas: and God saw that it was good. And God said, Let the earth bring forth grass, the herb yielding seed, and the fruit tree yielding fruit after his kind, whose seed is in itself, upon the earth: and it was so. And the earth brought forth grass, and herb yielding seed after his kind, and the tree yielding fruit, whose seed was in itself, after his kind: and God saw that it was good. And the evening and the morning were the third day. And God said, Let there be lights in the firmament of the heaven to divide the day from the night; and let them be for signs, and for seasons, and for days, and years: And let them be for lights in the firmament of the heaven to give light upon the earth: and it was so. And God made two great lights; the greater light to rule the day, and the lesser light to rule the night: he made the stars also. And God set them in the firmament of the heaven to give light upon the earth, And to rule over the day and over the night, and to divide the light from the darkness: and God saw that it was good. And the evening and the morning were the fourth day. And God said, Let the waters bring forth abundantly the moving creature that hath life, and fowl that may fly above the earth in the open firmament of heaven. And God created great whales, and every living creature that moveth, which the waters brought forth abundantly, after their kind, and every winged fowl after his kind: and God saw that it was good. And God blessed them, saying, Be fruitful, and multiply, and fill the waters in the seas, and let fowl multiply in the earth. And the evening and the morning were the fifth day. And God said, Let the earth bring forth the living creature after his kind, cattle, and creeping thing, and beast of the earth after his kind: and it was so. And God made the beast of the earth after his kind, and cattle after their kind, and every thing that creepeth upon the earth after his kind: and God saw that it was good. And God said, Let us make man in our image, after our likeness: and let them have dominion over the fish of the sea, and over the fowl of the air, and over the cattle, and over all the earth, and over every creeping thing that creepeth upon the earth. So God created man in his own image, in the image of God created he him; male and female created he them. And God blessed them, and God said unto them, Be fruitful, and multiply, and replenish the earth, and subdue it: and have dominion over the fish of the sea, and over the fowl of the air, and over every living thing that moveth upon the earth. And God said, Behold, I have given you every herb bearing seed, which is upon the face of all the earth, and every tree, in the which is the fruit of a tree yielding seed; to you it shall be for meat. And to every beast of the earth, and to every fowl of the air, and to every thing that creepeth upon the earth, wherein there is life, I have given every green herb for meat: and it was so. And God saw every thing that he had made, and, behold, it was very good. And the evening and the morning were the sixth day.

Genesis Chapter 2

Thus the heavens and the earth were finished, and all the host of them. And on the seventh day God ended his work which he had made; and he rested on the seventh day from all his work which he had made. And God blessed the seventh day, and sanctified it: because that in it he had rested from all his work which God created and made. These are the generations of the heavens and of the earth when they were created, in the day that the LORD God made the earth and the heavens, And every plant of the field before it was in the earth, and every herb of the field before it grew: for the LORD God had not caused it to rain upon the earth, and there was not a man to till the ground. But there went up a mist from the earth, and watered the whole face of the ground. And the LORD God formed man of the dust of the ground, and breathed into his nostrils the breath of life; and man became a living soul. And the LORD God planted a garden eastward in Eden; and there he put the man whom he had formed. And out of the ground made the LORD God to grow every tree that is pleasant to the sight, and good for food; the tree of life also in the midst of the garden, and the tree of knowledge of good and evil. And a river went out of Eden to water the garden; and from thence it was parted…

[…]

And the LORD God took the man, and put him into the garden of Eden to dress it and to keep it. And the LORD God commanded the man, saying, Of every tree of the garden thou mayest freely eat: But of the tree of the knowledge of good and evil, thou shalt not eat of it: for in the day that thou eatest thereof thou shalt surely die. And the LORD God said, It is not good that the man should be alone; I will make him an help meet for him. And out of the ground the LORD God formed every beast of the field, and every fowl of the air; and brought them unto Adam to see what he would call them: and whatsoever Adam called every living creature, that was the name thereof. And Adam gave names to all cattle, and to the fowl of the air, and to every beast of the field; but for Adam there was not found an help meet for him. And the LORD God caused a deep sleep to fall upon Adam, and he slept: and he took one of his ribs, and closed up the flesh instead thereof; And the rib, which the LORD God had taken from man, made he a woman, and brought her unto the man. And Adam said, This is now bone of my bones, and flesh of my flesh: she shall be called Woman, because she was taken out of Man. Therefore shall a man leave his father and his mother, and shall cleave unto his wife: and they shall be one flesh. And they were both naked, the man and his wife, and were not ashamed.

Genesis Chapter 3

Now the serpent was more subtle than any beast of the field which the LORD God had made. And he said unto the woman, Yea, hath God said, Ye shall not eat of every tree of the garden? And the woman said unto the serpent, We may eat of the fruit of the trees of the garden: But of the fruit of the tree which is in the midst of the garden, God hath said, Ye shall not eat of it, neither shall ye touch it, lest ye die. And the serpent said unto the woman, Ye shall not surely die: For God doth know that in the day ye eat thereof, then your eyes shall be opened, and ye shall be as gods, knowing good and evil. And when the woman saw that the tree was good for food, and that it was pleasant to the eyes, and a tree to be desired to make one wise, she took of the fruit thereof, and did eat, and gave also unto her husband with her; and he did eat. And the eyes of them both were opened, and they knew that they were naked; and they sewed fig leaves together, and made themselves aprons. And they heard the voice of the LORD God walking in the garden in the cool of the day: and Adam and his wife hid themselves from the presence of the LORD God amongst the trees of the garden. And the LORD God called unto Adam, and said unto him, Where art thou? And he said, I heard thy voice in the garden, and I was afraid, because I was naked; and I hid myself. And he said, Who told thee that thou wast naked? Hast thou eaten of the tree, whereof I commanded thee that thou shouldest not eat? And the man said, The woman whom thou gavest to be with me, she gave me of the tree, and I did eat. And the LORD God said unto the woman, What is this that thou hast done? And the woman said, The serpent beguiled me, and I did eat. And the LORD God said unto the serpent, Because thou hast done this, thou art cursed above all cattle, and above every beast of the field; upon thy belly shalt thou go, and dust shalt thou eat all the days of thy life: And I will put enmity between thee and the woman, and between thy seed and her seed; it shall bruise thy head, and thou shalt bruise his heel. Unto the woman he said, I will greatly multiply thy sorrow and thy conception; in sorrow thou shalt bring forth children; and thy desire shall be to thy husband, and he shall rule over thee. And unto Adam he said, Because thou hast hearkened unto the voice of thy wife, and hast eaten of the tree, of which I commanded thee, saying, Thou shalt not eat of it: cursed is the ground for thy sake; in sorrow shalt thou eat of it all the days of thy life; Thorns also and thistles shall it bring forth to thee; and thou shalt eat the herb of the field; In the sweat of thy face shalt thou eat bread, till thou return unto the ground; for out of it wast thou taken: for dust thou art, and unto dust shalt thou return. And Adam called his wife's name Eve; because she was the mother of all living. Unto Adam also and to his wife did the LORD God make coats of skins, and clothed them. And the LORD God said, Behold, the man is become as one of us, to know good and evil: and now, lest he put forth his hand, and take also of the tree of life, and eat, and live for ever: Therefore the LORD God sent him forth from the garden of Eden, to till the ground from whence he was taken. So he drove out the man; and he placed at the east of the garden of Eden Cherubims, and a flaming sword which turned every way, to keep the way of the tree of life.

[...]

Genesis Chapter 15

After these things the word of the LORD came unto Abram in a vision, saying, Fear not, Abram: I am thy shield, and thy exceeding great reward. And Abram said, LORD God, what wilt thou give me, seeing I go childless, and the steward of my house is this Eliezer of Damascus? And Abram said, Behold, to me thou hast given no seed: and, lo, one born in my house is mine heir. And, behold, the word of the LORD came unto him, saying, This shall not be thine heir; but he that shall come forth out of thine own bowels shall be thine heir. And he brought him forth abroad, and said, Look now toward heaven, and tell the stars, if thou be able to number them: and he said unto him, So shall thy seed be. And he believed in the LORD; and he counted it to him for righteousness.

[…]

In the same day the LORD made a covenant with Abram, saying, Unto thy seed have I given this land, from the river of Egypt unto the great river, the river Euphrates…

[…]

Genesis Chapter 16

Now Sarai Abram's wife bare him no children: and she had an handmaid, an Egyptian, whose name was Hagar. And Sarai said unto Abram, Behold now, the LORD hath restrained me from bearing: I pray thee, go in unto my maid; it may be that I may obtain children by her. And Abram hearkened to the voice of Sarai. And Sarai Abram's wife took Hagar her maid the Egyptian, after Abram had dwelt ten years in the land of Canaan, and gave her to her husband Abram to be his wife. And he went in unto Hagar, and she conceived: and when she saw that she had conceived, her mistress was despised in her eyes. And Sarai said unto Abram, My wrong be upon thee: I have given my maid into thy bosom; and when she saw that she had conceived, I was despised in her eyes: the LORD judge between me and thee. But Abram said unto Sarai, Behold, thy maid is in thine hand; do to her as it pleaseth thee. And when Sarai dealt hardly with her, she fled from her face. And the angel of the LORD found her by a fountain of water in the wilderness, by the fountain in the way to Shur. And he said, Hagar, Sarai's maid, whence camest thou? and whither wilt thou go? And she said, I flee from the face of my mistress Sarai. And the angel of the LORD said unto her, Return to thy mistress, and submit thyself under her hands. And the angel of the LORD said unto her, I will multiply thy seed exceedingly, that it shall not be numbered for multitude. And the angel of the LORD said unto her, Behold, thou art with child and shalt bear a son, and shalt call his name Ishmael; because the LORD hath heard thy affliction. And he will be a wild man; his hand will be against every man, and every man's hand against him; and he shall dwell in the presence of all his brethren. And she called the name of the LORD that spake unto her, Thou God seest me: for she said, Have I also here looked after him that seeth me? Wherefore the well was called Beerlahairoi; behold, it is between Kadesh and Bered. And Hagar bare Abram a son: and Abram called his son's name, which Hagar bare, Ishmael. And Abram was fourscore and six years old, when Hagar bare Ishmael to Abram.

And when Abram was ninety years old and nine, the LORD appeared to Abram, and said unto him, I am the Almighty God; walk before me, and be thou perfect. And I will make my covenant between me and thee, and will multiply thee exceedingly. And Abram fell on his face: and God talked with him, saying, As for me, behold, my covenant is with thee, and thou shalt be a father of many nations. Neither shall thy name any more be called Abram, but thy name shall be Abraham; for a father of many nations have I made thee. And I will make thee exceeding fruitful, and I will make nations of thee, and kings shall come out of thee. And I will establish my covenant between me and thee and thy seed after thee in their generations for an everlasting covenant, to be a God unto thee, and to thy seed after thee. And I will give unto thee, and to thy seed after thee, the land wherein thou art a stranger, all the land of Canaan, for an everlasting possession; and I will be their God. And God said unto Abraham, Thou shalt keep my covenant therefore, thou, and thy seed after thee in their generations. This is my covenant, which ye shall keep, between me and you and thy seed after thee; Every man child among you shall be circumcised. And ye shall circumcise the flesh of your foreskin; and it shall be a token of the covenant betwixt me and you. And he that is eight days old shall be circumcised among you, every man child in your generations, he that is born in the house, or bought with money of any stranger, which is not of thy seed. He that is born in thy house, and he that is bought with thy money, must needs be circumcised: and my covenant shall be in your flesh for an everlasting covenant. And the uncircumcised man child whose flesh of his foreskin is not circumcised, that soul shall be cut off from his people; he hath broken my covenant. And God said unto Abraham, As for Sarai thy wife, thou shalt not call her name Sarai, but Sarah shall her name be. And I will bless her, and give thee a son also of her: yea, I will bless her, and she shall be a mother of nations; kings of people shall be of her. Then Abraham fell upon his face, and laughed, and said in his heart, Shall a child be born unto him that is an hundred years old? and shall Sarah, that is ninety years old, bear? And Abraham said unto God, O that Ishmael might live before thee! And God said, Sarah thy wife shall bear thee a son indeed; and thou shalt call his name Isaac: and I will establish my covenant with him for an everlasting covenant, and with his seed after him. And as for Ishmael, I have heard thee: Behold, I have blessed him, and will make him fruitful, and will multiply him exceedingly; twelve princes shall he beget, and I will make him a great nation. But my covenant will I establish with Isaac, which Sarah shall bear unto thee at this set time in the next year. And he left off talking with him, and God went up from Abraham. And Abraham took Ishmael his son, and all that were born in his house, and all that were bought with his money, every male among the men of Abraham's house; and circumcised the flesh of their foreskin in the selfsame day, as God had said unto him. And Abraham was ninety years old and nine, when he was circumcised in the flesh of his foreskin. And Ishmael his son was thirteen years old, when he was circumcised in the flesh of his foreskin. In the selfsame day was

Abraham circumcised, and Ishmael his son. And all the men of his house, born in the house, and bought with money of the stranger, were circumcised with him.

[…]

Exodus Chapter 1

[…]

And all the souls that came out of the loins of Jacob were seventy souls: for Joseph was in Egypt already. And Joseph died, and all his brethren, and all that generation. And the children of Israel were fruitful, and increased abundantly, and multiplied, and waxed exceeding mighty; and the land was filled with them. Now there arose up a new king over Egypt, which knew not Joseph. And he said unto his people, Behold, the people of the children of Israel are more and mightier than we: Come on, let us deal wisely with them; lest they multiply, and it come to pass, that, when there falleth out any war, they join also unto our enemies, and fight against us, and so get them up out of the land. Therefore they did set over them taskmasters to afflict them with their burdens. And they built for Pharaoh treasure cities, Pithom and Raamses. But the more they afflicted them, the more they multiplied and grew. And they were grieved because of the children of Israel. And the Egyptians made the children of Israel to serve with rigour: And they made their lives bitter with hard bondage, in morter, and in brick, and in all manner of service in the field: all their service, wherein they made them serve, was with rigour. And the king of Egypt spake to the Hebrew midwives, of which the name of the one was Shiphrah, and the name of the other Puah: And he said, When ye do the office of a midwife to the Hebrew women, and see them upon the stools; if it be a son, then ye shall kill him: but if it be a daughter, then she shall live. But the midwives feared God, and did not as the king of Egypt commanded them, but saved the men children alive. And the king of Egypt called for the midwives, and said unto them, Why have ye done this thing, and have saved the men children alive? And the midwives said unto Pharaoh, Because the Hebrew women are not as the Egyptian women; for they are lively, and are delivered ere the midwives come in unto them. Therefore God dealt well with the midwives: and the people multiplied, and waxed very mighty. And it came to pass, because the midwives feared God, that he made them houses. And Pharaoh charged all his people, saying, Every son that is born ye shall cast into the river, and every daughter ye shall save alive.

Exodus Chapter 2

And there went a man of the house of Levi, and took to wife a daughter of Levi. And the woman conceived, and bare a son: and when she saw him that he was a goodly child, she hid him three months. And when she could not longer hide him, she took for him an ark of bulrushes, and daubed it with slime and with pitch, and put the child therein; and she laid it in the flags by the river's brink. And his sister stood afar off, to wit what would be done to him. And the daughter of Pharaoh came down to wash herself at the river; and her maidens walked along by the river's side; and when she saw the ark among the flags, she sent her maid to fetch it. And when she had opened it, she saw the child: and, behold, the babe wept. And she had compassion on him, and said, This is one of the Hebrews' children. Then said his sister to Pharaoh's daughter, Shall I go and call to thee a nurse of the Hebrew women, that she may nurse the child for thee? And Pharaoh's daughter said to her, Go. And the maid went and called the child's mother. And Pharaoh's daughter said unto her, Take this child away, and nurse it for me, and I will give thee thy wages. And the women took the child, and nursed it. And the child grew, and she brought him unto Pharaoh's daughter, and he became her son. And she called his name Moses: and she said, Because I drew him out of the water. And it came to pass in those days, when Moses was grown, that he went out unto his brethren, and looked on their burdens: and he spied an Egyptian smiting an Hebrew, one of his brethren. And he looked this way and that way, and when he saw that there was no man, he slew the Egyptian, and hid him in the sand. And when he went out the second day, behold, two men of the Hebrews strove together: and he said to him that did the wrong, Wherefore smitest thou thy fellow? And he said, Who made thee a prince and a judge over us? intendest thou to kill me, as thou killedst the Egyptian? And Moses feared, and said, Surely this thing is known. Now when Pharaoh heard this thing, he sought to slay Moses. But Moses fled from the face of Pharaoh, and dwelt in the land of Midian: and he sat down by a well. Now the priest of Midian had seven daughters: and they came and drew water, and filled the troughs to water their father's flock. And the shepherds came and drove them away: but Moses stood up and helped them, and watered their flock. And when they came to Reuel their father, he said, How is it that ye are come so soon to day? And they said, An Egyptian delivered us out of the hand of the shepherds, and also drew water enough for us, and watered the flock. And he said unto his daughters, And where is he? why is it that ye have left the man? call him, that he may eat bread. And Moses was content to dwell with the man: and he gave Moses Zipporah his daughter. And she bare him a son, and he called his name Gershom: for he said, I have been a stranger in a strange land. And it came to pass in process of time, that the king of Egypt died: and the children of Israel sighed by reason of the bondage, and they cried, and their cry came up unto God by reason of the bondage. And God heard their groaning, and God remembered his covenant with Abraham, with Isaac, and with Jacob. And God looked upon the children of Israel, and God had respect unto them.

Exodus Chapter 3

Now Moses kept the flock of Jethro his father in law, the priest of Midian: and he led the flock to the backside of the desert, and came to the mountain of God, even to Horeb.

And the angel of the LORD appeared unto him in a flame of fire out of the midst of a bush: and he looked, and, behold, the bush burned with fire, and the bush was not consumed. And Moses said, I will now turn aside, and see this great sight, why the bush is not burnt. And when the LORD saw that he turned aside to see, God called unto him out of the midst of the bush, and said, Moses, Moses. And he said, Here am I. And he said, Draw not nigh hither: put off thy shoes from off thy feet, for the place whereon thou standest is holy ground. Moreover he said, I am the God of thy father, the God of Abraham, the God of Isaac, and the God of Jacob. And Moses hid his face; for he was afraid to look upon God. And the LORD said, I have surely seen the affliction of my people which are in Egypt, and have heard their cry by reason of their taskmasters; for I know their sorrows; And I am come down to deliver them out of the hand of the Egyptians, and to bring them up out of that land unto a good land and a large, unto a land flowing with milk and honey; unto the place of the Canaanites, and the Hittites, and the Amorites, and the Perizzites, and the Hivites, and the Jebusites. Now therefore, behold, the cry of the children of Israel is come unto me: and I have also seen the oppression wherewith the Egyptians oppress them. Come now therefore, and I will send thee unto Pharaoh, that thou mayest bring forth my people the children of Israel out of Egypt. And Moses said unto God, Who am I, that I should go unto Pharaoh, and that I should bring forth the children of Israel out of Egypt? And he said, Certainly I will be with thee; and this shall be a token unto thee, that I have sent thee: When thou hast brought forth the people out of Egypt, ye shall serve God upon this mountain. And Moses said unto God, Behold, when I come unto the children of Israel, and shall say unto them, The God of your fathers hath sent me unto you; and they shall say to me, What is his name? what shall I say unto them? And God said unto Moses, I AM THAT I AM: and he said, Thus shalt thou say unto the children of Israel, I AM hath sent me unto you. And God said moreover unto Moses, Thus shalt thou say unto the children of Israel, the LORD God of your fathers, the God of Abraham, the God of Isaac, and the God of Jacob, hath sent me unto you: this is my name for ever, and this is my memorial unto all generations. Go, and gather the elders of Israel together, and say unto them, The LORD God of your fathers, the God of Abraham, of Isaac, and of Jacob, appeared unto me, saying, I have surely visited you, and seen that which is done to you in Egypt: And I have said, I will bring you up out of the affliction of Egypt unto the land of the Canaanites, and the Hittites, and the Amorites, and the Perizzites, and the Hivites, and the Jebusites, unto a land flowing with milk and honey. And they shall hearken to thy voice: and thou shalt come, thou and the elders of Israel, unto the king of Egypt, and ye shall say unto him, The LORD God of the Hebrews hath met with us: and now let us go, we beseech thee, three days' journey into the wilderness, that we may sacrifice to the LORD our God. And I am sure that the king of Egypt will not let you go, no, not by a mighty hand. And I will stretch out my hand, and smite Egypt with all my wonders which I will do in the midst thereof: and after that he will let you go. And I will give this people favour in the sight of the Egyptians: and it shall come to pass, that, when ye go, ye shall not go empty. But every woman shall borrow of her neighbour, and of her that sojourneth in her house, jewels of silver, and jewels of gold, and raiment: and ye shall put them upon your sons, and upon your daughters; and ye shall spoil the Egyptians.

Exodus Chapter 4

And Moses answered and said, But, behold, they will not believe me, nor hearken unto my voice: for they will say, The LORD hath not appeared unto thee. And the LORD said unto him, What is that in thine hand? And he said, A rod. And he said, Cast it on the ground. And he cast it on the ground, and it became a serpent; and Moses fled from before it. And the LORD said unto Moses, Put forth thine hand, and take it by the tail. And he put forth his hand, and caught it, and it became a rod in his hand: That they may believe that the LORD God of their fathers, the God of Abraham, the God of Isaac, and the God of Jacob, hath appeared unto thee. And the LORD said furthermore unto him, Put now thine hand into thy bosom. And he put his hand into his bosom: and when he took it out, behold, his hand was leprous as snow. And he said, Put thine hand into thy bosom again. And he put his hand into his bosom again; and plucked it out of his bosom, and, behold, it was turned again as his other flesh. And it shall come to pass, if they will not believe thee, neither hearken to the voice of the first sign, that they will believe the voice of the latter sign. And it shall come to pass, if they will not believe also these two signs, neither hearken unto thy voice, that thou shalt take of the water of the river, and pour it upon the dry land: and the water which thou takest out of the river shall become blood upon the dry land. And Moses said unto the LORD, O my LORD, I am not eloquent, neither heretofore, nor since thou hast spoken unto thy servant: but I am slow of speech, and of a slow tongue. And the LORD said unto him, Who hath made man's mouth? or who maketh the dumb, or deaf, or the seeing, or the blind? have not I the LORD? Now therefore go, and I will be with thy mouth, and teach thee what thou shalt say. And he said, O my LORD, send, I pray thee, by the hand of him whom thou wilt send. And the anger of the LORD was kindled against Moses, and he said, Is not Aaron the Levite thy brother? I know that he can speak well. And also, behold, he cometh forth to meet thee: and when he seeth thee, he will be glad in his heart. And thou shalt speak unto him, and put words in his mouth: and I will be with thy mouth, and with his mouth, and will teach you what ye shall do. And he shall be thy spokesman unto the people: and he shall be, even he shall be to thee instead of a mouth, and thou shalt be to him instead of God. And thou shalt take this rod in thine hand, wherewith thou shalt do signs. And Moses went and returned to Jethro his father in law, and said unto him, Let me go, I pray thee, and return unto my brethren which are in Egypt, and see whether they be yet alive. And Jethro said to Moses, Go in peace. And the LORD said unto Moses in Midian, Go, return into Egypt: for all the men are dead which sought thy life. And Moses took his wife and his sons, and set them upon an ass, and he returned to the land of Egypt: and Moses took the rod of God in his hand. And the LORD said unto Moses, When thou goest to return into Egypt, see that thou do all those wonders before Pharaoh, which I have put in thine hand: but I will harden his heart, that he shall not let the people go. And thou shalt say unto Pharaoh, Thus saith the LORD, Israel is my son, even my firstborn: And I say unto thee, Let my son go, that he may serve me: and if thou refuse to let him go, behold, I will slay thy son, even thy firstborn. And it came to pass by the way in the inn, that the LORD met him, and sought to kill him. Then Zipporah took a sharp stone, and cut off the foreskin of her son, and cast it at his feet, and said, Surely a bloody husband art thou to me. So he let him go: then she said, A bloody husband thou art, because of the circumcision. And the LORD said to Aaron, Go into the wilderness to meet Moses. And he went, and met him in the mount of God, and kissed him. And Moses told Aaron all the words of the LORD who had sent him, and all the signs which he had commanded him. And Moses and Aaron went and gathered together all the elders of the children of Israel: And Aaron spake all the words which the LORD had spoken unto Moses, and did the signs in the sight of the people. And the people believed: and when they heard that the LORD had visited the children of Israel, and that he had looked upon their affliction, then they bowed their heads and worshipped.

Exodus Chapter 5

And afterward Moses and Aaron went in, and told Pharaoh, Thus saith the LORD God of Israel, Let my people go, that they may hold a feast unto me in the wilderness. And Pharaoh said, Who is the LORD, that I should obey his voice to let Israel go? I know not the LORD, neither will I let Israel go. And they said, The God of the Hebrews hath met with us: let us go, we pray thee, three days' journey into the desert, and sacrifice unto the LORD our God; lest he fall upon us with pestilence, or with the sword. And the king of Egypt said unto them, Wherefore do ye, Moses and Aaron, let the people from their works? get you unto your burdens. And Pharaoh said, Behold, the people of the land now are many, and ye make them rest from their burdens. And Pharaoh commanded the same day the taskmasters of the people, and their officers, saying, Ye shall no more give the people straw to make brick, as heretofore: let them go and gather straw for themselves. And the tale of the bricks, which they did make heretofore, ye shall lay upon them; ye shall not diminish ought thereof: for they be idle; therefore they cry, saying, Let us go and sacrifice to our God. Let there more work be laid upon the men, that they may labour therein; and let them not regard vain words. And the taskmasters of the people went out, and their officers, and they spake to the people, saying, Thus saith Pharaoh, I will not give you straw. Go ye, get you straw where ye can find it: yet not ought of your work shall be diminished. So the people were scattered abroad throughout all the land of Egypt to gather stubble instead of straw. And the taskmasters hasted them, saying, Fulfil your works, your daily tasks, as when there was straw. And the officers of the children of Israel, which Pharaoh's taskmasters had set over them, were beaten, and demanded, Wherefore have ye not fulfilled your task in making brick both yesterday and today, as heretofore? Then the officers of the children of Israel came and cried unto Pharaoh, saying, Wherefore dealest thou thus with thy servants? There is no straw given unto thy servants, and they say to us, Make brick: and, behold, thy servants are beaten; but the fault is in thine own people. But he said, Ye are idle, ye are idle: therefore ye say, Let us go and do sacrifice to the LORD. Go therefore now, and work; for there shall no straw be given you, yet shall ye deliver the tale of bricks. And the officers of the children of Israel did see that they were in evil case, after it was said, Ye shall not minish ought from your bricks of your daily task. And they met Moses and Aaron, who stood in the way, as they came forth from Pharaoh: And they said unto them, The LORD look upon you, and judge; because ye have made our savour to be abhorred in the eyes of Pharaoh, and in the eyes of his servants, to put a sword in their hand to slay us. And Moses returned unto the LORD, and said, LORD, wherefore hast thou so evil entreated this people? why is it that thou hast sent me? For since I came to Pharaoh to speak in thy name, he hath done evil to this people; neither hast thou delivered thy people at all.

Exodus Chapter 6

Then the LORD said unto Moses, Now shalt thou see what I will do to Pharaoh: for with a strong hand shall he let them go, and with a strong hand shall he drive them out of his land. And God spake unto Moses, and said unto him, I am the LORD: And I appeared unto Abraham, unto Isaac, and unto Jacob, by the name of God Almighty, but by my name JEHOVAH was I not known to them. And I have also established my covenant with them, to give them the land of Canaan, the land of their pilgrimage, wherein they were strangers. And I have also heard the groaning of the children of Israel, whom the Egyptians keep in bondage; and I have remembered my covenant. Wherefore say unto the children of Israel, I am the LORD, and I will bring you out from under the burdens of the Egyptians, and I will rid you out of their bondage, and I will redeem you with a stretched out arm, and with great judgments: And I will take you to me for a people, and I will be to you a God: and ye shall know that I am the LORD your God, which bringeth you out from under the burdens of the Egyptians. And I will bring you in unto the land, concerning the which I did swear to give it to Abraham, to Isaac, and to Jacob; and I will give it you for an heritage: I am the LORD. And Moses spake so unto the children of Israel: but they hearkened not unto Moses for anguish of spirit, and for cruel bondage. And the LORD spake unto Moses, saying, Go in, speak unto Pharaoh king of Egypt, that he let the children of Israel go out of his land.

[…]

Exodus Chapter 12

And the LORD spake unto Moses and Aaron in the land of Egypt saying: This month shall be unto you the beginning of months: it shall be the first month of the year to you.

Speak ye unto all the congregation of Israel, saying, In the tenth day of this month they shall take to them every man a lamb, according to the house of their fathers, a lamb for an house: And if the household be too little for the lamb, let him and his neighbour next unto his house take it according to the number of the souls; every man according to his eating shall make your count for the lamb. Your lamb shall be without blemish, a male of the first year: ye shall take it out from the sheep, or from the goats: And ye shall keep it up until the fourteenth day of the same month: and the whole assembly of the congregation of Israel shall kill it in the evening. And they shall take of the blood, and strike it on the two side posts and on the upper door post of the houses, wherein they shall eat it. And they shall eat the flesh in that night, roast with fire, and unleavened bread; and with bitter herbs they shall eat it. Eat not of it raw, nor sodden at all with water, but roast with fire; his head with his legs, and with the purtenance thereof. And ye shall let nothing of it remain until the morning; and that which remaineth of it until the morning ye shall burn with fire. And thus shall ye eat it; with your loins girded, your shoes on your feet, and your staff in your hand; and ye shall eat it in haste: it is the LORD's passover. For I will pass through the land of Egypt this night, and will smite all the firstborn in the land of Egypt, both man and beast; and against all the gods of Egypt I will execute judgment: I am the LORD. And the blood shall be to you for a token upon the houses where ye are: and when I see the blood, I will pass over you, and the plague shall not be upon you to destroy you, when I smite the land of Egypt. And this day shall be unto you for a memorial; and ye shall keep it a feast to the LORD throughout your generations; ye shall keep it a feast by an ordinance for ever. Seven days shall ye eat unleavened bread; even the first day ye shall put away leaven out of your houses: for whosoever eateth leavened bread from the first day until the seventh day, that soul shall be cut off from Israel. And in the first day there shall be an holy convocation, and in the seventh day there shall be an holy convocation to you; no manner of work shall be done in them, save that which every man must eat, that only may be done of you. And ye shall observe the feast of unleavened bread; for in this selfsame day have I brought your armies out of the land of Egypt: therefore shall ye observe this day in your generations by an ordinance for ever. In the first month, on the fourteenth day of the month at even, ye shall eat unleavened bread, until the one and twentieth day of the month at even. Seven days shall there be no leaven found in your houses: for whosoever eateth that which is leavened, even that soul shall be cut off from the congregation of Israel, whether he be a stranger, or born in the land. Ye shall eat nothing leavened; in all your habitations shall ye eat unleavened bread. Then Moses called for all the elders of Israel, and said unto them, Draw out and take you a lamb according to your families, and kill the passover. And ye shall take a bunch of hyssop, and dip it in the blood that is in the bason, and strike the lintel and the two side posts with the blood that is in the bason; and none of you shall go out at the door of his house until the morning. For the LORD will pass through to smite the Egyptians; and when he seeth the blood upon the lintel, and on the two side posts, the LORD will pass over the door, and will not suffer the destroyer to come in unto your houses to smite you. And ye shall observe this thing for an ordinance to thee and to thy sons for ever. And it shall come to pass, when ye be come to the land which the LORD will give you, according as he hath promised, that ye shall keep this service. And it shall come to pass, when your children shall say unto you, What mean ye by this service? That ye shall say, It is the sacrifice of the LORD's passover, who passed over the houses of the children of Israel in Egypt, when he smote the Egyptians, and delivered our houses. And the people bowed the head and worshipped. And the children of Israel went away, and did as the LORD had commanded Moses and Aaron, so did they. And it came to pass, that at midnight the LORD smote all the firstborn in the land of Egypt, from the firstborn of Pharaoh that sat on his throne unto the firstborn of the captive that was in the dungeon; and all the firstborn of cattle. And Pharaoh rose up in the night, he, and all his servants, and all the Egyptians; and there was a great cry in Egypt; for there was not a house where there was not one dead. And he called for Moses and Aaron by night, and said, Rise up, and get you forth from among my people, both ye and the children of Israel; and go, serve the LORD, as ye have said. Also take your flocks and your herds, as ye have said, and be gone; and bless me also. And the Egyptians were urgent upon the people, that they might send them out of the land in haste; for they said, We be all dead men. And the people took their dough before it was leavened, their kneading troughs being bound up in their clothes upon their shoulders. And the children of Israel did according to the word of Moses; and they borrowed of the Egyptians jewels of silver, and jewels of gold, and raiment: And the LORD gave the people favour in the sight of the Egyptians, so that they lent unto them such things as they required. And they spoiled the Egyptians. And the children of Israel journeyed from Rameses to Succoth, about six hundred thousand on foot that were men, beside children. And a mixed multitude went up also with them; and flocks, and herds, even very much cattle. And they baked unleavened cakes of the dough which they brought forth out of Egypt, for it was not leavened; because they were thrust out of Egypt, and could not tarry, neither had they prepared for themselves any victual. Now the sojourning of the children of Israel, who dwelt in Egypt, was four hundred and thirty years. And it came to pass at the end of the four hundred and thirty years, even the selfsame day it came to pass, that all the hosts of the LORD went out from the land of Egypt. It is a night to be much observed unto the LORD for bringing them out from the land of Egypt: this is that night of the LORD to be observed of all the children of Israel in their generations. And the LORD said unto Moses and Aaron, This is the ordinance of the passover: There shall no stranger eat thereof: But every man's servant that is bought for money, when thou hast circumcised him, then shall he eat thereof. A foreigner and an hired servant shall not eat thereof. In one house shall it be eaten; thou shalt not carry forth ought of the flesh abroad out of the house; neither shall ye break a bone thereof. All the congregation of Israel shall keep it. And when a stranger shall sojourn with thee, and will keep the passover to the LORD, let all his males be circumcised, and then let him come near and keep it; and he shall be as one that is born in the land: for no uncircumcised person shall eat thereof. One law shall be to him that is home born, and unto the stranger that sojourneth among you. Thus did all the children of Israel; as the LORD commanded Moses and Aaron, so did they. And it came to pass the selfsame day, that the LORD did bring the children of Israel out of the land of Egypt by their armies.

[…]

Exodus Chapter 14

And the LORD spake unto Moses, saying, Speak unto the children of Israel, that they turn and encamp before Pihahiroth, between Migdol and the sea, over against Baalzephon: before it shall ye encamp by the sea. For Pharaoh will say of the children of Israel, They are entangled in the land, the wilderness hath shut them in. And I will harden Pharaoh's heart, that he shall follow after them; and I will be honoured upon Pharaoh, and upon all his host; that the Egyptians may know that I am the LORD. And they did so. And it was told the king of Egypt that the people fled: and the heart of Pharaoh and of his servants was turned against the people, and they said, Why have we done this, that we have let Israel go from serving us? And he made ready his chariot, and took his people with him: And he took six hundred chosen chariots, and all the chariots of Egypt, and captains over every one of them. And the LORD hardened the heart of Pharaoh king of Egypt, and he pursued after the children of Israel: and the children of Israel went out with an high hand. But the Egyptians pursued after them, all the horses and chariots of Pharaoh, and his horsemen, and his army, and overtook them encamping by the sea, beside Pihahiroth, before Baalzephon.

And when Pharaoh drew nigh, the children of Israel lifted up their eyes, and, behold, the Egyptians marched after them; and they were sore afraid: and the children of Israel cried out unto the LORD. And they said unto Moses, Because there were no graves in Egypt, hast thou taken us away to die in the wilderness? Wherefore hast thou dealt thus with us, to carry us forth out of Egypt? Is not this the word that we did tell thee in Egypt, saying, Let us alone, that we may serve the Egyptians? For it had been better for us to serve the Egyptians, than that we should die in the wilderness. And Moses said unto the people, Fear ye not, stand still, and see the salvation of the LORD, which he will shew to you to day: for the Egyptians whom ye have seen to day, ye shall see them again no more for ever. The LORD shall fight for you, and ye shall hold your peace. And the LORD said unto Moses, Wherefore criest thou unto me? speak unto the children of Israel, that they go forward: But lift thou up thy rod, and stretch out thine hand over the sea, and divide it: and the children of Israel shall go on dry ground through the midst of the sea. And I, behold, I will harden the hearts of the Egyptians, and they shall follow them: and I will get me honour upon Pharaoh, and upon all his host, upon his chariots, and upon his horsemen. And the Egyptians shall know that I am the LORD, when I have gotten me honour upon Pharaoh, upon his chariots, and upon his horsemen. And the angel of God, which went before the camp of Israel, removed and went behind them; and the pillar of the cloud went from before their face, and stood behind them: And it came between the camp of the Egyptians and the camp of Israel; and it was a cloud and darkness to them, but it gave light by night to these: so that the one came not near the other all the night. And Moses stretched out his hand over the sea; and the LORD caused the sea to go back by a strong east wind all that night, and made the sea dry land, and the waters were divided. And the children of Israel went into the midst of the sea upon the dry ground: and the waters were a wall unto them on their right hand, and on their left. And the Egyptians pursued, and went in after them to the midst of the sea, even all Pharaoh's horses, his chariots, and his horsemen. And it came to pass, that in the morning watch the LORD looked unto the host of the Egyptians through the pillar of fire and of the cloud, and troubled the host of the Egyptians, And took off their chariot wheels, that they drave them heavily: so that the Egyptians said, Let us flee from the face of Israel; for the LORD fighteth for them against the Egyptians. And the LORD said unto Moses, Stretch out thine hand over the sea, that the waters may come again upon the Egyptians, upon their chariots, and upon their horsemen. And Moses stretched forth his hand over the sea, and the sea returned to his strength when the morning appeared; and the Egyptians fled against it; and the LORD overthrew the Egyptians in the midst of the sea. And the waters returned, and covered the chariots, and the horsemen, and all the host of Pharaoh that came into the sea after them; there remained not so much as one of them. But the children of Israel walked upon dry land in the midst of the sea; and the waters were a wall unto them on their right hand, and on their left. Thus the LORD saved Israel that day out of the hand of the Egyptians; and Israel saw the Egyptians dead upon the sea shore. And Israel saw that great work which the LORD did upon the Egyptians: and the people feared the LORD, and believed the LORD, and his servant Moses.

[...]

Exodus Chapter 16

And they took their journey from Elim, and all the congregation of the children of Israel came unto the wilderness of Sin, which is between Elim and Sinai, on the fifteenth day of the second month after their departing out of the land of Egypt. And the whole congregation of the children of Israel murmured against Moses and Aaron in the wilderness: And the children of Israel said unto them, Would to God we had died by the hand of the LORD in the land of Egypt, when we sat by the flesh pots, and when we did eat bread to the full; for ye have brought us forth into this wilderness, to kill this whole assembly with hunger. Then said the LORD unto Moses, Behold, I will rain bread from heaven for you; and the people shall go out and gather a certain rate every day, that I may prove them, whether they will walk in my law, or no. And it shall come to pass, that on the sixth day they shall prepare that which they bring in; and it shall be twice as much as they gather daily. And Moses and Aaron said unto all the children of Israel, At even, then ye shall know that the LORD hath brought you out from the land of Egypt: And in the morning, then ye shall see the glory of the LORD; for that he heareth your murmurings against the LORD: and what are we, that ye murmur against us? And Moses said, This shall be, when the LORD shall give you in the evening flesh to eat, and in the morning bread to the full; for that the LORD heareth your murmurings which ye murmur against him: and what are we? Your murmurings are not against us, but against the LORD. And Moses spake unto Aaron, Say unto all the congregation of the children of Israel, Come near before the LORD: for he hath heard your murmurings. And it came to pass, as Aaron spake unto the whole congregation of the children of Israel, that they looked toward the wilderness, and, behold, the glory of the LORD appeared in the cloud. And the LORD spake unto Moses, saying, I have heard the murmurings of the children of Israel: speak unto them, saying, At even ye shall eat flesh, and in the morning ye shall be filled with bread; and ye shall know that I am the LORD your God. And it came to pass, that at even the quails came up, and covered the camp: and in the morning the dew lay round about the host. And when the dew that lay was gone up, behold, upon the face of the wilderness there lay a small round thing, as small as the hoar frost on the ground. And when the children of Israel saw it, they said one to another, It is manna: for they wist not what it was. And Moses said unto them, This is the bread which the LORD hath given you to eat. This is the thing which the LORD hath commanded, Gather of it every man according to his eating, an omer for every man, according to the number of your persons; take ye every man for them which are in his tents. And the children of Israel did so, and gathered, some more, some less. And when they did mete it with an omer, he that gathered much had nothing over, and he that gathered little had no lack; they gathered every man according to his eating. And Moses said, Let no man leave of it till the morning. Notwithstanding they hearkened not unto Moses; but some of them left of it until the morning, and it bred worms, and stank: and Moses was wroth with them. And they gathered it every morning, every man according to his eating: and when the sun waxed hot, it melted. And it came to pass, that on the sixth day they gathered twice as much bread, two omers for one man: and all the rulers of the congregation came and told Moses. And he said unto them, This is that which the LORD hath said, To morrow is the rest of the holy sabbath unto the LORD: bake that which ye will bake to day, and seethe that ye will seethe; and that which remaineth over lay up for you to be kept until the morning. And they laid it up till the morning, as Moses bade: and it did not stink, neither was there any worm therein. And Moses said, Eat that to day; for to day is a sabbath unto the LORD: to day ye shall not find it in the field. Six days ye shall gather it; but on the seventh day, which is the sabbath, in it there shall be none. And it came to pass, that there went out some of the people on the seventh day for to gather, and they found none. And the LORD said unto Moses, How long refuse ye to keep my commandments and my laws? See, for that the LORD hath given you the sabbath, therefore he giveth you on the sixth day the bread of two days; abide ye every man in his place, let no man go out of his place on the seventh day. So the people rested on the seventh day. And the house of Israel called the name thereof Manna: and it was like coriander seed, white; and the taste of it was like wafers made with honey. And Moses said, This is the thing which the LORD commandeth, Fill an omer of it to be kept for your generations; that they may see the bread wherewith I have fed you in the wilderness, when I brought you forth from the land of Egypt. And Moses said unto Aaron, Take a pot, and put an omer full of manna therein, and lay it up before the LORD, to be kept for your generations. As the LORD commanded Moses, so Aaron laid it up before the Testimony, to be kept. And the children of Israel did eat manna forty years, until they came to a land inhabited; they did eat manna, until they came unto the borders of the land of Canaan.

[…]

Exodus Chapter 20

And God spake all these words, saying, I am the LORD thy God, which have brought thee out of the land of Egypt, out of the house of bondage. Thou shalt have no other gods before me. Thou shalt not make unto thee any graven image, or any likeness of any thing that is in heaven above, or that is in the earth beneath, or that is in the water under the earth. Thou shalt not bow down thyself to them, nor serve them: for I the LORD thy God am a jealous God, visiting the iniquity of the fathers upon the children unto the third and fourth generation of them that hate me; And shewing mercy unto thousands of them that love me, and keep my commandments. Thou shalt not take the name of the LORD thy God in vain; for the LORD will not hold him guiltless that taketh his name in vain. Remember the sabbath day, to keep it holy. Six days shalt thou labour, and do all thy work: But the seventh day is the sabbath of the LORD thy God: in it thou shalt not do any work, thou, nor thy son, nor thy daughter, thy manservant, nor thy maidservant, nor thy cattle, nor thy stranger that is within thy gates: For in six days the LORD made heaven and earth, the sea, and all that in them is, and rested the seventh day: wherefore the LORD blessed the sabbath day, and hallowed it. Honour thy father and thy mother: that thy days may be long upon the land which the LORD thy God giveth thee. Thou shalt not kill. Thou shalt not commit adultery. Thou shalt not steal. Thou shalt not bear false witness against thy neighbour. Thou shalt not covet thy neighbour's house, thou shalt not covet thy neighbour's wife, nor his manservant, nor his maidservant, nor his ox, nor his ass, nor any thing that is thy neighbour's. And all the people saw the thunderings, and the lightnings, and the noise of the trumpet, and the mountain smoking: and when the people saw it, they removed, and stood afar off. And they said unto Moses, Speak thou with us, and we will hear: but let not God speak with us, lest we die. And Moses said unto the people, Fear not: for God is come to prove you, and that his fear may be before your faces, that ye sin not. And the people stood afar off, and Moses drew near unto the thick darkness where God was. And the LORD said unto Moses, Thus thou shalt say unto the children of Israel, Ye have seen that I have talked with you from heaven. Ye shall not make with me gods of silver, neither shall ye make unto you gods of gold. An altar of earth thou shalt make unto me, and shalt sacrifice thereon thy burnt offerings, and thy peace offerings, thy sheep, and thine oxen: in all places where I record my name I will come unto thee, and I will bless thee. And if thou wilt make me an altar of stone, thou shalt not build it of hewn stone: for if thou lift up thy tool upon it, thou hast polluted it. Neither shalt thou go up by steps unto mine altar, that thy nakedness be not discovered thereon.

[…]

Deuteronomy Chapter 34

And Moses went up from the plains of Moab unto the mountain of Nebo, to the top of Pisgah, that is over against Jericho. And the LORD shewed him all the land of Gilead, unto Dan, And all Naphtali, and the land of Ephraim, and Manasseh, and all the land of Judah, unto the utmost sea, And the south, and the plain of the valley of Jericho, the city of palm trees, unto Zoar. And the LORD said unto him, This is the land which I sware unto Abraham, unto Isaac, and unto Jacob, saying, I will give it unto thy seed: I have caused thee to see it with thine eyes, but thou shalt not go over thither. So Moses the servant of the LORD died there in the land of Moab, according to the word of the LORD. And he buried him in a valley in the land of Moab, over against Bethpeor: but no man knoweth of his sepulchre unto this day. And Moses was an hundred and twenty years old when he died: his eye was not dim, nor his natural force abated. And the children of Israel wept for Moses in the plains of Moab thirty days: so the days of weeping and mourning for Moses were ended. And Joshua the son of Nun was full of the spirit of wisdom; for Moses had laid his hands upon him: and the children of Israel hearkened unto him, and did as the LORD commanded Moses. And there arose not a prophet since in Israel like unto Moses, whom the LORD knew face to face, In all the signs and the wonders, which the LORD sent him to do in the land of Egypt to Pharaoh, and to all his servants, and to all his land, And in all that mighty hand, and in all the great terror which Moses shewed in the sight of all Israel.

[…]

Jeremiah Chapter 1

The words of Jeremiah the son of Hilkiah, of the priests that were in Anathoth in the land of Benjamin: To whom the word of the LORD came in the days of Josiah the son of Amon king of Judah, in the thirteenth year of his reign. It came also in the days of

Jehoiakim the son of Josiah king of Judah, unto the end of the eleventh year of Zedekiah the son of Josiah king of Judah, unto the carrying away of Jerusalem captive in the fifth month. Then the word of the LORD came unto me, saying, Before I formed thee in the belly I knew thee; and before thou camest forth out of the womb I sanctified thee, and I ordained thee a prophet unto the nations. Then said I, Ah, Lord GOD! behold, I cannot speak: for I am a child. But the LORD said unto me, Say not, I am a child: for thou shalt go to all that I shall send thee, and whatsoever I command thee thou shalt speak. Be not afraid of their faces: for I am with thee to deliver thee, saith the LORD. Then the LORD put forth his hand, and touched my mouth. And the LORD said unto me, Behold, I have put my words in thy mouth. See, I have this day set thee over the nations and over the kingdoms, to root out, and to pull down, and to destroy, and to throw down, to build, and to plant. Moreover the word of the LORD came unto me, saying, Jeremiah, what seest thou? And I said, I see a rod of an almond tree. Then said the LORD unto me, Thou hast well seen: for I will hasten my word to perform it. And the word of the LORD came unto me the second time, saying, What seest thou? And I said, I see a seething pot; and the face thereof is toward the north. Then the LORD said unto me, Out of the north an evil shall break forth upon all the inhabitants of the land. For, lo, I will call all the families of the kingdoms of the north, saith the LORD; and they shall come, and they shall set every one his throne at the entering of the gates of Jerusalem, and against all the walls thereof round about, and against all the cities of Judah. And I will utter my judgments against them touching all their wickedness, who have forsaken me, and have burned incense unto other gods, and worshipped the works of their own hands. Thou therefore gird up thy loins, and arise, and speak unto them all that I command thee: be not dismayed at their faces, lest I confound thee before them. For, behold, I have made thee this day a defenced city, and an iron pillar, and brasen walls against the whole land, against the kings of Judah, against the princes thereof, against the priests thereof, and against the people of the land. And they shall fight against thee; but they shall not prevail against thee; for I am with thee, saith the LORD, to deliver thee.

Jeremiah Chapter 2

Moreover the word of the LORD came to me, saying, Go and cry in the ears of Jerusalem, saying, Thus saith the LORD; I remember thee, the kindness of thy youth, the love of thine espousals, when thou wentest after me in the wilderness, in a land that was not sown. Israel was holiness unto the LORD, and the first fruits of his increase: all that devour him shall offend; evil shall come upon them, saith the LORD. Hear ye the word of the LORD, O house of Jacob, and all the families of the house of Israel: Thus saith the LORD, What iniquity have your fathers found in me, that they are gone far from me, and have walked after vanity, and are become vain? Neither said they, Where is the LORD that brought us up out of the land of Egypt, that led us through the wilderness, through a land of deserts and of pits, through a land of drought, and of the shadow of death, through a land that no man passed through, and where no man dwelt? And I brought you into a plentiful country, to eat the fruit thereof and the goodness thereof; but when ye entered, ye defiled my land, and made mine heritage an abomination. The priests said not, Where is the LORD? And they that handle the law knew me not: the pastors also transgressed against me, and the prophets prophesied by Baal, and walked after things that do not profit. Wherefore I will yet plead with you, saith the LORD, and with your children's children will I plead. For pass over the isles of Chittim, and see; and send unto Kedar, and consider diligently, and see if there be such a thing. Hath a nation changed their gods, which are yet no gods? But my people have changed their glory for that which doth not profit. Be astonished, O ye heavens, at this, and be horribly afraid, be ye very desolate, saith the LORD. For my people have committed two evils; they have forsaken me the fountain of living waters, and hewed them out cisterns, broken cisterns, that can hold no water. Is Israel a servant? Is he a homeborn slave? Why is he spoiled? The young lions roared upon him, and yelled, and they made his land waste: his cities are burned without inhabitant. Also the children of Noph and Tahapanes have broken the crown of thy head. Hast thou not procured this unto thyself, in that thou hast forsaken the LORD thy God, when he led thee by the way? And now what hast thou to do in the way of Egypt, to drink the waters of Sihor? Or what hast thou to do in the way of Assyria, to drink the waters of the river? Thine own wickedness shall correct thee, and thy backslidings shall reprove thee: know therefore and see that it is an evil thing and bitter, that thou hast forsaken the LORD thy God, and that my fear is not in thee, saith the Lord GOD of hosts. For of old time I have broken thy yoke, and burst thy bands; and thou saidst, I will not transgress; when upon every high hill and under every green tree thou wanderest, playing the harlot. Yet I had planted thee a noble vine, wholly a right seed: how then art thou turned into the degenerate plant of a strange vine unto me? For though thou wash thee with nitre, and take thee much soap, yet thine iniquity is marked before me, saith the Lord GOD. How canst thou say, I am not polluted, I have not gone after Baalim? See thy way in the valley, know what thou hast done: thou art a swift dromedary traversing her ways; a wild ass used to the wilderness, that snuffeth up the wind at her pleasure; in her occasion who can turn her away? All they that seek her will not weary themselves; in her month they shall find her. Withhold thy foot from being unshod, and thy throat from thirst: but thou saidst, There is no hope: no; for I have loved strangers, and after them will I go. As the thief is ashamed when he is found, so is the house of Israel ashamed; they, their kings, their princes, and their priests, and their prophets. Saying to a stock, Thou art my father; and to a stone, Thou hast brought me forth: for they have turned their back unto me, and not their face: but in the time of their trouble they will say, Arise, and save us. But where are thy gods that thou hast made thee? Let them arise, if they can save thee in the time of thy trouble: for according to the number of thy cities are thy gods, O Judah. Wherefore will ye plead with me? Ye all have transgressed against me, saith the LORD. In vain have I smitten your children; they received no correction: your own sword hath devoured your prophets, like a destroying lion. O generation, see ye the word of the LORD. Have I been a wilderness unto Israel?

a land of darkness? Wherefore say my people, We are lords; we will come no more unto thee? Can a maid forget her ornaments, or a bride her attire? Yet my people have forgotten me days without number. Why trimmest thou thy way to seek love? Therefore hast thou also taught the wicked ones thy ways. Also in thy skirts is found the blood of the souls of the poor innocents: I have not found it by secret search, but upon all these. Yet thou sayest, Because I am innocent, surely his anger shall turn from me. Behold, I will plead with thee, because thou sayest, I have not sinned. Why gaddest thou about so much to change thy way? Thou also shalt be ashamed of Egypt, as thou wast ashamed of Assyria. Yea, thou shalt go forth from him, and thine hands upon thine head: for the LORD hath rejected thy confidences, and thou shalt not prosper in them.

[…]

Jeremiah Chapter 52

Zedekiah was one and twenty years old when he began to reign, and he reigned eleven years in Jerusalem. And his mother's name was Hamutal the daughter of Jeremiah of Libnah. And he did that which was evil in the eyes of the LORD, according to all that Jehoiakim had done. For through the anger of the LORD it came to pass in Jerusalem and Judah, till he had cast them out from his presence, that Zedekiah rebelled against the king of Babylon. And it came to pass in the ninth year of his reign, in the tenth month, in the tenth day of the month, that Nebuchadrezzar king of Babylon came, he and all his army, against Jerusalem, and pitched against it, and built forts against it round about. So the city was besieged unto the eleventh year of king Zedekiah. And in the fourth month, in the ninth day of the month, the famine was sore in the city, so that there was no bread for the people of the land. Then the city was broken up, and all the men of war fled, and went forth out of the city by night by the way of the gate between the two walls, which was by the king's garden; (now the Chaldeans were by the city round about:) and they went by the way of the plain. But the army of the Chaldeans pursued after the king, and overtook Zedekiah in the plains of Jericho; and all his army was scattered from him. Then they took the king, and carried him up unto the king of Babylon to Riblah in the land of Hamath; where he gave judgment upon him. And the king of Babylon slew the sons of Zedekiah before his eyes: he slew also all the princes of Judah in Riblah. Then he put out the eyes of Zedekiah; and the king of Babylon bound him in chains, and carried him to Babylon, and put him in prison till the day of his death. Now in the fifth month, in the tenth day of the month, which was the nineteenth year of Nebuchadrezzar king of Babylon, came Nebuzaradan, captain of the guard, which served the king of Babylon, into Jerusalem, And burned the house of the LORD, and the king's house; and all the houses of Jerusalem, and all the houses of the great men, burned he with fire: And all the army of the Chaldeans, that were with the captain of the guard, brake down all the walls of Jerusalem round about. Then Nebuzaradan the captain of the guard carried away captive certain of the poor of the people, and the residue of the people that remained in the city, and those that fell away, that fell to the king of Babylon, and the rest of the multitude. But Nebuzaradan the captain of the guard left certain of the poor of the land for vinedressers and for husbandmen. Also the pillars of brass that were in the house of the LORD, and the bases, and the brasen sea that was in the house of the LORD, the Chaldeans brake, and carried all the brass of them to Babylon. The caldrons also, and the shovels, and the snuffers, and the bowls, and the spoons, and all the vessels of brass wherewith they ministered, took they away. And the basons, and the firepans, and the bowls, and the caldrons, and the candlesticks, and the spoons, and the cups; that which was of gold in gold, and that which was of silver in silver, took the captain of the guard away. The two pillars, one sea, and twelve brasen bulls that were under the bases, which king Solomon had made in the house of the LORD: the brass of all these vessels was without weight. And concerning the pillars, the height of one pillar was eighteen cubits; and a fillet of twelve cubits did compass it; and the thickness thereof was four fingers: it was hollow. And a chapiter of brass was upon it; and the height of one chapiter was five cubits, with network and pomegranates upon the chapiters round about, all of brass. The second pillar also and the pomegranates were like unto these. And there were ninety and six pomegranates on a side; and all the pomegranates upon the network were an hundred round about. And the captain of the guard took Seraiah the chief priest, and Zephaniah the second priest, and the three keepers of the door: He took also out of the city an eunuch, which had the charge of the men of war; and seven men of them that were near the king's person, which were found in the city; and the principal scribe of the host, who mustered the people of the land; and threescore men of the people of the land, that were found in the midst of the city. So Nebuzaradan the captain of the guard took them, and brought them to the king of Babylon to Riblah. And the king of Babylon smote them, and put them to death in Riblah in the land of Hamath. Thus Judah was carried away captive out of his own land. This is the people whom Nebuchadrezzar carried away captive: in the seventh year three thousand Jews and three and twenty: In the eighteenth year of Nebuchadrezzar he carried away captive from Jerusalem eight hundred thirty and two persons: In the three and twentieth year of Nebuchadrezzar, Nebuzaradan the captain of the guard carried away captive of the Jews seven hundred forty and five persons: all the persons were four thousand and six hundred. And it came to pass in the seven and thirtieth year of the captivity of Jehoiachin king of Judah, in the twelfth month, in the five and twentieth day of the month, that Evilmerodach king of Babylon in the first year of his reign lifted up the head of Jehoiachin king of Judah, and brought him forth out of prison. And spake kindly unto him, and set his throne above the throne of the kings that were with him in Babylon, And changed his prison garments: and he did continually eat bread before him all the days of his life. And for his diet, there was a continual diet given him of the king of Babylon, every day a portion until the day of his death, all the days of his life.

[…]

The LORD is my shepherd; I shall not want. He maketh me to lie down in green pastures: he leadeth me beside the still waters. He restoreth my soul: he leadeth me in the paths of righteousness for his name's sake. Yea, though I walk through the valley of the shadow of death, I will fear no evil: for thou art with me; thy rod and thy staff they comfort me. Thou preparest a table before me in the presence of mine enemies: thou anointest my head with oil; my cup runneth over. Surely goodness and mercy shall follow me all the days of my life: and I will dwell in the house of the LORD for ever.

[...]

Psalms Chapter 117

O praise the LORD, all ye nations: praise him, all ye people. For his merciful kindness is great toward us: and the truth of the LORD endureth for ever. Praise ye the LORD.

[...]

Psalms Chapter 137

By the rivers of Babylon, there we sat down, yea, we wept, when we remembered Zion. We hanged our harps upon the willows in the midst thereof. For there they that carried us away captive required of us a song; and they that wasted us required of us mirth, saying, Sing us one of the songs of Zion. How shall we sing the LORD's song in a strange land? If I forget thee, O Jerusalem, let my right hand forget her cunning. If I do not remember thee, let my tongue cleave to the roof of my mouth; if I prefer not Jerusalem above my chief joy. Remember, O LORD, the children of Edom in the day of Jerusalem; who said, Rase it, rase it, even to the foundation thereof. O daughter of Babylon, who art to be destroyed; happy shall he be, that rewardeth thee as thou hast served us. Happy shall he be, that taketh and dasheth thy little ones against the stones.

[...]

Proverbs Chapter 8

Doth not wisdom cry? And understanding put forth her voice? She standeth in the top of high places, by the way in the places of the paths. She crieth at the gates, at the entry of the city, at the coming in at the doors. Unto you, O men, I call; and my voice is to the sons of man. O ye simple, understand wisdom: and, ye fools, be ye of an understanding heart. Hear; for I will speak of excellent things; and the opening of my lips shall be right things. For my mouth shall speak truth; and wickedness is an abomination to my lips. All the words of my mouth are in righteousness; there is nothing froward or perverse in them. They are all plain to him that understandeth, and right to them that find knowledge. Receive my instruction, and not silver; and knowledge rather than choice gold. For wisdom is better than rubies; and all the things that may be desired are not to be compared to it. I wisdom dwell with prudence, and find out knowledge of witty inventions. The fear of the LORD is to hate evil: pride, and arrogancy, and the evil way, and the froward mouth, do I hate. Counsel is mine, and sound wisdom: I am understanding; I have strength. By me kings reign, and princes decree justice. By me princes rule, and nobles, even all the judges of the earth. I love them that love me; and those that seek me early shall find me. Riches and honour are with me; yea, durable riches and righteousness. My fruit is better than gold, yea, than fine gold; and my revenue than choice silver. I lead in the way of righteousness, in the midst of the paths of judgment: That I may cause those that love me to inherit substance; and I will fill their treasures. The LORD possessed me in the beginning of his way, before his works of old. I was set up from everlasting, from the beginning, or ever the earth was. When there were no depths, I was brought forth; when there were no fountains abounding with water. Before the mountains were settled, before the hills was I brought forth: While as yet he had not made the earth, nor the fields, nor the highest part of the dust of the world. When he prepared the heavens, I was there: when he set a compass upon the face of the depth: When he established the clouds above: when he strengthened the fountains of the deep: When he gave to the sea his decree, that the waters should not pass his commandment: when he appointed the foundations of the earth: Then I was by him, as one brought up with him: and I was daily his delight, rejoicing always before him; Rejoicing in the habitable part of his earth; and my delights were with the sons of men. Now therefore hearken unto me, O ye children: for blessed are they that keep my ways. Hear instruction, and be wise, and refuse it not. Blessed is the man that heareth me, watching daily at my gates, waiting at the posts of my doors. For whoso findeth me findeth life, and shall obtain favour of the LORD. But he that sinneth against me wrongeth his own soul: all they that hate me love death.

Chapter 6
Christianity

The New Testament of the Christian Bible

The Christian Bible is structured into a longer Old Testament, written before the time of Jesus; and a shorter New Testament, written after the time of Jesus. The Old Testament is composed of books of the Tanakh (although following a somewhat different order). We considered the Tanakh in the section on Jewish scripture. Here, we focus on the New Testament.

The New Testament begins with four books, or Gospels, about the life of Jesus Christ. This is followed by other books, including the Acts of the Apostles, The Epistles (or Letters), most of which were written by Paul of Tarsus. The final book of the Christian Bible is the Book of Revelation (alternatively referred to as the Book of the Apocalypse).

Of the four Gospels, three (Matthew, Mark and Luke) are sometimes referred to as "synoptics" (literally seen together) because of their similarities. While the first three focus more on the humanity of Jesus, the Gospel of John, the last of the four to be written, emphasizes Jesus as the Messiah.

The Gospel of Matthew begins with the human provenance of Jesus, going back to Abraham, tracing 42 generations. We read of the birth of Jesus, the visit of the Magi and, in a scene adumbrated in the Old Testament, the infant Jesus escapes from King Herod, who had wanted to kill him. After this, Mary and Joseph bring the baby Jesus to Nazareth.

We then pick up the life of Jesus as a grown man of some 30 years. He spends 40 days in the desert where he faces temptations from the Devil. He is baptized by John the Baptist in the River Jordan. These events mark the beginning of Jesus's public ministry.

Jesus quickly garners followers. The first of the Apostles, we learn, are two pairs of brothers: first Andrew and Peter, then James and John. Jesus travels throughout Galilee, preaching, teaching, and healing the sick.

In Chapter 5 of Matthew, we encounter what may be the most famous public oratory in all history—The Sermon on the Mount. It is organized around "beatitudes" or blessed virtues. Jesus articulates a vision of righteousness quite distinct from worldly success.

Jesus delivers many of his teachings in parables. In the middle chapters of Matthew's Gospel, Jesus explains why he does this, and holds forth with one parable after another.

Jesus returns to his home town of Nazareth where, ironically, he is not greeted with the enthusiasm or respect he had encountered to that point in much of his public ministry. It is here that he makes the often quoted declaration: "A prophet is not without honor, save in his own country..."

The final chapters chronicle many of the events at the dramatic end of Jesus's public ministry. We read of the Last Supper. Much of the blessing Jesus gives is used to this day for the consecration prayers for the Eucharist in many Christian services.

We then read of the passion and death of Jesus, and of some of the surrounding events, including his betrayal. Jesus dies on the cross and on the third day, subsequently celebrated as Easter, Jesus rises from the dead. The Gospel of Matthew ends with the "Great Commission," where a risen Jesus visits the Apostles and exhorts them to "Go and make disciples of all nations."

We next consider a brief but powerful opening of the Gospel of John. Brother of James and the youngest of the 12, John was the only one of the Apostles to die of natural causes. His was the last of the Gospels to be written, perhaps as late as 90 A.D.

In contrast with Matthew's focus on the human ancestry of Jesus, John places the emphasis on Jesus's divine nature. The Gospel opens with an explosion of potent imagery: "In the beginning was the Word...the Word became flesh and made his dwelling among us."

We consider as well the Epistle of Paul to the Philippians. This is one of the "prison epistles" written from his jail cell in Rome, about ten years after he had been instrumental in the founding of the church at Philippi in the middle of the First Century. He encourages the Christian community to think on the most uplifting things: "...whatever is true, whatever is noble, whatever is right, whatever is pure..."

Let us now turn to the New Testament of the Christian Bible...

Matthew Chapter 1

The book of the generation of Jesus Christ, the son of David, the son of Abraham. Abraham begat Isaac; and Isaac begat Jacob; and Jacob begat...

[...]

And Jesse begat David the king; and David the king begat Solomon

[...]

...begat Joseph the husband of Mary, of whom was born Jesus, who is called Christ. So all the generations from Abraham to David are fourteen generations; and from David until the carrying away into Babylon are fourteen generations; and from the carrying away into Babylon unto Christ are fourteen generations. Now the birth of Jesus Christ was on this wise: When as his mother Mary was espoused to Joseph, before they came together, she was found with child of the Holy Ghost. Then Joseph her husband, being a just man, and not willing to make her a publick example, was minded to put her away privily. But while he thought on these things, behold, the angel of the LORD appeared unto him in a dream, saying, Joseph, thou son of David, fear not to take unto thee Mary thy wife: for that which is conceived in her is of the Holy Ghost. And she shall bring forth a son, and thou shalt call his name JESUS: for he shall save his people from their sins. Now all this was done, that it might be fulfilled which was spoken of the Lord by the prophet, saying, Behold, a virgin shall be with child, and shall bring forth a son, and they shall call his name Emmanuel, which being interpreted is, God with us. Then Joseph being raised from sleep did as the angel of the Lord had bidden him, and took unto him his wife: And knew her not till she had brought forth her firstborn son: and he called his name JESUS.

Matthew Chapter 2

Now when Jesus was born in Bethlehem of Judaea in the days of Herod the king, behold, there came wise men from the east to Jerusalem, Saying, Where is he that is born King of the Jews? for we have seen his star in the east, and are come to worship him. When Herod the king had heard these things, he was troubled, and all Jerusalem with him. And when he had gathered all the chief priests and scribes of the people together, he demanded of them where Christ should be born. And they said unto him, In Bethlehem of Judaea: for thus it is written by the prophet, And thou Bethlehem, in the land of Juda, art not the least among the princes of Juda: for out of thee shall come a Governor, that shall rule my people Israel. Then Herod, when he had privily called the wise men, enquired of them diligently what time the star appeared. And he sent them to Bethlehem, and said, Go and search diligently for the young child; and when ye have found him, bring me word again, that I may come and worship him also. When they had heard the king, they departed; and, lo, the star, which they saw in the east, went before them, till it came and stood over where the young child was. When they saw the star, they rejoiced with exceeding great joy. And when they were come into the house, they saw the young child with Mary his mother, and fell down, and worshipped him: and when they had opened their treasures, they presented unto him gifts; gold, and frankincense and myrrh. And being warned of God in a dream that they should not return to Herod, they departed into their own country another way. And when they were departed, behold, the angel of the Lord appeareth to Joseph in a dream, saying, Arise, and take the young child and his mother, and flee into Egypt, and be thou there until I bring thee word: for Herod will seek the young child to destroy him. When he arose, he took the young child and his mother by night, and departed into Egypt: And was there until the death of Herod: that it might be fulfilled which was spoken of the Lord by the prophet, saying, Out of Egypt have I called my son. Then Herod, when he saw that he was mocked of the wise men, was exceeding wroth, and sent forth, and slew all the children that were in Bethlehem, and in all the coasts thereof, from two years old and under, according to the time which he had diligently enquired of the wise men. Then was fulfilled that which was spoken by Jeremy the prophet, saying, In Rama was there a voice heard, lamentation, and weeping, and great mourning, Rachel weeping for her children, and would not be comforted, because they are not. But when Herod was dead, behold, an angel of the Lord appeareth in a dream to Joseph in Egypt, Saying, Arise, and take the young child and his mother, and go into the land of Israel: for they are dead which sought the young child's life. And he arose, and took the young child and his mother, and came into the land of Israel. But when he heard that Archelaus did reign in Judaea in the room of his father Herod, he was afraid to go thither: notwithstanding, being warned of God in a dream, he turned aside into the parts of Galilee: And he came and dwelt in a city called Nazareth: that it might be fulfilled which was spoken by the prophets, He shall be called a Nazarene.

Matthew Chapter 3

In those days came John the Baptist, preaching in the wilderness of Judaea, And saying, Repent ye: for the kingdom of heaven is at hand. For this is he that was spoken of by the prophet Esaias, saying, The voice of one crying in the wilderness, Prepare ye the way of the Lord, make his paths straight. And the same John had his raiment of camel's hair, and a leathern girdle about his loins; and his meat was locusts and wild honey. Then went out to him Jerusalem, and all Judaea, and all the region round about Jordan, And were baptized of him in Jordan, confessing their sins. But when he saw many of the Pharisees and Sadducees come to his baptism, he said unto them, O generation of vipers, who hath warned you to flee from the wrath to come? Bring forth therefore fruits meet for repentance: And think not to say within yourselves, We have Abraham to our father: for I say unto you, that God is able of these stones to raise up children unto Abraham. And now also the axe is laid unto the root of the trees: therefore every tree which bringeth not forth good fruit is hewn down, and cast into the fire. I indeed baptize you with water unto repentance. but he that cometh after me is mightier than I, whose shoes I am not worthy to bear: he shall baptize you with the Holy Ghost, and with fire: Whose fan is in his hand, and he will throughly purge his floor, and gather his wheat into the garner; but he will burn up the chaff with unquenchable fire. Then cometh Jesus from Galilee to Jordan unto John, to be baptized of him. But John forbad him, saying, I have need to be baptized of thee, and comest thou to me? And Jesus answering said unto him, Suffer it to be so now: for thus it becometh us to fulfil all righteousness. Then he suffered him. And Jesus, when he was baptized, went up straightway out of the water: and, lo, the heavens were opened unto him, and he saw the Spirit of God descending like a dove, and lighting upon him: And lo a voice from heaven, saying, This is my beloved Son, in whom I am well pleased.

Matthew Chapter 4

Then was Jesus led up of the spirit into the wilderness to be tempted of the devil. And when he had fasted forty days and forty nights, he was afterward an hungred. And when the tempter came to him, he said, If thou be the Son of God, command that these stones be made bread. But he answered and said, It is written, Man shall not live by bread alone, but by every word that proceedeth out of the mouth of God. Then the devil taketh him up into the holy city, and setteth him on a pinnacle of the temple, And saith unto him, If thou be the Son of God, cast thyself down: for it is written, He shall give his angels charge concerning thee: and in their hands they shall bear thee up, lest at any time thou dash thy foot against a stone. Jesus said unto him, It is written again, Thou shalt not tempt the Lord thy God. Again, the devil taketh him up into an exceeding high mountain, and sheweth him all the kingdoms of the world, and the glory of them; And saith unto him, All these things will I give thee, if thou wilt fall down and worship me. Then saith Jesus unto him, Get thee hence, Satan: for it is written, Thou shalt worship the Lord thy God, and him only shalt thou serve. Then the devil leaveth him, and, behold, angels came and ministered unto him. Now when Jesus had heard that John was cast into prison, he departed into Galilee; And leaving Nazareth, he came and dwelt in Capernaum, which is upon the sea coast, in the borders of Zabulon and Nephthalim: That it might be fulfilled which was spoken by Esaias the prophet, saying, The land of Zabulon, and the land of Nephthalim, by the way of the sea, beyond Jordan, Galilee of the Gentiles; The people which sat in darkness saw great light; and to them which sat in the region and shadow of death light is sprung up. From that time Jesus began to preach, and to say, Repent: for the kingdom of heaven is at hand. And Jesus, walking by the sea of Galilee, saw two brethren, Simon called Peter, and Andrew his brother, casting a net into the sea: for they were fishers. And he saith unto them, Follow me, and I will make you fishers of men. And they straightway left their nets, and followed him. And going on from thence, he saw other two brethren, James the son of Zebedee, and John his brother, in a ship with Zebedee their father, mending their nets; and he called them. And they immediately left the ship and their father, and followed him. And Jesus went about all Galilee, teaching in their synagogues, and preaching the gospel of the kingdom, and healing all manner of sickness and all manner of disease among the people. And his fame went throughout all Syria: and they brought unto him all sick people that were taken with divers diseases and torments, and those which were possessed with devils, and those which were lunatick, and those that had the palsy; and he healed them. And there followed him great multitudes of people from Galilee, and from Decapolis, and from Jerusalem, and from Judaea, and from beyond Jordan.

Matthew Chapter 5

And seeing the multitudes, he went up into a mountain: and when he was set, his disciples came unto him: And he opened his mouth, and taught them, saying, Blessed are the poor in spirit: for theirs is the kingdom of heaven. Blessed are they that mourn: for they shall be comforted. Blessed are the meek: for they shall inherit the earth. Blessed are they which do hunger and thirst after righteousness: for they shall be filled. Blessed are the merciful: for they shall obtain mercy. Blessed are the pure in heart: for they shall see God. Blessed are the peacemakers: for they shall be called the children of God. Blessed are they which are persecuted for righteousness' sake: for theirs is the kingdom of heaven. Blessed are ye, when men shall revile you, and persecute you, and shall say all manner of evil against you falsely, for my sake. Rejoice, and be exceeding glad: for great is your reward in heaven: for so persecuted they the prophets which were before you. Ye are the salt of the earth: but if the salt have lost his savour, wherewith shall it be salted? It is thenceforth good for nothing, but to be cast out, and to be trodden under foot of men. Ye are the light of the world. A city that is set on an hill cannot be hid. Neither do men light a candle, and put it under a bushel, but on a candlestick; and it giveth light unto all that are in the house. Let your light so shine before men, that they may see your good works, and glorify your Father which is in heaven. Think not that I am come to destroy the law, or the prophets: I am not come to destroy, but to fulfil. For verily I say unto you, till heaven and earth pass, one jot or one tittle shall in no wise pass from the law, till all be fulfilled. Whosoever therefore shall break one of these least commandments, and shall teach men so, he shall be called the least in the kingdom of heaven: but whosoever shall do and teach them, the same shall be called great in the kingdom of heaven. For I say unto you, that except your righteousness shall exceed the righteousness of the scribes and Pharisees, ye shall in no case enter into the kingdom of heaven. Ye have heard that it was said of them of old time, Thou shalt not kill; and whosoever shall kill shall be in danger of the judgment: But I say unto you, that whosoever is angry with his brother without a cause shall be in danger of the judgment: and whosoever shall say to his brother, Raca, shall be in danger of the council: but whosoever shall say, Thou fool, shall be in danger of hell fire. Therefore if thou bring thy gift to the altar, and there rememberest that thy brother hath ought against thee; leave there thy gift before the altar, and go thy way; first be reconciled to thy brother, and then come and offer thy gift. Agree with thine adversary quickly, whiles thou art in the way with him; lest at any time the adversary deliver thee to the judge, and the judge deliver thee to the officer, and thou be cast into prison. Verily I say unto thee, thou shalt by no means come out thence, till thou hast paid the uttermost farthing. Ye have heard that it was said by them of old time, Thou shalt not commit adultery: But I say unto you, that whosoever looketh on a woman to lust after her hath committed adultery with her already in his heart. And if thy right eye offend thee, pluck it out, and cast it from thee: for it is profitable for thee that one of thy members should perish, and not that thy whole body should be cast into hell. And if thy right hand offend thee, cut it off, and cast it from thee: for it is profitable for thee that one of thy members should perish, and not that thy whole body should be cast into hell. It hath been said, Whosoever shall put away his wife, let him give her a writing of divorcement: But I say unto you, that whosoever shall put away his wife, saving for the cause of fornication, causeth her to commit adultery: and whosoever shall marry her that is divorced committeth adultery. Again, ye have heard that it hath been said by them of old time, Thou shalt not forswear thyself, but shalt perform unto the Lord thine oaths: But I say unto you, swear not at all; neither by heaven; for it is God's throne: nor by the earth; for it is his footstool: neither by Jerusalem; for it is the city of the great King. Neither shalt thou swear by thy head, because thou canst not make one hair white or black. But let your communication be, Yea, yea; Nay, nay: for whatsoever is more than these cometh of evil. Ye have heard that it hath been said, An eye for an eye, and a tooth for a tooth: But I say unto you, that ye resist not evil: but whosoever shall smite thee on thy right cheek, turn to him the other also. And if any man will sue thee at the law, and take away thy coat, let him have thy cloak also. And whosoever shall compel thee to go a mile, go with him twain. Give to him that asketh thee, and from him that would borrow of thee turn not thou away. Ye have heard that it hath been said, Thou shalt love thy neighbour, and hate thine enemy. But I say unto you, love your enemies, bless them that curse you, do good to them that hate you, and pray for them which despitefully use you, and persecute you; that ye may be the children of your Father which is in heaven: for he maketh his sun to rise on the evil and on the good, and sendeth rain on the just and on the unjust. For if ye love them which love you, what reward have ye? Do not even the publicans the same? And if ye salute your brethren only, what do ye more than others? Do not even the publicans so? Be ye therefore perfect, even as your Father which is in heaven is perfect.

Matthew Chapter 6

Take heed that ye do not your alms before men, to be seen of them: otherwise ye have no reward of your Father which is in heaven. Therefore when thou doest thine alms, do not sound a trumpet before thee, as the hypocrites do in the synagogues and in the streets, that they may have glory of men. Verily I say unto you, they have their reward. But when thou doest alms, let not thy left hand know what thy right hand doeth: that thine alms may be in secret: and thy Father which seeth in secret himself shall reward thee openly. And when thou prayest, thou shalt not be as the hypocrites are: for they love to pray standing in the synagogues and in the corners of the streets, that they may be seen of men. Verily I say unto you, they have their reward. But thou, when thou prayest, enter into thy closet, and when thou hast shut thy door, pray to thy Father which is in secret; and thy Father which seeth in secret shall reward thee openly. But when ye pray, use not vain repetitions, as the heathen do: for they think that they shall be heard for their much speaking. Be not ye therefore like unto them: for your Father knoweth what things ye have need of, before ye ask him. After this manner therefore pray ye: Our Father which art in heaven, Hallowed be thy name. Thy kingdom come, Thy will be done in earth, as it is in heaven. Give us this day our daily bread. And forgive us our debts, as we forgive our debtors. And lead us not into temptation, but deliver us from evil: For thine is the kingdom, and the power, and the glory, for ever. Amen. For if ye forgive men their trespasses, your heavenly Father will also forgive you: but if ye forgive not men their trespasses, neither will your Father forgive your trespasses. Moreover when ye fast, be not, as the hypocrites, of a sad countenance: for they disfigure their faces, that they may appear unto men to fast. Verily I say unto you, they have their reward. But thou, when thou fastest, anoint thine head, and wash thy face; that thou appear not unto men to fast, but unto thy Father which is in secret: and thy Father, which seeth in secret, shall reward thee openly. Lay not up for yourselves treasures upon earth, where moth and rust doth corrupt, and where thieves break through and steal: but lay up for yourselves treasures in heaven, where neither moth nor rust doth corrupt, and where thieves do not break through nor steal: for where your treasure is, there will your heart be also. The light of the body is the eye: if therefore thine eye be single, thy whole body shall be full of light. But if thine eye be evil, thy whole body shall be full of darkness. If therefore the light that is in thee be darkness, how great is that darkness! No man can serve two masters: for either he will hate the one, and love the other; or else he will hold to the one, and despise the other. Ye cannot serve God and mammon. Therefore I say unto you, take no thought for your life, what ye shall eat, or what ye shall drink; nor yet for your body, what ye shall put on. Is not the life more than meat, and the body than raiment? Behold the fowls of the air: for they sow not, neither do they reap, nor gather into barns; yet your heavenly Father feedeth them. Are ye not much better than they? Which of you by taking thought can add one cubit unto his stature? And why take ye thought for raiment? Consider the lilies of the field, how they grow; they toil not, neither do they spin: And yet I say unto you, that even Solomon in all his glory was not arrayed like one of these. Wherefore, if God so clothe the grass of the field, which to day is, and to morrow is cast into the oven, shall he not much more clothe you, O ye of little faith? Therefore take no thought, saying, What shall we eat? or, What shall we drink? or, Wherewithal shall we be clothed? (For after all these things do the Gentiles seek:) for your heavenly Father knoweth that ye have need of all these things. But seek ye first the kingdom of God, and his righteousness; and all these things shall be added unto you. Take therefore no thought for the morrow: for the morrow shall take thought for the things of itself. Sufficient unto the day is the evil thereof.

Judge not, that ye be not judged. For with what judgment ye judge, ye shall be judged: and with what measure ye mete, it shall be measured to you again. And why beholdest thou the mote that is in thy brother's eye, but considerest not the beam that is in thine own eye? Or how wilt thou say to thy brother, Let me pull out the mote out of thine eye; and, behold, a beam is in thine own eye? Thou hypocrite, first cast out the beam out of thine own eye; and then shalt thou see clearly to cast out the mote out of thy brother's eye. Give not that which is holy unto the dogs, neither cast ye your pearls before swine, lest they trample them under their feet, and turn again and rend you. Ask, and it shall be given you; seek, and ye shall find; knock, and it shall be opened unto you: For every one that asketh receiveth; and he that seeketh findeth; and to him that knocketh it shall be opened. Or what man is there of you, whom if his son ask bread, will he give him a stone? Or if he ask a fish, will he give him a serpent? If ye then, being evil, know how to give good gifts unto your children, how much more shall your Father which is in heaven give good things to them that ask him? Therefore all things whatsoever ye would that men should do to you, do ye even so to them: for this is the law and the prophets. Enter ye in at the strait gate: for wide is the gate, and broad is the way, that leadeth to destruction, and many there be which go in thereat: because strait is the gate, and narrow is the way, which leadeth unto life, and few there be that find it. Beware of false prophets, which come to you in sheep's clothing, but inwardly they are ravening wolves. Ye shall know them by their fruits. Do men gather grapes of thorns, or figs of thistles? Even so every good tree bringeth forth good fruit; but a corrupt tree bringeth forth evil fruit. A good tree cannot bring forth evil fruit, neither can a corrupt tree bring forth good fruit. Every tree that bringeth not forth good fruit is hewn down, and cast into the fire. Wherefore by their fruits ye shall know them. Not every one that saith unto me, Lord, Lord, shall enter into the kingdom of heaven; but he that doeth the will of my Father which is in heaven. Many will say to me in that day, Lord, Lord, have we not prophesied in thy name? And in thy name have cast out devils? And in thy name done many wonderful works? And then will I profess unto them, I never knew you: depart from me, ye that work iniquity. Therefore whosoever heareth these sayings of mine, and doeth them, I will liken him unto a wise man, which built his house upon a rock: and the rain descended, and the floods came, and the winds blew, and beat upon that house; and it fell not: for it was founded upon a rock. And every one that heareth these sayings of mine, and doeth them not, shall be likened unto a foolish man, which built his house upon the sand: and the rain descended, and the floods came, and the winds blew, and beat upon that house; and it fell: and great was the fall of it. And it came to pass, when Jesus had ended these sayings, the people were astonished at his doctrine: for he taught them as one having authority, and not as the scribes.

<...>

The same day went Jesus out of the house, and sat by the sea side. And great multitudes were gathered together unto him, so that he went into a ship, and sat; and the whole multitude stood on the shore. And he spake many things unto them in parables, saying, Behold, a sower went forth to sow; And when he sowed, some seeds fell by the way side, and the fowls came and devoured them up: Some fell upon stony places, where they had not much earth: and forthwith they sprung up, because they had no deepness of earth: And when the sun was up, they were scorched; and because they had no root, they withered away. And some fell among thorns; and the thorns sprung up, and choked them: But other fell into good ground, and brought forth fruit, some an hundredfold, some sixtyfold, some thirtyfold. Who hath ears to hear, let him hear. And the disciples came, and said unto him, Why speakest thou unto them in parables? He answered and said unto them, Because it is given unto you to know the mysteries of the kingdom of heaven, but to them it is not given. For whosoever hath, to him shall be given, and he shall have more abundance: but whosoever hath not, from him shall be taken away even that he hath. Therefore speak I to them in parables: because they seeing see not; and hearing they hear not, neither do they understand. And in them is fulfilled the prophecy of Esaias, which saith, By hearing ye shall hear, and shall not understand; and seeing ye shall see, and shall not perceive: For this people's heart is waxed gross, and their ears are dull of hearing, and their eyes they have closed; lest at any time they should see with their eyes and hear with their ears, and should understand with their heart, and should be converted, and I should heal them. But blessed are your eyes, for they see: and your ears, for they hear. For verily I say unto you, that many prophets and righteous men have desired to see those things which ye see, and have not seen them; and to hear those things which ye hear, and have not heard them. Hear ye therefore the parable of the sower. When any one heareth the word of the kingdom, and understandeth it not, then cometh the wicked one, and catcheth away that which was sown in his heart. This is he which received seed by the way side. But he that received the seed into stony places, the same is he that heareth the word, and anon with joy receiveth it; Yet hath he not root in himself, but dureth for a while: for when tribulation or persecution ariseth because of the word, by and by he is offended. He also that received seed among the thorns is he that heareth the word; and the care of this world, and the deceitfulness of riches, choke the word, and he becometh unfruitful. But he that received seed into the good ground is he that heareth the word, and understandeth it; which also beareth fruit, and bringeth forth, some an hundredfold, some sixty, some thirty. Another parable put he forth unto them, saying, The kingdom of heaven is likened unto a man which sowed good seed in his field: but while men slept, his enemy came and sowed tares among the wheat, and went his way. But when the blade was sprung up, and brought forth fruit, then appeared the tares also. So the servants of the householder came and said unto him, Sir, didst not thou sow good seed in thy field? From whence then hath it tares? He said unto them, An enemy hath done this. The servants said unto him, Wilt thou then that we go and gather them up? But he said, Nay; lest while ye gather up the tares, ye root up also the wheat with them. Let both grow together until the harvest: and in the time of harvest I will say to the reapers, Gather ye together first the tares, and bind them in bundles to burn them: but gather the wheat into my barn. Another parable put he forth unto them, saying, The kingdom of heaven is like to a grain of mustard seed, which a man took, and sowed in his field: Which indeed is the least of all seeds: but when it is grown, it is the greatest among herbs, and becometh a tree, so that the birds of the air come and lodge in the branches thereof. Another parable spake he unto them; The kingdom of heaven is like unto leaven, which a woman took, and hid in three measures of meal, till the whole was leavened. All these things spake Jesus unto the multitude in parables; and without a parable spake he not unto them: That it might be fulfilled which was spoken by the prophet, saying, I will open my mouth in parables; I will utter things which have been kept secret from the foundation of the world. Then Jesus sent the multitude away, and went into the house: and his disciples came unto him, saying, Declare unto us the parable of the tares of the field. He answered and said unto them, He that soweth the good seed is the Son of man; the field is the world; the good seed are the children of the kingdom; but the tares are the children of the wicked one; the enemy that sowed them is the devil; the harvest is the end of the world; and the reapers are the angels. As therefore the tares are gathered and burned in the fire; so shall it be in the end of this world. The Son of man shall send forth his angels, and they shall gather out of his kingdom all things that offend, and them which do iniquity; and shall cast them into a furnace of fire: there shall be wailing and gnashing of teeth. Then shall the righteous shine forth as the sun in the kingdom of their Father. Who hath ears to hear, let him hear. Again, the kingdom of heaven is like unto treasure hid in a field; the which when a man hath found, he hideth, and for joy thereof goeth and selleth all that he hath, and buyeth that field. Again, the kingdom of heaven is like unto a merchant man, seeking goodly pearls: who, when he had found one pearl of great price, went and sold all that he had, and bought it. Again, the kingdom of heaven is like unto a net, that was cast into the sea, and gathered of every kind: which, when it was full, they drew to shore, and sat down, and gathered the good into vessels, but cast the bad away. So shall it be at the end of the world: the angels shall come forth, and sever the wicked from among the just, and shall cast them into the furnace of fire: there shall be wailing and gnashing of teeth. Jesus saith unto them, Have ye understood all these things? They say unto him, Yea, Lord. Then said he unto them, Therefore every scribe which is instructed unto the kingdom of heaven is like unto a man that is an householder, which bringeth forth out of his treasure things new and old. And it came to pass, that when Jesus had finished these parables, he departed thence. And when he was come into his own country, he taught them in their synagogue, insomuch that they were astonished, and said, Whence hath this man this wisdom, and these mighty works? Is not this the carpenter's son? Is not his mother called Mary? And his brethren, James, and Joses, and Simon, and Judas? And his sisters, are they not all with us? Whence then hath this man all these things? And they were offended in him. But Jesus said unto them, A prophet is not without honour, save in his own country, and in his own house. And he did not many mighty works there because of their unbelief.

Matthew Chapter 14

At that time Herod the tetrarch heard of the fame of Jesus, And said unto his servants, This is John the Baptist; he is risen from the dead; and therefore mighty works do shew forth themselves in him. For Herod had laid hold on John, and bound him, and put him in prison for Herodias' sake, his brother Philip's wife. For John said unto him, It is not lawful for thee to have her. And when he would have put him to death, he feared the multitude, because they counted him as a prophet. But when Herod's birthday was kept, the daughter of Herodias danced before them, and pleased Herod. Whereupon he promised with an oath to give her whatsoever she would ask. And she, being before instructed of her mother, said, Give me here John Baptist's head in a charger. And the king was sorry: nevertheless for the oath's sake, and them which sat with him at meat, he commanded it to be given her. And he sent, and beheaded John in the prison. And his head was brought in a charger, and given to the damsel: and she brought it to her mother. And his disciples came, and took up the body, and buried it, and went and told Jesus. When Jesus heard of it, he departed thence by ship into a desert place apart: and when the people had heard thereof, they followed him on foot out of the cities. And Jesus went forth, and saw a great multitude, and was moved with compassion toward them, and he healed their sick. And when it was evening, his disciples came to him, saying, This is a desert place, and the time is now past; send the multitude away, that they may go into the villages, and buy themselves victuals. But Jesus said unto them, They need not depart; give ye them to eat. And they say unto him, We have here but five loaves, and two fishes. He said, Bring them hither to me. And he commanded the multitude to sit down on the grass, and took the five loaves, and the two fishes, and looking up to heaven, he blessed, and brake, and gave the loaves to his disciples, and the disciples to the multitude. And they did all eat, and were filled: and they took up of the fragments that remained twelve baskets full. And they that had eaten were about five thousand men, beside women and children. And straightway Jesus constrained his disciples to get into a ship, and to go before him unto the other side, while he sent the multitudes away. And when he had sent the multitudes away, he went up into a mountain apart to pray: and when the evening was come, he was there alone. But the ship was now in the midst of the sea, tossed with waves: for the wind was contrary. And in the fourth watch of the night Jesus went unto them, walking on the sea. And when the disciples saw him walking on the sea, they were troubled, saying, It is a spirit; and they cried out for fear. But straightway Jesus spake unto them, saying, Be of good cheer; it is I; be not afraid. And Peter answered him and said, Lord, if it be thou, bid me come unto thee on the water. And he said, Come. And when Peter was come down out of the ship, he walked on the water, to go to Jesus. But when he saw the wind boisterous, he was afraid; and beginning to sink, he cried, saying, Lord, save me. And immediately Jesus stretched forth his hand, and caught him, and said unto him, O thou of little faith, wherefore didst thou doubt? And when they were come into the ship, the wind ceased. Then they that were in the ship came and worshipped him, saying, Of a truth thou art the Son of God. And when they were gone over, they came into the land of Gennesaret. And when the men of that place had knowledge of him, they sent out into all that country round about, and brought unto him all that were diseased; And besought him that they might only touch the hem of his garment: and as many as touched were made perfectly whole.

[…]

Matthew Chapter 17

And after six days Jesus taketh Peter, James, and John his brother, and bringeth them up into an high mountain apart, And was transfigured before them: and his face did shine as the sun, and his raiment was white as the light. And, behold, there appeared unto them Moses and Elias talking with him. Then answered Peter, and said unto Jesus, Lord, it is good for us to be here: if thou wilt, let us make here three tabernacles; one for thee, and one for Moses, and one for Elias. While he yet spake, behold, a bright cloud overshadowed them: and behold a voice out of the cloud, which said, This is my beloved Son, in whom I am well pleased; hear ye him. And when the disciples heard it, they fell on their face, and were sore afraid. And Jesus came and touched them, and said, Arise, and be not afraid. And when they had lifted up their eyes, they saw no man, save Jesus only. And as they came down from the mountain, Jesus charged them, saying, Tell the vision to no man, until the Son of man be risen again from the dead. And his disciples asked him, saying, Why then say the scribes that Elias must first come? And Jesus answered and said unto them, Elias truly shall first come, and restore all things. But I say unto you, that Elias is come already, and they knew him not, but have done unto him whatsoever they listed. Likewise shall also the Son of man suffer of them. Then the disciples understood that he spake unto them of John the Baptist. And when they were come to the multitude, there came to him a certain man, kneeling down to him, and saying, Lord, have mercy on my son: for he is lunatick, and sore vexed: for ofttimes he falleth into the fire, and oft into the water. And I brought him to thy disciples, and they could not cure him. Then Jesus answered and said, O faithless and perverse generation, how long shall I be with you? How long shall I suffer you? Bring him hither to me. And Jesus rebuked the devil; and he departed out of him: and the child was cured from that very hour. Then came the disciples to Jesus apart, and said, Why could not we cast him out? And Jesus said unto them, Because of your unbelief: for verily I say unto you, if ye have faith as a grain of mustard seed, ye shall say unto this mountain, Remove hence to yonder place; and it shall remove; and nothing shall be impossible unto you. Howbeit this kind goeth not out but by prayer and fasting. And while they abode in

Galilee, Jesus said unto them, The Son of man shall be betrayed into the hands of men: And they shall kill him, and the third day he shall be raised again. And they were exceeding sorry. And when they were come to Capernaum, they that received tribute money came to Peter, and said, Doth not your master pay tribute? He saith, Yes. And when he was come into the house, Jesus prevented him, saying, What thinkest thou, Simon? Of whom do the kings of the earth take custom or tribute? Of their own children, or of strangers? Peter saith unto him, Of strangers. Jesus saith unto him, Then are the children free. Notwithstanding, lest we should offend them, go thou to the sea, and cast an hook, and take up the fish that first cometh up; and when thou hast opened his mouth, thou shalt find a piece of money: that take, and give unto them for me and thee.

<...>

Matthew Chapter 24

And Jesus went out, and departed from the temple: and his disciples came to him for to shew him the buildings of the temple. And Jesus said unto them, See ye not all these things? Verily I say unto you, there shall not be left here one stone upon another, that shall not be thrown down. And as he sat upon the mount of Olives, the disciples came unto him privately, saying, Tell us, when shall these things be? And what shall be the sign of thy coming, and of the end of the world? And Jesus answered and said unto them, Take heed that no man deceive you. For many shall come in my name, saying, I am Christ; and shall deceive many. And ye shall hear of wars and rumours of wars: see that ye be not troubled: for all these things must come to pass, but the end is not yet. For nation shall rise against nation, and kingdom against kingdom: and there shall be famines, and pestilences, and earthquakes, in divers places. All these are the beginning of sorrows. Then shall they deliver you up to be afflicted, and shall kill you: and ye shall be hated of all nations for my name's sake. And then shall many be offended, and shall betray one another, and shall hate one another. And many false prophets shall rise, and shall deceive many. And because iniquity shall abound, the love of many shall wax cold. But he that shall endure unto the end, the same shall be saved. And this gospel of the kingdom shall be preached in all the world for a witness unto all nations; and then shall the end come. When ye therefore shall see the abomination of desolation, spoken of by Daniel the prophet, stand in the holy place, (whoso readeth, let him understand.) Then let them which be in Judaea flee into the mountains: Let him which is on the housetop not come down to take any thing out of his house: Neither let him which is in the field return back to take his clothes. And woe unto them that are with child, and to them that give suck in those days! But pray ye that your flight be not in the winter, neither on the sabbath day: For then shall be great tribulation, such as was not since the beginning of the world to this time, no, nor ever shall be. And except those days should be shortened, there should no flesh be saved: but for the elect's sake those days shall be shortened.

Then if any man shall say unto you, Lo, here is Christ, or there; believe it not. For there shall arise false Christs, and false prophets, and shall shew great signs and wonders; insomuch that, if it were possible, they shall deceive the very elect. Behold, I have told you before. Wherefore if they shall say unto you, Behold, he is in the desert; go not forth: behold, he is in the secret chambers; believe it not. For as the lightning cometh out of the east, and shineth even unto the west; so shall also the coming of the Son of man be. For wheresoever the carcass is, there will the eagles be gathered together. Immediately after the tribulation of those days shall the sun be darkened, and the moon shall not give her light, and the stars shall fall from heaven, and the powers of the heavens shall be shaken: And then shall appear the sign of the Son of man in heaven: and then shall all the tribes of the earth mourn, and they shall see the Son of man coming in the clouds of heaven with power and great glory. And he shall send his angels with a great sound of a trumpet, and they shall gather together his elect from the four winds, from one end of heaven to the other. Now learn a parable of the fig tree; When his branch is yet tender, and putteth forth leaves, ye know that summer is nigh: So likewise ye, when ye shall see all these things, know that it is near, even at the doors. Verily I say unto you, This generation shall not pass, till all these things be fulfilled. Heaven and earth shall pass away, but my words shall not pass away. But of that day and hour knoweth no man, no, not the angels of heaven, but my Father only. But as the days of Noe were, so shall also the coming of the Son of man be. For as in the days that were before the flood they were eating and drinking, marrying and giving in marriage, until the day that Noe entered into the ark, and knew not until the flood came, and took them all away; so shall also the coming of the Son of man be. Then shall two be in the field; the one shall be taken, and the other left. Two women shall be grinding at the mill; the one shall be taken, and the other left. Watch therefore: for ye know not what hour your Lord doth come. But know this, that if the goodman of the house had known in what watch the thief would come, he would have watched, and would not have suffered his house to be broken up. Therefore be ye also ready: for in such an hour as ye think not the Son of man cometh. Who then is a faithful and wise servant, whom his lord hath made ruler over his household, to give them meat in due season? Blessed is that servant, whom his lord when he cometh shall find so doing. Verily I say unto you, that he shall make him ruler over all his goods. But and if that evil servant shall say in his heart, My lord delayeth his coming; and shall begin to smite his fellow servants, and to eat and drink with the drunken; the lord of that servant shall come in a day when he looketh not for him, and in an hour that he is not aware of, and shall cut him asunder, and appoint him his portion with the hypocrites: there shall be weeping and gnashing of teeth.

Matthew Chapter 25

Then shall the kingdom of heaven be likened unto ten virgins, which took their lamps, and went forth to meet the bridegroom. And five of them were wise, and five were foolish. They that were foolish took their lamps, and took no oil with them: But the wise took oil in their vessels with their lamps. While the bridegroom tarried, they all slumbered and slept. And at midnight there was a cry made, Behold, the bridegroom cometh; go ye out to meet him. Then all those virgins arose, and trimmed their lamps. And the foolish said unto the wise, Give us of your oil; for our lamps are gone out. But the wise answered, saying, Not so; lest there be not enough for us and you: but go ye rather to them that sell, and buy for yourselves. And while they went to buy, the bridegroom came; and they that were ready went in with him to the marriage: and the door was shut. Afterward came also the other virgins, saying, Lord, Lord, open to us. But he answered and said, Verily I say unto you, I know you not. Watch therefore, for ye know neither the day nor the hour wherein the Son of man cometh. For the kingdom of heaven is as a man travelling into a far country, who called his own servants, and delivered unto them his goods. And unto one he gave five talents, to another two, and to another one; to every man according to his several ability; and straightway took his journey. Then he that had received the five talents went and traded with the same, and made them other five talents. And likewise he that had received two, he also gained other two. But he that had received one went and digged in the earth, and hid his lord's money. After a long time the lord of those servants cometh, and reckoneth with them. And so he that had received five talents came and brought other five talents, saying, Lord, thou deliveredst unto me five talents: behold, I have gained beside them five talents more. His lord said unto him, Well done, thou good and faithful servant: thou hast been faithful over a few things, I will make thee ruler over many things: enter thou into the joy of thy lord. He also that had received two talents came and said, Lord, thou deliveredst unto me two talents: behold, I have gained two other talents beside them. His lord said unto him, Well done, good and faithful servant; thou hast been faithful over a few things, I will make thee ruler over many things: enter thou into the joy of thy lord. Then he which had received the one talent came and said, Lord, I knew thee that thou art an hard man, reaping where thou hast not sown, and gathering where thou hast not strawed: And I was afraid, and went and hid thy talent in the earth: lo, there thou hast that is thine. His lord answered and said unto him, Thou wicked and slothful servant, thou knewest that I reap where I sowed not, and gather where I have not strawed: Thou oughtest therefore to have put my money to the exchangers, and then at my coming I should have received mine own with usury. Take therefore the talent from him, and give it unto him which hath ten talents. For unto every one that hath shall be given, and he shall have abundance: but from him that hath not shall be taken away even that which he hath. And cast ye the unprofitable servant into outer darkness: there shall be weeping and gnashing of teeth. When the Son of man shall come in his glory, and all the holy angels with him, then shall he sit upon the throne of his glory: And before him shall be gathered all nations: and he shall separate them one from another, as a shepherd divideth his sheep from the goats: And he shall set the sheep on his right hand, but the goats on the left. Then shall the King say unto them on his right hand, Come, ye blessed of my Father, inherit the kingdom prepared for you from the foundation of the world: For I was an hungred, and ye gave me meat: I was thirsty, and ye gave me drink: I was a stranger, and ye took me in: naked, and ye clothed me: I was sick, and ye visited me: I was in prison, and ye came unto me. Then shall the righteous answer him, saying, Lord, when saw we thee an hungred, and fed thee? or thirsty, and gave thee drink? When saw we thee a stranger, and took thee in? or naked, and clothed thee? Or when saw we thee sick, or in prison, and came unto thee? And the King shall answer and say unto them, Verily I say unto you, inasmuch as ye have done it unto one of the least of these my brethren, ye have done it unto me. Then shall he say also unto them on the left hand, Depart from me, ye cursed, into everlasting fire, prepared for the devil and his angels: For I was an hungred, and ye gave me no meat: I was thirsty, and ye gave me no drink: I was a stranger, and ye took me not in: naked, and ye clothed me not: sick, and in prison, and ye visited me not. Then shall they also answer him, saying, Lord, when saw we thee an hungred, or athirst, or a stranger, or naked, or sick, or in prison, and did not minister unto thee? Then shall he answer them, saying, Verily I say unto you, inasmuch as ye did it not to one of the least of these, ye did it not to me. And these shall go away into everlasting punishment: but the righteous into life eternal.

Matthew Chapter 26

And it came to pass, when Jesus had finished all these sayings, he said unto his disciples, Ye know that after two days is the feast of the Passover, and the Son of man is betrayed to be crucified. Then assembled together the chief priests, and the scribes, and the elders of the people, unto the palace of the high priest, who was called Caiaphas, And consulted that they might take Jesus by subtlety, and kill him. But they said, Not on the feast day, lest there be an uproar among the people. Now when Jesus was in Bethany, in the house of Simon the leper, there came unto him a woman having an alabaster box of very precious ointment, and poured it on his head, as he sat at meat. But when his disciples saw it, they had indignation, saying, To what purpose is this waste? For this ointment might have been sold for much, and given to the poor. When Jesus understood it, he said unto them, Why trouble ye the woman? For she hath wrought a good work upon me. For ye have the poor always with you; but me ye have not always. For in that she hath poured this ointment on my body, she did it for my burial. Verily I say unto you, Wheresoever this gospel shall be preached in the whole world, there shall also this, that this woman hath done, be told for a memorial of her. Then one of the twelve, called Judas Iscariot, went unto the chief priests, And said unto them, What will ye give me, and I will deliver him unto you? And they covenanted with him for thirty pieces of silver. And from that time he sought opportunity to betray him. Now the first day of the feast of unleavened bread the disciples came to Jesus, saying unto him, Where wilt thou that we prepare for thee to eat the Passover? And he said, Go into the city to such a man, and say unto him, The Master saith, My time is at hand; I will keep the Passover at thy house with my disciples. And the disciples did as Jesus had appointed them; and they made ready the passover. Now when the even was come, he sat down with the twelve. And as they did eat, he said, Verily I say unto you, that one of you shall betray me. And they were exceeding sorrowful, and began every one of them to say unto him, Lord, is it I? And he answered and said, He that dippeth his hand with me in the dish, the same shall betray me. The Son of man goeth as it is written of him: but woe unto that man by whom the Son of man is betrayed! It had been good for that man if he had not been born. Then Judas, which betrayed him, answered and said, Master, is it I? He said unto him, Thou hast said. And as they were eating, Jesus took bread, and blessed it, and brake it, and gave it to the disciples, and said, Take, eat; this is my body. And he took the cup, and gave thanks, and gave it to them, saying, Drink ye all of it; for this is my blood of the new testament, which is shed for many for the remission of sins. But I say unto you, I will not drink henceforth of this fruit of the vine, until that day when I drink it new with you in my Father's kingdom. And when they had sung an hymn, they went out into the mount of Olives. Then saith Jesus unto them, All ye shall be offended because of me this night: for it is written, I will smite the shepherd, and the sheep of the flock shall be scattered abroad. But after I am risen again, I will go before you into Galilee. Peter answered and said unto him, Though all men shall be offended because of thee, yet will I never be offended. Jesus said unto him, Verily I say unto thee, that this night, before the cock crow, thou shalt deny me thrice. Peter said unto him, though I should die with thee, yet will I not deny thee. Likewise also said all the disciples. Then cometh Jesus with them unto a place called Gethsemane, and saith unto the disciples, sit ye here, while I go and pray yonder. And he took with him Peter and the two sons of Zebedee, and began to be sorrowful and very heavy. Then saith he unto them, my soul is exceeding sorrowful, even unto death: tarry ye here, and watch with me. And he went a little farther, and fell on his face, and prayed, saying, O my Father, if it be possible, let this cup pass from me: nevertheless not as I will, but as thou wilt. And he cometh unto the disciples, and findeth them asleep, and saith unto Peter, What, could ye not watch with me one hour? Watch and pray, that ye enter not into temptation: the spirit indeed is willing, but the flesh is weak. He went away again the second time, and prayed, saying, O my Father, if this cup may not pass away from me, except I drink it, thy will be done. And he came and found them asleep again: for their eyes were heavy. And he left them, and went away again, and prayed the third time, saying the same words. Then cometh he to his disciples, and saith unto them, Sleep on now, and take your rest: behold, the hour is at hand, and the Son of man is betrayed into the hands of sinners. Rise, let us be going: behold, he is at hand that doth betray me. And while he yet spake, lo, Judas, one of the twelve, came, and with him a great multitude with swords and staves, from the chief priests and elders of the people. Now he that betrayed him gave them a sign, saying, Whomsoever I shall kiss, that same is he: hold him fast. And forthwith he came to Jesus, and said, Hail, master; and kissed him. And Jesus said unto him, Friend, wherefore art thou come? Then came they, and laid hands on Jesus and took him. And, behold, one of them which were with Jesus stretched out his hand, and drew his sword, and struck a servant of the high priest's, and smote off his ear. Then said Jesus unto him, Put up again thy sword into his place: for all they that take the sword shall perish with the sword. Thinkest thou that I cannot now pray to my Father, and he shall presently give me more than twelve legions of angels? But how then shall the scriptures be fulfilled, that thus it must be? In that same hour said Jesus to the multitudes, Are ye come out as against a thief with swords and staves for to take me? I sat daily with you teaching in the temple, and ye laid no hold on me. But all this was done, that the scriptures of the prophets might be fulfilled. Then all the disciples forsook him, and fled. And they that had laid hold on Jesus led him away to Caiaphas the high priest, where the scribes and the elders were assembled. But Peter followed him afar off unto the high priest's palace, and went in, and sat with the servants, to see the end. Now the chief priests, and elders, and all the council, sought false witness against Jesus, to put him to death; But found none: yea, though many false witnesses came, yet found they none. At the last came two false witnesses, and said, This fellow said, I am able to destroy the temple of God, and to build it in three days. And the high priest arose, and said unto him, Answerest thou nothing? What is it which these witness against thee? But Jesus held his peace, And the high priest answered and said unto him, I adjure thee by the living God, that thou tell us whether thou be the Christ, the Son of God. Jesus saith unto him, Thou hast said: nevertheless I say unto you, hereafter shall ye see the Son of man sitting on the right hand of power, and coming in the clouds of heaven. Then the high priest rent his clothes, saying, he hath spoken blasphemy; what further need have we of witnesses? Behold, now ye have heard his blasphemy. What think ye? They answered and said, he is guilty of death. Then did they spit in his face, and buffeted him; and others smote him with the palms of their hands, saying, Prophesy unto us, thou Christ, Who is he that smote thee? Now Peter sat without in the palace: and a damsel came unto him, saying, Thou also wast with Jesus of Galilee. But he denied before them all, saying, I know not what thou sayest. And when he was gone out into the porch, another maid saw him, and said unto them that were there, This fellow was also with Jesus of Nazareth. And again he denied with an oath, I do not know the man. And after a while came unto him they that stood by, and said to Peter, Surely thou also art one of them; for thy speech betrayeth thee. Then began he to curse and to swear, saying, I know not the man. And immediately the cock crew. And Peter remembered the word of Jesus, which said unto him, Before the cock crow, thou shalt deny me thrice. And he went out, and wept bitterly.

Matthew Chapter 27

When the morning was come, all the chief priests and elders of the people took counsel against Jesus to put him to death: And when they had bound him, they led him away, and delivered him to Pontius Pilate the governor. Then Judas, which had betrayed him, when he saw that he was condemned, repented himself, and brought again the thirty pieces of silver to the chief priests and elders, Saying, I have sinned in that I have betrayed the innocent blood. And they said, What is that to us? See thou to that. And he cast down the pieces of silver in the temple, and departed, and went and hanged himself. And the chief priests took the silver pieces, and said, It is not lawful for to put them into the treasury, because it is the price of blood. And they took counsel, and bought with them the potter's field, to bury strangers in. Wherefore that field was called, The Field of Blood, unto this day. Then was fulfilled that which was spoken by Jeremy the prophet, saying, And they took the thirty pieces of silver, the price of him that was valued, whom they of the children of Israel did value; And gave them for the potter's field, as the Lord appointed me. And Jesus stood before the governor: and the governor asked him, saying, Art thou the King of the Jews? And Jesus said unto him, Thou sayest. And when he was accused of the chief priests and elders, he answered nothing. Then said Pilate unto him, Hearest thou not how many things they witness against thee? And he answered him to never a word; insomuch that the governor marvelled greatly. Now at that feast the governor was wont to release unto the people a prisoner, whom they would. And they had then a notable prisoner, called Barabbas. Therefore when they were gathered together, Pilate said unto them, Whom will ye that I release unto you? Barabbas, or Jesus which is called Christ? For he knew that for envy they had delivered him. When he was set down on the judgment seat, his wife sent unto him, saying, Have thou nothing to do with that just man: for I have suffered many things this day in a dream because of him. But the chief priests and elders persuaded the multitude that they should ask Barabbas, and destroy Jesus. The governor answered and said unto them, Whether of the twain will ye that I release unto you? They said, Barabbas. Pilate saith unto them, What shall I do then with Jesus which is called Christ? They all say unto him, Let him be crucified. And the governor said, Why, what evil hath he done? But they cried out the more, saying, Let him be crucified. When Pilate saw that he could prevail nothing, but that rather a tumult was made, he took water, and washed his hands before the multitude, saying, I am innocent of the blood of this just person: see ye to it. Then answered all the people, and said, His blood be on us, and on our children. Then released he Barabbas unto them: and when he had scourged Jesus, he delivered him to be crucified. Then the soldiers of the governor took Jesus into the common hall, and gathered unto him the whole band of soldiers. And they stripped him, and put on him a scarlet robe. And when they had platted a crown of thorns, they put it upon his head, and a reed in his right hand: and they bowed the knee before him, and mocked him, saying, Hail, King of the Jews! And they spit upon him, and took the reed, and smote him on the head. And after that they had mocked him, they took the robe off from him, and put his own raiment on him, and led him away to crucify him. And as they came out, they found a man of Cyrene, Simon by name: him they compelled to bear his cross. And when they were come unto a place called Golgotha, that is to say, a place of a skull, they gave him vinegar to drink mingled with gall: and when he had tasted thereof, he would not drink. And they crucified him, and parted his garments, casting lots: that it might be fulfilled which was spoken by the prophet, They parted my garments among them, and upon my vesture did they cast lots. And sitting down they watched him there; And set up over his head his accusation written, THIS IS JESUS THE KING OF THE JEWS.

Then were there two thieves crucified with him, one on the right hand, and another on the left. And they that passed by reviled him, wagging their heads, And saying, Thou that destroyest the temple, and buildest it in three days, save thyself. If thou be the Son of God, come down from the cross. Likewise also the chief priests mocking him, with the scribes and elders, said, He saved others; himself he cannot save. If he be the King of Israel, let him now come down from the cross, and we will believe him. He trusted in God; let him deliver him now, if he will have him: for he said, I am the Son of God. The thieves also, which were crucified with him, cast the same in his teeth. Now from the sixth hour there was darkness over all the land unto the ninth hour. And about the ninth hour Jesus cried with a loud voice, saying, Eli, Eli, lama sabachthani? that is to say, My God, my God, why hast thou forsaken me? Some of them that stood there, when they heard that, said, This man calleth for Elias. And straightway one of them ran, and took a spunge, and filled it with vinegar, and put it on a reed, and gave him to drink. The rest said, Let be, let us see whether Elias will come to save him. Jesus, when he had cried again with a loud voice, yielded up the ghost. And, behold, the veil of the temple was rent in twain from the top to the bottom; and the earth did quake, and the rocks rent; And the graves were opened; and many bodies of the saints which slept arose, And came out of the graves after his resurrection, and went into the holy city, and appeared unto many. Now when the centurion, and they that were with him, watching Jesus, saw the earthquake, and those things that were done, they feared greatly, saying, Truly this was the Son of God. And many women were there beholding afar off, which followed Jesus from Galilee, ministering unto him: Among which was Mary Magdalene, and Mary the mother of James and Joses, and the mother of Zebedees children. When the even was come, there came a rich man of Arimathaea, named Joseph, who also himself was Jesus' disciple: He went to Pilate, and begged the body of Jesus. Then Pilate commanded the body to be delivered. And when Joseph had taken the body, he wrapped it in a clean linen cloth, And laid it in his own new tomb, which he had hewn out in the rock: and he rolled a great stone to the door of the sepulchre, and departed. And there was Mary Magdalene, and the other Mary, sitting over against the sepulchre. Now the next day, that followed the day of the preparation, the chief priests and Pharisees came together unto Pilate, saying, Sir, we remember that that deceiver said, while he was yet alive, After three days I will rise again. Command therefore that the sepulchre be made sure until the third day, lest his disciples come by night, and steal him away, and say unto the people, He is risen from the dead: so the last error shall be worse than the first. Pilate said unto them, Ye have a watch: go your way, make it as sure as ye can. So they went, and made the sepulchre sure, sealing the stone, and setting a watch.

Matthew Chapter 28

In the end of the sabbath, as it began to dawn toward the first day of the week, came Mary Magdalene and the other Mary to see the sepulchre. And, behold, there was a great earthquake: for the angel of the Lord descended from heaven, and came and rolled back the stone from the door, and sat upon it. His countenance was like lightning, and his raiment white as snow: And for fear of him the keepers did shake, and became as dead men. And the angel answered and said unto the women, Fear not ye: for I know that ye seek Jesus, which was crucified. He is not here: for he is risen, as he said. Come, see the place where the Lord lay. And go quickly, and tell his disciples that he is risen from the dead; and, behold, he goeth before you into Galilee; there shall ye see him: lo, I have told you. And they departed quickly from the sepulchre with fear and great joy; and did run to bring his disciples word. And as they went to tell his disciples, behold, Jesus met them, saying, All hail. And they came and held him by the feet, and worshipped him. Then said Jesus unto them, Be not afraid: go tell my brethren that they go into Galilee, and there shall they see me. Now when they were going, behold, some of the watch came into the city, and shewed unto the chief priests all the things that were done. And when they were assembled with the elders, and had taken counsel, they gave large money unto the soldiers, Saying, Say ye, His disciples came by night, and stole him away while we slept. And if this come to the governor's ears, we will persuade him, and secure you. So they took the money, and did as they were taught: and this saying is commonly reported among the Jews until this day. Then the eleven disciples went away into Galilee, into a mountain where Jesus had appointed them. And when they saw him, they worshipped him: but some doubted. And Jesus came and spake unto them, saying, All power is given unto me in heaven and in earth. Go ye therefore, and teach all nations, baptizing them in the name of the Father, and of the Son, and of the Holy Ghost: Teaching them to observe all things whatsoever I have commanded you: and, lo, I am with you always, even unto the end of the world. Amen.

[…]

John Chapter 1

In the beginning was the Word, and the Word was with God, and the Word was God. The same was in the beginning with God. All things were made by him; and without him was not any thing made that was made. In him was life; and the life was the light of men. And the light shineth in darkness; and the darkness comprehended it not. There was a man sent from God, whose name was John. The same came for a witness, to bear witness of the Light, that all men through him might believe. He was not that Light, but was sent to bear witness of that Light. That was the true Light, which lighteth every man that cometh into the world. He was in the world, and the world was made by him, and the world knew him not. He came unto his own, and his own received him not. But as many as received him, to them gave he power to become the sons of God, even to them that believe on his name: Which were born, not of blood, nor of the will of the flesh, nor of the will of man, but of God. And the Word was made flesh, and dwelt among us, (and we beheld his glory, the glory as of the only begotten of the Father,) full of grace and truth. John bare witness of him, and cried, saying, This was he of whom I spake, He that cometh after me is preferred before me: for he was before me. And of his fulness have all we received, and grace for grace. For the law was given by Moses, but grace and truth came by Jesus Christ.

<...>

Philippians Chapter 1

Paul and Timotheus, the servants of Jesus Christ, to all the saints in Christ Jesus which are at Philippi, with the bishops and deacons: Grace be unto you, and peace, from God our Father, and from the Lord Jesus Christ. I thank my God upon every remembrance of you, Always in every prayer of mine for you all making request with joy, For your fellowship in the gospel from the first day until now; Being confident of this very thing, that he which hath begun a good work in you will perform it until the day of Jesus Christ: Even as it is meet for me to think this of you all, because I have you in my heart; inasmuch as both in my bonds, and in the defence and confirmation of the gospel, ye all are partakers of my grace. For God is my record, how greatly I long after you all in the bowels of Jesus Christ. And this I pray, that your love may abound yet more and more in knowledge and in all judgment; That ye may approve things that are excellent; that ye may be sincere and without offence till the day of Christ. Being filled with the fruits of righteousness, which are by Jesus Christ, unto the glory and praise of God. But I would ye should understand, brethren, that the things which happened unto me have fallen out rather unto the furtherance of the gospel; So that my bonds in Christ are manifest in all the palace, and in all other places; And many of the brethren in the Lord, waxing confident by my bonds, are much more bold to speak the word without fear. Some indeed preach Christ even of envy and strife; and some also of good will: The one preach Christ of contention, not sincerely, supposing to add affliction to my bonds: But the other of love, knowing that I am set for the defence of the gospel. What then? Notwithstanding, every way, whether in pretence, or in truth, Christ is preached; and I therein do rejoice, yea, and will rejoice. For I know that this shall turn to my salvation through your prayer, and the supply of the Spirit of Jesus Christ, According to my earnest expectation and my hope, that in nothing I shall be ashamed, but that with all boldness, as always, so now also Christ shall be magnified in my body, whether it be by life, or by death. For to me to live is Christ, and to die is gain. But if I live in the flesh, this is the fruit of my labour: yet what I shall choose I wot not. For I am in a strait betwixt two, having a desire to depart, and to be with Christ; which is far better: Nevertheless to abide in the flesh is more needful for you. And having this confidence, I know that I shall abide and continue with you all for your furtherance and joy of faith; That your rejoicing may be more abundant in Jesus Christ for me by my coming to you again. Only let your conversation be as it becometh the gospel of Christ:

that whether I come and see you, or else be absent, I may hear of your affairs, that ye stand fast in one spirit, with one mind striving together for the faith of the gospel; And in nothing terrified by your adversaries: which is to them an evident token of perdition, but to you of salvation, and that of God. For unto you it is given in the behalf of Christ, not only to believe on him, but also to suffer for his sake; Having the same conflict which ye saw in me, and now hear to be in me.

<...>

Philippians Chapter 4

Therefore, my brethren dearly beloved and longed for, my joy and crown, so stand fast in the Lord, my dearly beloved. I beseech Euodias, and beseech Syntyche, that they be of the same mind in the Lord. And I intreat thee also, true yokefellow, help those women which laboured with me in the gospel, with Clement also, and with other my fellow labourers, whose names are in the book of life. Rejoice in the Lord alway: and again I say, Rejoice. Let your moderation be known unto all men. The Lord is at hand. Be careful for nothing; but in every thing by prayer and supplication with thanksgiving let your requests be made known unto God. And the peace of God, which passeth all understanding, shall keep your hearts and minds through Christ Jesus. Finally, brethren, whatsoever things are true, whatsoever things are honest, whatsoever things are just, whatsoever things are pure, whatsoever things are lovely, whatsoever things are of good report; if there be any virtue, and if there be any praise, think on these things. Those things, which ye have both learned, and received, and heard, and seen in me, do: and the God of peace shall be with you. But I rejoiced in the Lord greatly, that now at the last your care of me hath flourished again; wherein ye were also careful, but ye lacked opportunity. Not that I speak in respect of want: for I have learned, in whatsoever state I am, therewith to be content. I know both how to be abased, and I know how to abound: every where and in all things I am instructed both to be full and to be hungry, both to abound and to suffer need. I can do all things through Christ which strengtheneth me. Notwithstanding ye have well done, that ye did communicate with my affliction. Now ye Philippians know also, that in the beginning of the gospel, when I departed from Macedonia, no church communicated with me as concerning giving and receiving, but ye only. For even in Thessalonica ye sent once and again unto my necessity. Not because I desire a gift: but I desire fruit that may abound to your account. But I have all, and abound: I am full, having received of Epaphroditus the things which were sent from you, an odour of a sweet smell, a sacrifice acceptable, well-pleasing to God. But my God shall supply all your need according to his riches in glory by Christ Jesus. Now unto God and our Father be glory for ever and ever. Amen. Salute every saint in Christ Jesus. The brethren which are with me greet you. All the saints salute you, chiefly they that are of Caesar's household. The grace of our Lord Jesus Christ be with you all. Amen.

Chapter 7
Islam

The Qur'an

Muslims believe the Qur'an to have been given by God (Allah) to the Prophet Muhammad during the early part of the Seventh Century of the Common Era. Organized into 114 Chapters or Surahs (typically with a provenance from Mecca or Medina), the Qur'an opens with the most recited of prayers among Muslims, The Opening Prayer. One of the Pillars of Islam is to face Islam's site in Mecca and pray five times daily. Parts of the Qur'an, particularly the Opening Prayer, are prominent in this regard.

After the First Surah, or brief Opening Prayer, the Surahs of the Qur'an are lengthy in the beginning (starting with the Second Surah) and gradually becoming shorter. Toward the end, the Surahs are quite brief, with some of them only being a few lines.

In this volume, we read the Opening Surah, and then two of the lengthy Surahs from the front, and two short Surahs from near the end. From early in the Qur'an, we consider Surahs III and IV.

Surah III is set against a backdrop of understanding some of the ideas of Judaism and Christianity. It considers the family of Jesus (whom Muslims consider a Prophet, but not the Messiah), ideas about the Resurrection, and refers to other "People of the Book" (Jews and Christians—both monotheistic and honoring God's Covenant with Abraham).

This Surah explores a theme that will resonate throughout the Qur'an—the absolute power and sovereignty of Allah. Underscoring a theme we saw earlier in other traditions (e.g. in the words of the Buddha and of Paul in the Christian New Testament), this Surah affirms that meditating on good things will be rewarded. On the other hand, thinking on bad things will bring evil.

Surah IV is one of the most quoted and cited sections of the Qur'an. It grapples with a number of the complexities of gender relations, giving a sense of the expectations of women and of children and men in an array of situations.

In this section is laid out guidelines of inheritance. As a general rule, for example, sons inherit twice as much as daughters. But this is followed by a number of nuances. What about if there are more than two girls? What about deceased children? This Surah addresses such questions and more.

Believers are exhorted to conduct themselves in good faith in all endeavors. Honesty is demanded in all things; hypocrisy is condemned.

Again in this Surah, there is attention to the Muslim view of major figures from Jewish and Christian history. While there is much in Islam that is in concert with the other Abrahamic traditions, there are some significant differences as well. In concert with the other Abrahamic traditions, the reader learns, for example, that God spoke directly to Moses. In contrast with the Christian tradition, Jesus, the son of Mary, is seen as "no more than an apostle." He is not seen as having been crucified, although the people "thought they did."

The Fourth Surah exhorts people to have faith and to do good works. Both faith and works are important. We see this theme throughout the Qur'an. We consider Surah XCII, on The Night, where the importance of putting faith into action through almsgiving is underscored. In fact, one of the Pillars of Islam focuses on almsgiving, and it is a central idea in Islam.

We consider next in Surah CXII a brief meditation on Oneness. Coming toward the end of the text, the 112th Surah is the shortest in the entire Qur'an. It is also one of the most poignant and powerful.

Let us now turn to the Qur'an…

The Opening Chapter

(Surah I. Mecca.)

In the name of the merciful and compassionate God.

Praise belongs to God, the Lord of the worlds, the merciful, the compassionate, the ruler of the day of judgment! Thee we serve and Thee we ask for aid. Guide us in the right path, the path of those Thou art gracious to; not of those Thou art wroth with; nor of those who err.

[…]

The Chapter of Imrân's Family

(Surah III. Medina.)

In the name of the merciful and compassionate God.

There is no god but He, the living, the self-subsistent. He has sent down to thee the Book in truth, confirming what was before it, and has revealed the law, and the gospel before for the guidance of men, and has revealed the Discrimination. Verily, those who disbelieve in the signs of God, for them is severe torment, for God is mighty and avenging. Verily, God, there is nothing hidden from Him in the earth, nor in the heaven; He it is who fashions you in the womb as He pleases. There is no God but He, the mighty, the wise.

He it is who has revealed to thee the Book, of which there are some verses that are decisive, they are the mother of the Book; and others ambiguous; but as for those in whose hearts is perversity, they follow what is ambiguous, and do crave for sedition, craving for (their own) interpretation of it; but none know the interpretation of it except God. But those who are well grounded in knowledge say, 'We believe in it; It is all from our Lord; but none will remember save those who possess minds.

'O Lord! Pervert not our hearts again when Thou hast guided them, and grant us mercy from Thee, for Thou art He who grants. O Lord! Thou shalt gather together men unto the day wherein is no doubt. Verily, God will not depart from His promise.' Verily, those who misbelieve, their wealth shall not help them, nor their children, against God at all; and they it is who are the fuel of the fire.

As was the wont of Pharaoh's people, and those before them, they said our signs were lies, and God caught them up in their sins, for God is severe to punish. Say to those who misbelieve, 'Ye shall be overcome and driven together to hell, an ill couch will it be.' 'Ye have had a sign in the two parties who met; one party fighting in the way of God, the other misbelieving; these saw twice the same number as themselves to the eyesight, for God aids with His help those whom He pleases.' Verily, in that is a lesson for those who have perception. Seemly unto men is a life of lusts, of women, and children, and hoarded talents of gold and silver, and of horses well-bred, and cattle, and tilth;—that is the provision for the life of this world; but God, with Him is the best resort.

Say, 'But shall we tell you of a better thing than this?' For those who fear are gardens with their Lord, beneath which rivers flow; they shall dwell therein for aye, and pure wives and grace from God; the Lord looks on His servants, who say, 'Lord, we believe, pardon Thou our sins and keep us from the torment of the fire,'—upon the patient, the truthful, the devout, and those who ask for pardon at the dawn. God bears witness that there is no god but He, and the angels, and those possessed of knowledge standing up for justice. There is no God but He, the mighty, the wise.

Verily, (the true) religion in God's sight is Islâm, and those to whom the Book was given disagreed not until after that there was given to them knowledge, through mutual envy. But whoso disbelieves in God's signs, truly God is quick at reckoning up. And if they would dispute with thee, then say, 'I turn my face with resignation unto God, and whoso follows me.' And say to those who have been given the Book, unto the Gentiles, 'Are ye, too, resigned?' And if they are resigned, then are they guided. But if they turn their backs, then thou hast only to preach, and God looks on his servants.

Verily, those who disbelieve in God's signs, and kill the prophets without right, and kill those from among men, who bid what is just,—to them give the glad tidings of grievous woe! These are they whose works are void in this world and the next, and helpers have they none. Did ye not see those who have been given a portion of the Book? They were called unto the Book of God to decide between them; and then a sect of them turned their backs and turned away;—that is because they say the fire shall not touch us save for a certain number of days. But that deceived them in their religion which they had invented. How will it be when we have gathered them together for a day whereof there is no doubt, when each soul shall be paid what it has earned, and they shall not be wronged?

Say, 'O God, Lord of the kingdom! Thou givest the kingdom to whomsoever Thou pleasest, and strippest the kingdom from whomsoever Thou pleasest; Thou honourest whom Thou pleasest, and abasest whom Thou pleasest; in Thy hand is good. Verily, Thou art mighty over all. Thou dost turn night to day, and dost turn day to night, and dost bring forth the living from the dead, and dost provide for whom Thou pleasest without taking count.' Those who believe shall not take misbelievers for their patrons, rather than believers, and he who does this has no part with God at all, unless, indeed, ye fear some danger from them. But God bids you beware of Himself, for unto Him your journey is.

Say, 'If ye hide that which is in your breasts, or if ye show it, God knows it: He knows what is in the heavens and what is in the earth, for God is mighty over all.' The day that every soul shall find what it has done of good present before it; and what it has done of evil, it would fain that there were between itself and that a wide interval. 'God bids you beware of Himself, but God is gentle with His servants.' Say, 'If ye would love God then follow me, and God will love you and forgive you your sins, for God is forgiving and merciful.' Say, 'Obey God and the Apostle; but if ye turn your backs God loves not misbelievers.'

Verily, God has chosen Adam, and Noah, and Abraham's people, and Imrân's people above the world,—a seed, of which one succeeds the other, but God both hears and knows. When Imrân's wife said, 'Lord! I have vowed to Thee what is within my womb, to be dedicated unto Thee, receive it then from me. Verily, Thou dost hear and know.' And when she brought it forth she said, 'Verily, I have brought it forth a female'—but God knew best what she brought forth; and a male is not like a female—'I have called her Mary, and I seek a refuge in Thee for her and for her seed from Satan the pelted.' And her Lord received her with a good reception, and made her grow up with a good growth, and Zachariah took care of her. Whenever Zachariah entered the chamber to her he found beside her a provision, and said, 'O Mary, how hast thou this?' She said, It is from God, for God provides for whom He pleases without count.' Therefore prayed Zachariah to his Lord, and said, 'Lord, grant me from Thee a good seed. Verily, Thou hearest prayer.' And an angel cried out to him as he was standing praying in the chamber (and said) that 'God gives thee the glad tidings of John, to confirm the Word from God,—of a chief and a chaste one, and a prophet from amongst the righteous.'

He said, 'My Lord, how can there be to me a boy when old age has reached me, and my wife is barren?' Said he, 'Thus God does what He pleaseth.' He said, 'My Lord, make for me a sign.' He said, 'Thy sign is that thou shalt not speak to men for three days, save by gesture; but remember thy Lord much, and celebrate His praises in the evening and the morning.' And when the angels said, 'O Mary! Verily, God has chosen thee, and has purified thee, and has chosen thee above the women of the world. O Mary! Be devout unto thy Lord, and adore and bow down with those who bow. That is (one) of the declarations of the unseen world which we reveal to thee, though thou wert not by them when they threw their lots for which of them should take care of Mary, nor were ye by them when they did dispute.'

When the angel said, 'O Mary! Verily, God gives thee the glad tidings of a Word from Him; his name shall be the Messiah Jesus the son of Mary, regarded in this world and the next and of those whose place is nigh to God. And he shall speak to people in his cradle, and when grown up, and shall be among the righteous.' She said, 'Lord! how can I have a son, when man has not yet touched me?' He said, 'Thus God creates what He pleaseth. When He decrees a matter He only says BE and it is; and He will teach him the Book, and wisdom, and the law, and the gospel, and he shall be a prophet to the people of Israel (saying), that I have come to you, with a sign from God, namely, that I will create for you out of clay as though it were the form of a bird, and I will blow thereon and it shall become a bird by God's permission; and I will heal the blind from birth, and lepers; and I will bring the dead to life by God's permission; and I will tell you what you eat and what ye store up in your houses. Verily, in that is a sign for you if ye be believers. And I will confirm what is before you of the law, and will surely make lawful for you some of that which was prohibited from you. I have come to you with a sign from your Lord, so fear God and follow me, for God is my Lord, and your Lord, so worship Him:—this is the right path.'

And when Jesus perceived their unbelief, He said, 'Who are my helpers for God?' Said the apostles, 'We are God's helpers. We believe in God, so bear witness that we are resigned. Lord, we have believed in what Thou hast revealed, and we have followed the Apostle, so write us down with those which bear witness.' But they (the Jews) were crafty, and God was crafty, for God is the best of crafty ones!

When God said, 'O Jesus! I will make Thee die and take Thee up again to me and will clear thee of those who misbelieve, and will make those who follow thee above those who misbelieve, at the day of judgment, then to me is your return. I will decide between you concerning that wherein ye disagree. And as for those who misbelieve, I will punish them with grievous punishment in this world and the next, and they shall have none to help them.'

But as for those who believe and do what is right, He will pay them their reward, for God loves not the unjust. That is what we recite to thee of the signs and of the wise reminder Verily, the likeness of Jesus with God is as the likeness of Adam. He created him from earth, then He said to him BE, and he was;—the truth from thy Lord, so be thou not of those who are in doubt. And whoso disputeth with thee after what has come to thee of knowledge, say, 'Come, let us call our sons and your sons, and our women and your women, and ourselves and yourselves: then we will imprecate and put God's curse on those who lie.'

Verily, those are the true stories, and there is no god but God, and, verily, God He is the mighty, the wise; but if they turn back, God knows the evildoers. Say, 'O ye people of the Book, come to a word laid down plainly between us and you, that we will not serve other than God, nor associate aught with him, nor take each other for lords rather than God.' But if they turn back then say, 'Bear witness that we are resigned.' O people of the Book, why do ye dispute about Abraham, when the law and the gospel were not revealed until after him? What! Do ye not understand? Here ye are, disputing about what ye have some knowledge of; why then do ye dispute about what ye have no knowledge of? God knows and ye know not.

Abraham was not a Jew, nor yet a Christian, but he was a "Hanîf resigned, and not of the idolaters. Verily, the people most worthy of Abraham are those who follow him and his prophets, and those who believe;—God is the patron of the believers. A sect of the people of the Book would fain they could lead you astray, but they only lead themselves astray, and they do not perceive. O people of the Book! Why do ye disbelieve in the signs of God, the while ye witness them? O people of the Book! Why do ye clothe the truth with falsehood and hide the truth the while ye know?

A sect of the people of the Book say, 'Believe in what was revealed to those who believed at the first appearance of the day, and disbelieve it at the end thereof,'—that (others) may perchance go back (from their faith)—'Do not believe save one who followeth your religion.' Say, 'Verily, the (true) guidance is the guidance of God, that one should be given like what ye are given.' Or would they dispute with you before your Lord, say, 'Grace is in the hand of God, He gives it to whom he pleases, for God both comprehends and knows. He specially favours with his mercy whom he pleases, for God is Lord of mighty grace.' And of the people of the Book, there are some of them who, if thou entrust them with a talent give it back to you; and some of them, if thou entrust them with a dînâr, he will not give it back to thee except so long as thou dost stand over him. That is because they say, 'We owe no duty to the Gentiles;' but they tell a lie against God, the while they know.

Yea, whoso fulfils his covenant and fears,—verily, God loves those who fear. Those who sell God's covenant and their oaths for a little price, these have no portion in the future life. God will not speak to them, and will not look upon them on the resurrection day, and will not purify them; but for them is grievous woe. And, verily, amongst them is a sect who twist their tongues concerning the Book, that ye may reckon it to be from the Book, but it is not from the Book. They say, 'It is from God,' but it is not from God, and they tell a lie against God, the while they know. It is not right for a man that God should give him a Book, and judgment, and prophecy, and that then he should say to men, 'Be ye servants of mine rather than of God' but be ye rather masters of teaching the Book and of what ye learn. He does not bid you take the angels and the prophets for your lords; shall He bid you misbelieve again when you are once resigned?'

And when God took the compact from the prophets '(This is) surely what we have given you of the Book and wisdom. Then shall come to you the Apostle confirming what is with you. Ye must believe in him and help him.' He said, moreover, 'Are ye resolved and have ye taken my compact on that (condition)?' They say, 'We are resolved.' He said, 'Then bear witness, for I am witness with you; but he who turns back after that, these are sinners.' What is it other than God's religion that they crave? When to Him is resigned whosoever is in the heavens and the earth, will he or nill he, and to him shall they return! Say, 'We believe in God, and what has been revealed to thee, and what was revealed to Abraham, and Ishmael, and Isaac, and Jacob, and the tribes, and what was given to Moses, and Jesus, and the prophets from their Lord,—we will make no distinction between any of them,—and we are unto Him resigned. Whosoever craves other than Islam for a religion, it shall surely not be accepted from him, and he shall, in the next world, be of those who lose.'

How shall God guide people who have disbelieved after believing and bearing witness that the Apostle is true, and after there come to them manifest signs? God guides the unjust folk. These, their reward is, that on them is the curse of God, and of the angels, and of men together; they shall dwell therein, for aye—the torment shall not be alleviated from them, nor shall they be respited; save those who repent after that, and act aright, for verily, God is forgiving and merciful. Verily, those who misbelieve after believing, and then increase in misbelief, their repentance shall not be accepted; these are those who err.

Verily, those who misbelieve and die in misbelief, there shall not be accepted from any one of them the earth-full of gold, though he should give it as a ransom. For them is grievous woe, and helpers have they none. Ye cannot attain to righteousness until ye expend in alms of what ye love. But what ye expend in alms, that God knows. All food was lawful to the children of Israel save what Israel made unlawful to himself before that the law was revealed. Say, 'Bring the law and recite it, if ye speak the truth.' But whoso forges against God a lie, after that, they are the unjust. Say, 'God speaks the truth, then follow the faith of Abraham, a ' 'Hanîf, who was not of the idolaters.'

Verily, the first House founded for men was surely that at Bekkah, for a blessing and a guidance to the worlds. Therein are manifest signs,—Abraham's station, and whosoever enters in is safe. There is due to God from man a pilgrimage unto the House, for whosoever can find his way there. But whoso misbelieves—God is independent of the worlds. Say, 'O people of the Book! Why do ye misbelieve in God's signs, while God is witness of what ye do?' Say, 'O people of the Book! Why do ye turn from the way of God him who believes, craving to make it crooked, while ye are witnesses? But God is not careless of what ye do.'

O ye who believe! If ye obey the sect of those to whom the Book was brought, they will turn you, after your faith, to unbelievers again. How can ye misbelieve while unto you are recited the signs of God, and among you is His Apostle? But whoso takes tight hold on God, he is guided into the right way. O ye who believe! Fear God with the fear that He deserves, and die not save ye be resigned. Take tight hold of God's rope altogether, and do not part in sects; but remember the favours of God towards you, when ye were enemies and He made friendship between your hearts, and on the morrow ye were, by His favour, brothers. Ye were on the edge of a pit of fire, but he rescued you therefrom. Thus does God show to you His signs, perchance ye may be guided; and that there may be of you a nation who shall invite to good, and bid what is reasonable, and forbid what is wrong; these are the prosperous. Be not like those who parted in sects and disagreed after there came to them manifest signs; for them is mighty woe, on the day when faces shall be whitened and faces shall be blackened. As for those whose faces are blackened,—'Did ye misbelieve after your faith, then taste the torment for your misbelief!' But as for those whose faces are whitened, they are in God's mercy, and they shall dwell therein for aye. These are the signs of God. We recite them to you in truth, for God desires not wrong unto the worlds.

God's is what is in the heavens and what is in the earth, and unto God affairs return. Ye were the best of nations brought forth unto man. Ye bid what is reasonable, and forbid what is wrong, believing in God. Had the people of the Book believed, it would have been better for them. There are believers among them, though most of them are sinners. They shall surely not harm you save a hurt; and if they fight you, they shall show you their backs, then they shall not be helped. They are smitten with abasement wherever they be found, save for the rope of God and the rope of man; and they draw on themselves wrath from God. They are smitten, too, with poverty; that is because they did disbelieve in God's signs, and kill the prophets undeservedly. That is because they did rebel and did transgress. They are not all alike. Of the people of the Book there is a nation upright, reciting God's signs throughout the night, as they adore the while. They believe in God, and in the last day, and bid what is reasonable, and forbid what is wrong, and vie in charity; these are among the righteous. What ye do of good surely God will not deny, for God knows those who fear.

Verily, those who misbelieve, their wealth is of no service to them, nor their children either, against God; they are the fellows of the Fire, and they shall dwell therein for aye. The likeness of what they expend in this life of the world, is as the likeness of wind wherein is a cold blast that falls upon a people's tilth who have wronged themselves and destroys it. It is not God who wrongs them, but it is themselves they wrong. O ye who believe! Take not to intimacy with others than yourselves; they will not fail to spoil you; they would fain ye came to trouble,—hatred is shown by their mouths; but what their breasts conceal is greater still. We have made manifest to you our signs, did ye but understand.

Ye it is who love them, but they love not you; and ye believe in the Book, all of it. But when they meet you they say, 'We believe;' and when they go aside they bite their finger tips at you through rage. Say, 'Die in your rage, for God doth know the nature of men's breasts.' If good luck touch you it is bad for them, but if bad luck befall you they rejoice therein; yet if ye are patient and fear, their tricks shall not harm you, for what they do God comprehends. When thou didst set forth early from thy people to settle for the believers a camp to fight;—but God both hears and knows;—when two companies of you were on the point of showing cowardice; but God was their guardian, for on God surely the believers do rely. Why! God gave you victory at Bedr when ye were in a poor way; fear God, then, haply ye may give thanks.

When thou didst say unto the believers, 'Is it not enough for you that your Lord assists you with three thousand of the angels sent down from on high? Yea, if ye are patient and fear God, and they come upon you on a sudden, now, your Lord will assist you with five thousand of His angels, (angels) of mark. God only made this as glad tidings for you to comfort your hearts withal,—for victory is but from God, the mighty, the wise;—to cut off the flank of those who misbelieve, or make them downcast, that they may retire disappointed.' Thou hast nothing to do with the affair at all, whether He turn towards them again or punish them; for, verily, they are unjust. God's is what is in the heavens and in the earth. He forgives whom He pleases, and punishes whom He pleases; for God is forgiving and merciful.

O ye who believe! Devour not usury doubly doubled, but fear God, perchance ye may be prosperous; fear the fire which is prepared for the unbelievers, and obey God and His Apostle, perchance ye may get mercy. And vie with one another for pardon from your Lord, and for Paradise, the breadth of which is as the heaven and the earth, prepared for those who fear;—for those who expend in alms, in prosperity and adversity, for those who repress their rage, and those who pardon men; God loves the kind. Those who when they do a crime, or wrong themselves, remember God, and ask forgiveness for their sins,—and who forgives sins save God?—and do not persevere in what they did, the while they know;—[130]—these have their reward:—pardon from their Lord, and gardens beneath which rivers flow, dwelling therein for aye; for pleasant is the hire of those who act like this. Incidents have passed before your time, go on then in the earth, and see what was the end of those who called (the prophets) liars. This is an explanation unto men, and a guidance and a warning unto those who fear. Do not give way nor grieve, for ye shall have the upper hand if ye but be believers.

If a sore touch you, a sore like it has touched people: these are days which we make to alternate amongst mankind that God may know who it is that believe, and may take from you witnesses, for God loves not the unjust; and that God may assay those who believe, and blot out the misbelievers. Do ye think that ye can enter Paradise and God not know those of you who have fought well, or know the patient? Why, ye longed for death before ye met it! Now ye have looked upon it and ye halt!

Mohammed is but an apostle; apostles have passed away before his time; what if he die or is killed, will ye retreat upon your heels? He who retreats upon his heels does no harm to God at all; but God will recompense the thankful. It is not for any soul to die, save by God's permission written down for an appointed time; but he who wishes for the reward of this world we will give him of it, and he who wishes for the reward of the future we will give him of it, and we will recompense the grateful.

How many prophets have myriads fought against! Yet they did not give way at what befel them in God's way! Nor were they weak, nor did they demean themselves:—God loves the patient. And their word was only to say, 'Lord, forgive us our sins and our

extravagance in our affairs; and make firm our footing and help us against the misbelieving folk!' And God gave them the reward of this world, and good reward for the
future too, for God doth love the kind.

O ye who believe! If ye obey those who misbelieve, they will turn you back upon
your heels, and ye will retreat the losers. Nay, God is your Lord, He is the best of helpers.
We will throw dread into the hearts of those who misbelieve, for that they associate that
with God. which He has sent down no power for; but their resort is fire, and evil is the
resort of the unjust.

God has truly kept His promise, when ye knocked them senseless by His permission,
until ye showed cowardice, and wrangled, and rebelled, after he had shown you what ye
loved. Amongst you are those who love this world, and amongst you are those who love
the next. Then He turned you away from them to try you; but He has pardoned you, for
God is Lord of grace unto believers,—when ye went up and looked not round upon any
one, although the Apostle was calling you from your rear. Therefore did God reward
you with trouble on trouble that ye should not grieve after what ye had missed, nor for
what befell you, for God is well aware of what ye do. Then He sent down upon you after
trouble safety,—drowsiness creeping over one company of you, and one company of
you getting anxious about themselves, suspecting about God other than the truth, with
the suspicion of the ignorant, and saying, 'Have we any chance in the affair?' Say, 'Verily,
the affair is God's.' They conceal in themselves what they will not show to thee, and say,
'If we had any chance in the affair we should not be killed here.' Say, 'If ye were in your
houses, surely those against whom slaughter was written down, would have gone forth
to fight even to where they are lying now; that God may try what is in your breasts and
assay what is in your hearts, for God doth know the nature of men's breasts.' Verily,
those of you who turned your backs on that day when the two armies met, it was but
Satan who made them slip for something they had earned. But God has now pardoned
them; verily, God is forgiving and clement.

O ye who believe! Be not like those who misbelieve, and say unto their brethren
when they knock about in the earth, or are upon a raid, 'Had they but been at home,
they had not died and had not been killed.' It was that God might make a sighing in
their hearts, for God gives life and death; and God on what ye do doth look. And if,
indeed, ye be killed in God's way or die, surely forgiveness from God and mercy is
better than what ye gather; and if ye die or be killed it is to God ye shall be assembled. It
was by a sort of mercy from God thou didst deal gently with them, for hadst thou been
rough and rude of heart they had dispersed from around thee. But pardon them, and
ask forgiveness for them, and take counsel with them in the affair. As for what thou hast
resolved, rely upon God; verily, God loves those who do rely. If God help you, there is
none can overcome you; but if He leave you in the lurch, who is there can help you after
Him? Upon God then let believers rely.

It is not for the prophet to cheat; and he who cheats shall bring what he has cheated on
the resurrection day. Then shall each soul be paid what it has earned, and they shall not
be wronged. Is he who follows the pleasure of God, like him who has drawn on himself

anger from God, whose resort is hell? An evil journey shall it be! These are degrees with God, and God sees what ye do. God was surely very gracious to the believers, when He sent amongst them an apostle from themselves, to recite to them His signs, and purify them, and teach them the Book and wisdom, although they surely were before his time in manifest error. Or when an accident befalls you, and ye have fallen on twice as much, ye say, 'How is this?' Say, 'It is from yourselves. Verily, God is mighty over all.'

And what befell you the day when the two armies met, it was by God's permission; that He might know the believers, and might know those who behaved hypocritically; for it was said to them, 'Come, fight in God's way,' or 'repel (the foe);' they said, 'If we knew how to fight we would surely follow you.' They were that day far nigher unto misbelief than they were to faith. They say with their mouths what is not in their hearts, but God doth know best what they hid. Those who said of their brethren, whilst they themselves stayed at home, 'Had they obeyed us they would not have been killed.' Say, 'Ward off from yourselves death, if ye do speak the truth.'

Count not those who are killed in the way of God as dead, but living with their Lord;—provided for, rejoicing in what God has brought them of His grace, and being glad for those who have not reached them yet,—those left behind them; there is no fear for them, and they shall not be grieved; glad at favour from God and grace, and that God wasteth not the hire of the believers. Whoso answered to the call of God and of His prophet after sorrow had befallen them, for those, if they do good and fear God, is a mighty hire. To whom when men said, 'Verily, men have gathered round you, fear then them,' it only increased their faith, and they said, 'God is enough for us, a good guardian is He.' Then they retired in favour from God and grace; no evil touched them; they followed the pleasure of God, and God is Lord of mighty grace. It is only that Satan who frightens his friends. Do not ye fear them, but fear me, if ye be believers.

Let them not grieve thee who vie with each other in misbelief. Verily, they cannot hurt God at all. God wills not to make for them a portion in the future life; but for them is mighty woe. Verily, those who purchase misbelief for faith, they do not hurt God at all, and for them is grievous woe. Let not those who misbelieve reckon that our letting them range is good for themselves. We only let them have their range that they may increase in sin. And for them is shameful woe. God would not leave believers in the state which ye are in, until He discerns the vile from the good. And God would not inform you of the unseen, but God chooses of His apostles whom He pleases. 'Wherefore believe ye in God and His Apostle; and if ye believe and fear, for you is mighty hire.'

And let not those who are niggard of what God has given them of His grace, count that it is best for them;—nay, it is worse for them. What they have been niggard of shall be a collar round their necks upon the resurrection day. And God's is the heritage of the heavens and the earth, and God of what ye do is, well aware. God heard the speech of those who said, 'Verily, God is poor and we are rich.' We will write down what they said, and how they killed the prophets undeservedly, and say, 'Taste ye the torment of burning;' this shall they suffer for what their hands have sent on before;—for, verily,

God is no unjust one to His servants,—who say, 'Verily, God has covenanted with us that we should not believe in an apostle until he gives us a sacrifice which fire devours.'

Say, 'There have come to you apostles before me with manifest signs, and with what ye talk about; why then did ye kill them, if ye speak the truth?' And if they did call thee a liar, apostles before thee have been called liars too, who came with manifest signs, and with scriptures, and with the illuminating Book. Every soul must taste of death; and ye shall only be paid your hire upon the resurrection day. But he who is forced away from the fire and brought into Paradise is indeed happy; but the life of this world is but a possession of deceit. Ye shall surely be tried in your wealth, and in your persons, and ye shall surely hear from those who have had the Book brought them before you, and from those who associate others with God, much harm. But if ye be patient and fear,—verily, that is one of the determined affairs. When God took the compact from those who have had the Book brought them that 'Ye shall of a surety manifest it unto men, and not hide it,' they cast it behind their backs, and bought therewith a little price,—but evil is what they buy.

Count not that those who rejoice in what they have produced, and love to be praised for what they have not done,—think not that they are in safety from woe,—for them is grievous woe! God's is the kingdom of the heavens and the earth, and God is mighty over all! Verily, in the creation of the heavens and the earth, and in the succession of night and day, are signs to those possessed of minds; who remember God standing and sitting or lying on their sides, and reflect on the creation of the heavens and the earth. 'O Lord! Thou hast not created this in vain. We celebrate Thy praise; then keep us from the torment of the fire! Lord! Verily, whomsoever Thou hast made to enter the fire, Thou hast disgraced him.; And the unjust shall have none to help them.

'Lord! Verily, we heard a crier calling to the faith, "Believe in your Lord," and we did believe. Lord! Forgive us our sins and cover our offences, and let us die with the righteous. Lord! And bring us what Thou hast promised us by Thy apostles, and disgrace us not upon the resurrection day; for, verily, Thou dost not break Thy promises!' And the Lord shall answer them, 'I waste not the works of a worker amongst you, be it male or female,—one of you is from the other. 'Those who fled, and were turned out of their houses, and were harmed in my way, and who fought and were killed, I will cover their offences, and I will make them enter into gardens beneath which rivers flow.' A reward from God; for God, with Him are the best of rewards.

Let it not deceive you that those who misbelieve go to and fro in the earth. It is a slight possession, and then their resort is Hell; an evil couch shall it be. But those who fear their Lord, for them are gardens beneath which rivers flow, and they shall dwell therein for aye,—an entertainment from God; and that which is with God is best for the righteous. Verily, of the people of the Book are some who do believe in God, and in what has been revealed to you, and what was revealed to them, humbling themselves before God, and selling not the signs of God for a little price. These shall have their reward with their Lord; verily, God is quick at reckoning up. O ye who believe! Be patient and vie in being patient, and be on the alert, and fear God, that haply ye may prosper.

(Surah IV. Medînah.)

In the name of the merciful and compassionate God.

O ye folk! Fear your Lord, who created you from one soul, and created therefrom its mate, and diffused from them twain many men and women. And fear God, in whose name ye beg of one another, and the wombs; verily, God over you doth watch. And give unto the orphans their property, and give them not the vile in exchange for the good, and devour not their property to your own property; verily, that were a great sin. But if ye fear that ye cannot do justice between orphans, then marry what seems good to you of women, by twos, or threes, or fours; and if ye fear that ye cannot be equitable, then only one, or what your right hands possess That keeps you nearer to not being partial. And give women their dowries freely; and if they are good enough to remit any of it of themselves, then devour it with good digestion and appetite. But do not give up to fools their property which God has made you to stand by; but maintain them from it, and clothe them, and speak to them with a reasonable speech.

Prove orphans until they reach a marriageable age, and if ye perceive in them right management, then hand over to them their property, and do not devour it extravagantly in anticipation of their growing up. And he who is rich, let him abstain; but he who is poor, let him devour in reason, and when ye hand over to them their property, then take witnesses against them; but God sufficeth for taking account. Men should have a portion of what their parents and kindred leave, and women should have a portion of what their parents and kindred leave, whether it be little or much, a determined portion. And when the next of kin and the orphans and the poor are present at the division, then maintain them out of it, and speak to them a reasonable speech.

And let these fear lest they leave behind them a weak seed, for whom they would be afraid; and let them fear God, and speak a straightforward speech. Verily, those who devour the property of orphans unjustly, only devour into their bellies fire, and they shall broil in flames. God instructs you concerning your children; for a male the like of the portion of two females, and if there be women above two, then let them have two-thirds of what (the deceased) leaves; and if there be but one, then let her have a half; and as to the parents, to each of them a sixth of what he leaves, if he has a son; but if he have no son, and his parents inherit, then let his mother have a third, and if he have brethren, let his mother have a sixth after payment of the bequest he bequeaths and of his debt.

Your parents or your children, ye know not which of them is nearest to you in usefulness:—an ordinance this from God; verily, God is knowing and wise! And ye shall have half of what your wives leave, if they have no son; but if they have a son, then ye shall have a fourth of what they leave, after payment of the bequests they bequeath or of their debts. And they shall have a fourth of what ye leave, if ye have no son; but if ye have a son, then let them have an eighth of what ye leave, after payment of the bequest ye bequeath and of your debts.

And if the man's or the woman's (property) be inherited by a kinsman who is neither parent nor child, and he have a brother or sister, then let each of these two have a sixth; but if they are more than that, let them share in a third after payment of the bequest he bequeaths and of his debts, without prejudice,—an ordinance this from God, and God is knowing and clement! These be God's bounds, and whoso obeys God and the Apostle He will make him enter into gardens beneath which rivers flow, and they shall dwell therein for aye;—that is the mighty happiness. But whoso rebels against God and His Apostle, and transgresses His bounds, He will make him enter into fire, and dwell therein for aye; and for him is shameful woe.

Against those of your women who commit adultery, call witnesses four in number from among yourselves; and if these bear witness, then keep the women in houses until death release them, or God shall make for them a way. And if two of you commit it, then hurt them both; but if they turn again and amend, leave them alone, verily, God is easily turned, compassionate.

God is only bound to turn again towards those who do evil through ignorance and then turn again, Surely, these will God turn again to, for God is knowing, wise. His turning again is not for those who do evil, until, when death comes before one of them, he says, 'Now I turn again;' nor yet for those who die in misbelief. For such as these have we prepared a grievous woe. O ye who believe! It is not lawful for you to inherit women's estates against their will; nor to hinder them, that ye may go off with part of what ye brought them, unless they commit fornication manifestly; but associate with them in reason, for if ye are averse from them, it may be that ye are averse from something wherein God has put much good for you. But if ye wish to exchange one wife for another, and have given one of them a talent, then take not from it anything. What! would you take it for a calumny and a manifest crime?

How can ye take it when one of you has gone in unto the other, and they have taken from you a rigid compact? And do not marry women your fathers married,—except bygones,—for it is abominable and hateful, and an evil way; unlawful for you are your mothers, and your daughters, and your sisters, and your paternal aunts and maternal aunts, and your brother's daughters, and your sister's daughters, and your foster mothers, and your foster sisters, and your wives' mothers, and your step daughters who are your wards, born of your wives to whom ye have gone in; but if ye have not gone in unto them, then it is no crime in you; and the lawful spouses of your sons from your own loins, and that ye form a connexion between two sisters,—except bygones,—verily, God is forgiving, merciful; and married women, save such as your right hands possess,—God's Book against you!—But lawful for you is all besides this, for you to seek them with your wealth, marrying them and not fornicating; but such of them as ye have enjoyed, give them their hire as a lawful due; for there is no crime in you about what ye agree between you after such lawful due, verily, God is knowing and wise. But whosoever of you cannot go the length of marrying marriageable women who believe, then take of what your right hands possess, of your maidens who believe;—though God knows best about your faith. Ye come one from the other; then marry them with the permission of their people, and give them their hire in reason, they being chaste and not fornicating, and not receivers of paramours.

But when they are married, if they commit fornication, then inflict upon them half the penalty for married women; that is for whomsoever of you fears wrong; but that ye should have patience is better for you, and God is forgiving and merciful. God wishes to explain to you and to guide you into the ordinances of those who were before you, and to turn towards you, for God is knowing, wise. God wishes to turn towards you, but those who follow their lusts wish that ye should swerve with a mighty swerving! God wishes to make it light for you, for man was created weak. O ye who believe! Devour not your property amongst yourselves vainly, unless it be a merchandise by mutual consent. And do not kill yourselves; verily, God is compassionate unto you. But whoso does that maliciously and unjustly, we will broil him with fire; for that is easy with God.

If ye avoid great sins from which ye are forbidden, we will cover your offences and make you enter with a noble entrance. And do not covet that by which God has preferred one of you over another. The men shall have a portion of what they earn, and the women a portion of what they earn; ask God for His grace, verily, God knows all. To every one have we appointed kinsfolk as heirs of what parents and relatives and those with whom ye have joined right hands leave; so give them their portion, for, verily, God is over all a witness.

Men stand superior to women in that God hath preferred some of them over others, and in that they expend of their wealth: and the virtuous women, devoted, careful (in their husbands') absence, as God has cared for them. But those whose perverseness ye fear, admonish them and remove them into bed-chambers and beat them; but if they submit to you, then do not seek a way against them; verily, God is high and great. And if ye fear a breach between the two, then send a judge from his people and a judge from her people. If they wish for reconciliation, God will arrange between them; verily, God is knowing and aware.

And serve God, and do not associate aught with Him; and to your parents show kindness, and to kindred, and orphans, and the poor, and the neighbour who is akin, and the neighbour who is a stranger, and the companion who is strange, and the son of the road, and what your right hands possess, verily, God loves not him who is proud and boastful; who are miserly and bid men be miserly too, and who hide what God has given them of His grace;—but we have prepared for the misbelievers shameful woe. And those who expend their wealth in alms for appearance sake before men, and who believe not in God nor in the last day;—but whosoever has Satan for his mate, an evil mate has he. What harm would it do them if they believed in God and in the last day, and expended in alms of what God has provided them with? But God knows about them. Verily, God would not wrong by the weight of an atom; and if it's a good work, He will double it and bring from Himself a mighty hire.

How then when we bring from every nation a witness, and bring thee as a witness against these on the day when those who misbelieve and rebel against the Apostle would fain that the earth were levelled with them? But they cannot hide the news from God.

O ye who believe! Approach not prayer while ye are drunk, until ye well know what ye say; nor yet while polluted,—unless ye be passing by the way,—until ye have washed yourselves. But if ye are sick, or on a journey, or one of you come from the privy, or if ye have touched a woman, and ye cannot find water, then use good surface sand and wipe your faces and your hands therewith; verily, God pardons and forgives. Do ye not see those who have been given a portion of the Book? They buy error, and they wish that ye may err from the way! But God knows best who your enemies are, and God suffices as a patron, and sufficient is God as a help. And those who are Jews, and those who pervert the words from their places, and say, 'We hear but we rebel, and do thou listen without hearing,' and (who say) 'râ'hinâ,' distorting it with their tongues and taunting about religion. But had they said, 'We hear and we obey, so listen and look upon us,' it would have been better for them and more upright;—but may God curse them in their misbelief, for they will not believe except a few.

O ye who have been given the Book! Believe in what we have revealed, confirming what ye had before; ere we deface your faces and turn them into hinder parts, or curse you as we cursed the fellows of the Sabbath when God's command was done. Verily, God pardons not associating aught with Him, but He pardons anything short of that to whomsoever He pleases; but he who associates aught with God, he hath devised a mighty sin. Do ye not see those who purify themselves? Nay, God purifies whom He will, and they shall not be wronged a straw. Behold, how they devise against God a lie, and that is manifest sin enough. Do ye not see those to whom a portion of the Book has been given? They believe in Gibt and Tâghût, and they say of those who misbelieve, 'These are better guided in the way than those who believe.'

These are those whom God has cursed, and whom God has cursed no helper shall he find. Shall they have a portion of the kingdom? Why even then they would not give to men a jot. Do they envy man for what God has given of His grace? We have given to Abraham's people the Book and wisdom, and we have given them a mighty kingdom: And of them are some who believe therein, and of them are some who turn from it, but Hell is flaming enough for them. Verily, those who disbelieve in our signs, we will broil them with fire; whenever their skins are well done, then we will change them for other skins, that they may taste the torment. Verily, God is glorious and wise.

But those who believe and do aright, we will make them enter gardens beneath which rivers flow, and they shall dwell therein for ever and aye, for them therein are pure wives, and we will make them enter into a shady shade. Verily, God bids you pay your trusts to their owners, and when ye judge between men to judge with justice. Verily, God, excellent is what He admonishes you with; verily, God both hears and sees. O ye who believe! Obey God, and obey the Apostle and those in authority amongst you; and if ye quarrel about anything, refer to God and the Apostle, if ye believe in God and the last day; that is better and fairer as a settlement. Do ye not see those who pretend that they believe in what has been revealed to them, and what was revealed before thee; they wish to refer their judgment to Tâghût, but they are bidden to disbelieve therein, and Satan wishes to lead them into a remote error. And when it is said to them, 'Come round to what God has sent down and unto the Apostle,' thou seest the hypocrites turning from thee, turning away.

How then when there befalls them a mischance through what their hands have sent on before? Then will they come to you, and swear by God, 'We meant naught but good and concord.' These, God knows what is in their hearts. Turn thou away from them and admonish them, and speak to them into their souls with a searching word. We have never sent an apostle save that he should be obeyed by the permission of God; and if they, when they have wronged themselves, come to thee and ask pardon of God, and the Apostle asks pardon for them, then they will find God easy to be turned, compassionate. But no! By thy Lord! They will not believe, until they have made thee judge of what they differ on; then they will not find in themselves aught to hinder what thou hast decreed, and they will submit with submission. But had we prescribed for them, 'Kill yourselves, or go ye forth out of your houses,' they would not have done it, save only a few of them but had they done what they are admonished, then it would have been better for them, and a more firm assurance.

And then we would surely have brought them from ourselves a mighty hire, and would have guided them into a right path. Whoso obeys God and the Apostle, these are with those God has been pleased with, of prophets and confessors and martyrs and the righteous;—a fair company are they. That is grace from God, and God knows well enough. O ye who believe! Take your precautions and sally in detachments or altogether. Verily, there is of you who tarries behind, and, if a mischance befalls you, says, 'God has been gracious to me, since I am not with them a martyr.'

But if there befalls you grace from God, he would say—as though there were no friendship between you and him—'O would that I had been with thee to attain this mighty happiness!' Let those then fight in God's way who sell this life of the world for the next; and whoso fights in God's way, then, be he killed or be he victorious, we will give him a mighty hire. What ails you that ye do not fight in God's way, and for the weak men and women and children, who say, 'Lord, bring us out of this town of oppressive folk, and make for us from Thee a patron, and make for us from Thee a help?' Those who believe fight in the way of God; and those who disbelieve fight in the way of Tâghût; fight ye then against the friends of Satan, verily, Satan's tricks are weak. Do ye not see those to whom it is said, 'Restrain your hands, and be steadfast in prayer and give alms;' and when it is prescribed for them to fight then a band of them fear men, as though it were the fear of God or a still stronger fear, and they say, 'O our Lord! why hast thou prescribed for us to fight, couldst thou not let us abide till our near appointed time?' Say, 'The enjoyment of this world is but slight, and the next is better for him who fears;'—but they shall not be wronged a straw.

Wheresoe'er ye be death will overtake you, though ye were in lofty towers. And if a good thing befall them, they say, 'This is from God,' but if a bad thing, they say, 'This is from thee.' Say, 'It is all from God.' What ails these people? They can hardly understand a tale. What befalls thee of good it is from God; and what befalls thee of bad it is from thyself. We have sent thee to mankind as an apostle, and God sufficeth for a witness.

Whoso obeys the prophet he has obeyed God; and he who turns back—we have not sent thee to watch over them. They say, 'Obedience!' But when they sally forth from you, a company of them brood by night over something else than that which thou hast said but God writes down that over which they brood. Turn then from them and rely on God, for God sufficeth for a guardian. Do they not meditate on the Qur'an? If it were from other than God they would find in it many a discrepancy.

And when there comes to them a matter of security or fear they publish it; but if they were to report it to the Apostle and to those in authority amongst them, then those of them who would elicit it from them would know it; but were it not for God's grace upon you and His mercy ye had followed Satan, save a few. Fight, then, in the way of God; impose not aught on any but thyself, and urge on the believers; it may be that God will restrain the violence of those who misbelieve, for God is more violent and more severe to punish. Whoso intercedes with a good intercession shall have a portion therefrom; but he who intercedes with a bad intercession shall have the like thereof, for God keeps watch over all things. And when ye are saluted with a salutation, salute with a better than it, or return it;—verily, God of all things takes account. God, there is no God but He! He will surely assemble you on the resurrection day, there is no doubt therein; who is truer than God in his discourse?

Why are ye two parties about the hypocrites, when God hath overturned them for what they earned? Do ye wish to guide those whom God hath led astray? Whoso God hath led astray ye shall not surely find for him a path. They would fain that ye misbelieve as they misbelieve, that ye might be alike; take ye not patrons from among them until they too flee in God's way; but if they turn their backs, then seize them and kill them wheresoever ye find them, and take from them neither patron nor help,—save those who reach a people betwixt whom and you is an alliance—or who come to you while their bosoms prevent them from fighting you or fighting their own people. But had God pleased He would have given you dominion over them, and they would surely have fought you. But if they retire from you and do not fight you, and offer you peace,—then God hath given you no way against them. Ye will find others who seek for quarter from you, and quarter from their own people; whenever they return to sedition they shall be overturned therein: but if they retire not from you, nor offer you peace, nor restrain their hands, then seize them and kill them wheresoever ye find them;—over these we have made for you manifest power.

It is not for a believer to kill a believer save by mistake; and whosoever kills a believer by mistake then let him free a believing neck; and the blood-money must be paid to his people save what they shall remit as alms. But if he be from a tribe hostile to you and yet a believer, then let him free a believing neck. And if it be a tribe betwixt whom and you there is an alliance, then let the blood-money be paid to his friends, and let him free a believing neck; but he who cannot find the means, then let him fast for two consecutive months—a penance this from God, for God is knowing, wise.

And whoso kills a believer purposely, his reward is hell, to dwell therein for aye; and God will be wrath with him, and curse him, and prepare for him a mighty woe. O ye who believe! When ye are knocking about in the way of God be discerning, and do not say to him who offers you a salutation, 'Thou art no believer,' craving after the chances of this world's life, for with God are many spoils! So were ye aforetime, but God was gracious to you, be ye then discerning; verily, God of what ye do is well aware.

Not alike are those of the believers who sit at home without harm, and those who are strenuous in God's way with their wealth and their persons. God hath preferred those who are strenuous with their wealth and their persons to those who sit still, by many degrees, and to each hath God promised good, but God hath preferred the strenuous for a mighty hire over those who sit still,—degrees from him, and pardon and mercy, for God is forgiving and merciful. Verily, the angels when they took the souls of those who had wronged themselves, said, 'What state were ye in?' They say, 'We were but weak in the earth;' they said, 'Was not God's earth wide enough for you to flee away therein?' These are those whose resort is hell, and a bad journey shall it be! Save for the weak men, and women, and children, who could not compass any stratagem, and were not guided to a way; these it may be God will pardon, for God both pardons and forgives.

Whosoever flees in the way of God shall find in the earth many a spacious refuge, and he who goes forth from his house, fleeing unto God and His prophet, and then death catches him up,—his hire devolves on God, and God is forgiving and merciful. And when ye knock about in the earth, it is no crime to you that ye come short in prayer, if ye fear that those who disbelieve will set upon you; verily, the misbelievers are your obvious foes. When thou art amongst them, and standest up to pray with them, then let a party of them stand up with thee, and let them take their arms; and when they adore, let them go behind you, and let another party who have not yet prayed come forward and pray with thee; and let them take their precautions and their arms. Fain would those who misbelieve that ye were careless of your arms and your baggage, that they might turn upon you with a single turning. And it is no crime to you if ye be annoyed with rain or be sick, that ye lay down your arms; but take your precautions,—verily, God has prepared for those who misbelieve a shameful woe. But when ye have fulfilled your prayer, remember God standing and sitting and lying on your sides; and when ye are in safety then be steadfast in prayer; verily, prayer is for the believers prescribed and timed!

And do not give way in pursuit of the people; if ye suffer they shall surely suffer too, even as ye suffer; and ye hope from God, but they hope not! And God is knowing, wise. Verily, we have revealed to thee the Book in truth that thou mayest judge between men of what God has shown thee; so be not with the treacherous a disputant; but ask God's pardon: verily, God is forgiving, merciful. And wrangle not for those who defraud themselves; for God loves not him who is a fraudulent sinner. They hide themselves from men; but they cannot hide themselves from God, for He is with them while they brood at night over speeches that please Him not;—but God doth compass what they do! Here are ye, wrangling for them about this world's life;—but who shall wrangle with God for them on the day of judgment, or who shall be a guardian over them?

Yet whoso does evil and wrongs himself, and then asks pardon of God, shall find God forgiving and merciful; and whoso commits a crime, he only commits it against himself, for God is knowing, wise. And whoso commits a fault or a sin and throws it on the innocent, he hath to bear a calumny and a manifest sin. Were it not for God's grace upon thee, and His mercy, a party of them would have tried to lead thee astray; but they only lead themselves astray; they shall not hurt you in aught: for God hath sent down upon thee the Book and the wisdom, and taught thee what thou didst not know, for God's grace was mighty on thee. There is no good in most of what they talk in private save in his who bids almsgiving, or kindness, or reconciliation between men; and whoso does this, craving the good pleasure of God, we will give to him a mighty hire.

But he who severs himself from the prophet after that we have made manifest to him the guidance, and follows other than the way of the believers, we will turn our backs on him as he hath turned his back; and we will make him reach hell, and a bad journey shall it be. Verily, God forgives not associating aught with Him, but He pardons anything short of that, to whomsoever He will; but whoso associates aught with God, he hath erred a wide error. Verily, they call not beside Him on aught save females; and they do not call on aught save a rebellious devil. God curse him! For he said, 'I will take from thy servants a portion due to me; and I will lead them astray; and I will stir up vain desires within them; and I will order them and they shall surely crop the ears of cattle; and I will order them and they shall surely alter God's creation;' But he who takes the devil for his patron instead of God, he loses with a manifest loss. He promises them, and stirs up vain desires within them; but the devil promises only to deceive.

These, their resort is hell; they shall not find an escape therefrom! But those who believe, and do what is right, we will make them enter into gardens beneath which rivers flow, to dwell therein for aye,—God's promise in truth; and who is truer than God in speech? Not for your vain desires, nor the vain desires of the people of the Book. He who doeth evil shall be recompensed therewith, and shall not find for him beside God a patron, or a help. But he who doeth good works,—be it male or female,—and believes, they shall enter into Paradise, and they shall not be wronged a jot. Who has a better religion than he who resigns his face to God, and does good, and follows the faith of Abraham, as a Hanîf?—For God took Abraham as a friend.

And God's is what is in the heavens and in the earth, and God encompasses all things! They will ask thee a decision about women; say, 'God decides for you about them, and that which is rehearsed to you in the Book; about orphan women to whom ye do not give what is prescribed for them, and whom ye are averse from marrying; and about weak children; and that ye stand fairly by orphans;—and what ye do of good, verily, that God knows.' And if a woman fears from her husband perverseness or aversion, it is no crime in them both that they should be reconciled to each other, for reconciliation is best. For souls are prone to avarice; but if ye act kindly and fear God, of what ye do He is aware. Ye are not able, it may be, to act equitably to your wives, even though ye covet it; do not however be quite partial, and leave one as it were in suspense; but if ye be reconciled and fear, then God is forgiving and merciful; but if they separate, God can make both independent out of His abundance; for God is abundant, wise.

God's is what is in the heavens and what is in the earth! We have ordained to those who have been given the Book before you, and to you too that ye fear God;—but if ye misbelieve, verily, God's is what is in the heavens and what is in the earth, and God is rich and to be praised! God's is what is in the heavens and what is in the earth! And God sufficeth for a guardian! If He will He can make ye pass away, O men! And can bring others;—God is able to do all that. He who wishes for a reward in this world,—with God is the reward of this world and of the next, and God both hears and sees. O ye who believe! Be ye steadfast in justice, witnessing before God though it be against yourselves, or your parents, or your kindred, be it rich or poor, for God is nearer akin than either. Follow not, then, lusts, so as to act partially; but if ye swerve or turn aside, God of what ye do is well aware.

O ye who believe! Believe in God and His apostles, and the Book which He hath re-vealed to His Apostle, and the Book which He sent down before; for whoso disbelieves in God, and His angels, and His Apostle, and the last day, has erred a wide error. Verily, those who believe and then misbelieve, and then believe and then misbelieve, and then increase in misbelief, God will never pardon them, nor will He guide them in the path. Give to the hypocrites the glad tidings that for them is grievous woe! Those who take the misbelievers for their patrons rather than believers,—do they crave honour from them? Verily, honour is altogether God's! He hath revealed this to you in the Book, that when ye hear the signs of God disbelieved in and mocked at, then sit ye not down with them until they plunge into another discourse, for verily, then ye would be like them. Verily, God will gather the hypocrites and misbelievers into hell together.

Those who lie in wait for you, and if the victory be yours from God, say, 'Were we not with you?' And if the misbelievers have a chance, they say, 'Did we not get the mastery over you, and defend you from the believers?' But God shall judge between you on the resurrection day; for God will not give the misbelievers a way against believers. Verily, the hypocrites seek to deceive God, but He deceives them; and when they rise up to pray, they rise up lazily to be seen of men, and do not remember God, except a few; wavering between the two, neither to these nor yet to those! But whomsoever God doth lead astray thou shall not find for him a way. O ye who believe! Take not misbelievers for patrons rather than believers; do ye wish to make for God a power against you? Verily, the hypocrites are in the lowest depths of hell-fire, and thou shalt not find for them a help.

Save those who turn again, and do right, and take tight hold on God, and are sincere in religion to God; these are with the believers, and God will give to the believers mighty hire. Why should God punish you, if ye are grateful and believe? For God is grateful and knowing. God loves not publicity of evil speech, unless one has been wronged; for God both hears and knows. If ye display good or hide it, or pardon evil, verily, God is pardoning and powerful! Verily, those who disbelieve in God and His apostles desire to make a distinction between God and His apostles, and say, 'We believe in part and disbelieve in part, and desire to take a midway course between the two:' these are the misbelievers, and we have prepared for misbelievers shameful woe! But those who believe in God and His apostles, and who do not make a distinction between any one of them,—to these we will give their hire, for God is forgiving and merciful!

The people of the Book will ask thee to bring down for them a book from heaven; but they asked Moses a greater thing than that, for they said, 'Show us God openly;' but the thunderbolt caught them in their injustice. Then they took the calf, after what had come to them of manifest signs; but we pardoned that, and gave Moses obvious authority. And we held over them the mountain at their compact, and said to them, 'Enter ye the door adoring;' and we said to them, 'Transgress not on the Sabbath day,' and we took from them a rigid compact.

But for that they broke their compact, and for their misbelief in God's signs, and for their killing the prophets undeservedly, and for their saying, 'Our hearts are uncircumcised,'—nay, God hath stamped on them their misbelief, so that they cannot believe except a few,—and for their misbelief, and for their saying about Mary a mighty calumny, and for their saying, 'Verily, we have killed the Messiah, Jesus the son of Mary, the apostle of God,' . . . . but they did not kill him, and they did not crucify him, but a similitude was made for them. And verily, those who differ about him are in doubt concerning him; they have no knowledge concerning him, but only follow an opinion. They did not kill him, for sure! Nay, God raised him up unto Himself; for God is mighty and wise!

And there shall not be one of the people of the Book but shall believe in him before his death; and on the day of judgment he shall be a witness against them. And for the injustice of those who are Jews have we forbidden them good things which we had made lawful for them, and for their obstructing so much the way of God, and for their taking usury when we had forbidden it, and for their devouring the wealth of people in vain,—but we have prepared for those of them who misbelieve a grievous woe.

But those amongst them who are firm in knowledge, and the believers who believe in what is revealed to thee, let what is revealed before thee, and the steadfast in prayer, and the givers of alms, and the believers in God and the last day,—unto these we will give a mighty hire. Verily, we have inspired thee as we inspired Noah and the prophets after him, and as we inspired Abraham, and Ishmael, and Jacob, and the tribes and Jesus, and Job, and Jonas, and Aaron, and Solomon; and to David did we give Psalms.

Of apostles we have already told thee of some before; and of apostles some we have not told thee of; But Moses did God speak to, speaking;—apostles giving glad tidings and warning, that men should have no argument against God, after the apostles for God is mighty, wise! But God bears witness to what He has revealed to thee: He revealed it in His knowledge, and the angels bear witness too; though God is witness enough.

Verily, those who misbelieve and obstruct the way of God, have erred a wide error. Verily, those who misbelieve and are unjust, God will not pardon them, nor will He guide them on the road—save the road to hell, to dwell therein for aye;—that is easy enough to God! O ye folk! The Apostle has come to you with truth from your Lord: believe then, for it is better for you. But if ye misbelieve, then God's is what is in the heavens and the earth, and God is knowing, wise. O ye people of the Book! Do not exceed in your religion, nor say against God aught save the truth. The Messiah, Jesus the son of Mary, is but the apostle of God and His Word, which He cast into Mary and a spirit from Him; believe then in God and His apostles, and say not 'Three.' Have done! It were better for you. God is only one God, celebrated be His praise that He should beget a Son! His is what is in the heavens and what is in the earth; and God sufficeth for a guardian.

The Messiah doth surely not disdain to be a servant of God, nor do the angels who are nigh to Him; and whosoever disdains His service and is too proud, He will gather them altogether to Himself. But as for those who believe and do what is right, He will pay their hire and will give increase to them of His grace. But as for those who disdain and are too proud, He will punish them with a grievous woe, and they shall not find for them other than God a patron or a help. O ye folk! Proof has come to you from your Lord, and we have sent down to you manifest light. As for those who believe in God, and take tight hold of Him, He will make them enter into mercy from Him and grace; and He will guide them to Himself by a right way.

They will ask thee for a decision; say, 'God will give you a decision concerning remote kinship.' If a man perish and have no child, but have a sister, let her have half of what he leaves; and he shall be her heir, if she have no son. But if there be two sisters, let them both have two thirds of what he leaves; and if there be brethren, both men and women, let the male have like the portion of two females. God makes this manifest to you lest ye err; for God all things doth know.

[…]

The Chapter of the Night

(Surah XCII. Mecca.)

In the name of the merciful and compassionate God.

By the night when it veils! And the day when it is displayed! And by what created male and female! Verily, your efforts are diverse! But as for him who gives alms and fears God, and believes in the best, we will send him easily to ease! But as for him who is niggardly, and longs for wealth, and calls the good a lie, we will send him easily to difficulty! And his wealth shall not avail him when he falls down (into hell)! Verily, it is for us to guide; and, verily, ours are the hereafter and the former life! And I have warned you of a fire that flames!

None shall broil thereon, but the most wretched, who says it is a lie and turns his back. But the pious shall be kept away from it, he who gives his wealth in alms, and who gives no favour to anyone for the sake of reward, but only craving the face of his Lord most high; in the end he shall be well pleased!

[...]

(Surah CXII. Place of origin doubtful.)

In the name of the merciful and compassionate God.

Say, 'He is God alone! God the Eternal! He begets not and is not begotten! Nor is there like unto Him any one!'

Chapter 8
Native Traditions

Stories from Native Traditions

Native Traditions have stories that are passed down by word of mouth. The ones here have been transcribed—put into writing when the people come into contact with larger, more powerful societies where the written word is the norm—but native religions have been, and remain, oriented around the oral rather than written word. Native Traditions thus typically do not have canonical texts, per se, although they have incredibly rich stories, some of which may be considered canonical.

The theorist of religions, Mircea Eliade, made an interesting and useful distinction between what he characterized as a cosmic orientation and an historical one. Religions that have spread throughout the world, and most particularly the Abrahamic faiths have a keen sense of history. God's covenant with Abraham, the giving of the law to Moses, the unique sacrifice of Jesus, and the revelation of the Qur'an to Muhammad, each are seen in the respective traditions as absolutely unique historical events.

Native traditions for Eliade are more bound in a sense of "cosmos" which is recreating itself throughout time. The native sense of time, then, is more oriented to the repeating cycles of nature. In fact, one of the things that these traditions have in common, regardless of where they are from in the world, is a keen sense of nature and a connectedness to it.

The other traditions in this volume tend to have an identifiable canon and trajectory of development. While they may have a presence throughout the world (think here of Christianity or Islam), their origins can be traced to a particular place (and in the cases of these two most populous faiths, a particular time as well). Native traditions also are associated, each with their own particular place. The stories here are from all over the world—the Americas, the Pacific, Africa, Europe, Asia and Australia.

We open, for example, with a story from the Hopi tradition in the southwestern United States about how life emerged the underworld. There is a kinship with natural things—with plants and animals, with the sun and the moon and the earth and the water. It is not unusual for people to see themselves as related to corn, or to have conversations with animals and spirits.

While the Western reader may be familiar with Rudyard Kipling's "Just So" stories of a century ago, it is the case that many native traditions have their own just so stories. We encounter one from the Aborigines of Australia in a story about how the native bear lost his tail. We consider as well, a Yoruba story from the African continent about a leopard-man.

We have stories where people try to make sense of corpses and spirits from different peoples and places, each apparently struggling with similar aspects of the human condition. We can consider how modern day Halloween (or the Yule or Easter season, for that matter) offers lessons on the workings of syncretism, even as we look at some of its "pagan" roots. The word pagan, incidentally, is an imprecise term that has come to mean any number of things, often pejorative. Originally, the term simply denoted a religion of the "countryside."

Here again, a profound connection to the forces and spirits of nature and the seasons is crucial. Rather than temples, native traditions tend to have special outdoor places to commune with nature, such as rock formations and oak groves. The feasts and many of the rituals corresponded to specific times of the yearly cycle.

Another thing we might notice, for example, is that native traditions tend to preponderate among foragers and horticultural peoples. Larger agrarian societies and, more recently since industrialization, "developed" societies, tend to favor historical religions. While it is a topic for another time, only in developed societies does there appear to be the occasional collapse of religion (and typically only a partial one at that) and a concomitant rise of the secular.

These are more general guidelines than hard and fast rules. People have always held and conveyed mythical ideas, particularly when talking and thinking about big things. And religion has and continues to be a vehicle for some of the most far-ranging and profound stories that people have.

Let us now consider some of those stories, from native traditions from around the world...

Truth of the Hopi (retold by Edmund Nequatewa, 1936)

How the People Came Out of the Underworld

ALAIKSAI!—Attention. Before anybody's memory the Hopi lived in the underworld, which was the original place of all human life. Here, in the beginning, all life and everything was good in peace and happy. The people were governed by the chiefs (*Mongwi*), village criers (*Chakmongwi*), priests (*Momwit*), and high priests and all their religious rites were ruled by the high priests. The people were classed as common, middle, and first class.

The time came when the common and middle class of people grew wise to the doings of the priests and the high priests. All the days of their lives these poor people had been cheated of their family rights by the upper classes of the people. At times the wives of the lower class were visited by these men and by the priests and high priests, while the poor husbands of the women were away. Now all this kept on from bad to worse.

By this time the wives of the priests and the higher class of men also grew wise to what had been going on for all these years, and they were greatly troubled. Then, gossip, quarreling and fighting started between the men and women. Some priests said that it was a joy to cheat and steal another man's wife and that they would pray hard and earnest for prosperity. The women in return said, "If this is so and true, would it be more joyful to you men if we did the same to you as you have done to us? Would you then pray harder still for prosperity?"

This question was, of course, asked by decent women brought up before guilty men and at this, every heart was troubled. The women turned their husbands away. They had no place to go but to their gathering places, called kivas, which were the underground houses—meeting places at times of ceremonies. In these kivas some hearts were sad and some did not seem to care so very much. They were all waiting and watching to see who would leave the kiva first to go to their houses to see if their wives would refuse to let them in. Some women had declared that they would not let their husbands in, so they put their belongings outside of their doors.

The men left the kiva one by one, going to their homes to try their wives, but finding their things outside, they had to go to the homes of their relatives. Even there, they were not welcomed and were not invited to eat, so they were forced to take two or three ears of corn to the kiva to roast. That was all they had for their meal on that day. The night came on. What were they going to do? This was the question. Some said they would stay in the kivas and live on roasted corn as long as they could, thinking that the women might get over this trouble and their anger.

While the wives were still feeling strong against their men, they called a council. Every woman was present. At this council it was decided that the men would be falsely forgiven and would be taken back by every wife. All this was followed out and the husbands were made happy. But knowing all this, the chief, Yai-hiwa, and village crier, and their families, were greatly troubled and were sad. A thought came to the chief's mind of what he should do and how he must punish his people. Now with all this he was troubled in mind. About this time, when the men had been falsely forgiven, the women were going around and running wild after the unmarried boys, so that they might break the hearts of their husbands and so be revenged. Their families were neglected and their fires and cookings were left unattended. Among both men and women there was not a soul who could be happy in such sinful days, for there was murder, suicide, and every other wicked thing that made the days darker and darker.

All this worry and sorrow was on the chief. What could be done? Nobody knew. So he went calling on his wise men (*Posi-wiwaimkum*) personally, and broken hearted as he was, he could not help but shed tears at every call. These wise men were named

Kotiwa, Tani, Sootiwa, Komay, Seytiwa, Nawiki, and Kowisa, and they were the best of all wise men, with high ideals. But everything was for the chief to say in those days, so he asked every wise man to come to his counsel on the fourth day, out at a distant place away from the people.

The day came and the chief was out early that morning. With his bag of tobacco and pipes he was waiting for his wise men to come to the appointed place. One by one they came, each with his bag of tobacco and his pipe. The village crier was the last to arrive, and now everyone had come who was expected. Here they kindled a fire and being weary and sad they were rather quiet, sitting around their fire. The chief filled up his pipe with tobacco, lit it and smoked, then passed it to Yai-owa, the village crier. He puffed the smoke four times, then looked up to the chief, saying, "Father." In return the chief said, "My son." The pipe was passed on around in the same manner to every man. After the chief's pipe was all smoked out, every man filled his own pipe. Every pipe was first handed to the chief. Here they had their fatherly and brotherly smoke.

When the smoking was done the chief said, "My dear fellowmen, I pray in hopes that the gods, our fathers, get the smell of our smoking that they may have mercy upon us. With their power, I pray we will succeed and win because of what I have planned to do. My dear fellowmen, it is this. We must find a new place somewhere and we must find some way to get out of this sinful land, either below or above. I am in hopes to save some of you people if you only could realize this and feel as grieved as I do, about the trouble we are having this very day. I pray you to help me." Everybody was silent, arms folded, heads down over their knees while the chief was speaking. Every word was heard.

Then they said, "Our father, our chief, we pray with all our hearts and we are ready to help you. We will stand with you. We will walk in your path and whatever you ask of us we will do."

"Very well," he said, "be watchful and look ahead in my path that I may not mislead you. I pray you all and hope that the words you have spoken are from the very hearts of you and are true."

"We pray you, chief, that the words we speak are from every heart, and they are true."

"Very well, my fellowmen, I thank you. We will get busy at once. Tomorrow we will make *pahos* (prayer offerings) for our gods asking for the mercy and blessings that they bring upon us. I, the chief, Yai-hiwa, again thank you all. Be here earlier tomorrow."

The men went to their homes with the hope of success in their hearts, for they were true, honest men and were loyal to their chief.

The next morning being the second day of the meeting, the chief and all his wise men came to the same place where they had met the day before and here they smoked, as usual. Every man had brought his material with which to make pahos, or prayer sticks.

"Now," said the chief, "my dear fellowmen, let us start our work, and let every heart be in earnest. Let no soul be discouraged for we must work till we succeed."

"Our father and chief, we are strong in heart to be with you. There is no thought in us to forsake you."

"Very well, I thank you all," said the chief.

So here they made their prayer sticks all the forenoon and part of the afternoon. The chief had done his cutting of the pahos first, then the rest had copied after his, for he knew every sort of cut for a certain god. All this was well done.

When they had finished their paho making, every man, with his tray or plaque full of prayer sticks held in front of him, again circled around the fire and filled his pipe with tobacco to smoke. With a Hopi, smoking a pipe is the most true and earnest way of showing himself in prayer. Here they let the smoke pass from their mouths onto the trays of their prayer offerings to let the gods know they were earnest. With the Hopi, the smell of the smoke is the most sincere message to the gods, and for this reason much smoking is done at the times of all ceremonies. Now the work was well done for that day, so the chief said, "This will be all for today, and tomorrow we will see again what we can do. Let us all leave our pahos here and four of you will stay to guard our things, while the rest of us will go home and get something to eat. Then we will all come back and will bring you something to eat, and from now on we will camp here to the finish."

This was the third day of their session. The four men stayed to watch, so that nothing would harm their prayer offerings, for they afraid that the witches and the wizards might send a spy to find out what was going on, for it has always been believed by the Hopi that the witches and wizards could change their form into anything—into wild animals or birds of any kind. The men who had gone home all came back and brought food for the rest that had stayed. Now they were to take turns that night in watching, so that nothing could come close enough to see what kind of pahos they had made. They did this and at last morning came and the watchmen had done well.

Then the chief called his men to come together and take their places in a circle, and their smoking started, asking for mercy and the blessings of the gods, and all this was done. And again the chief looked up and said, "My dear fellowmen, our work is done so far, but we must have someone—we must call somebody who is wiser than we are to do the rest, or to finish the work for us. So let us now sing the calling song." With this song they called the mocking bird, *Yapa*. Now when he came he asked them, "Why do you want me? What can I do for you?"

The chief said, "We are in great need of you for you are so much wiser than us all, and you know all the songs of our gods. We need your help. We want to be sure that we make no mistakes. This is why we have called for you to come, and so we did make some pahos for you."

The chief handed him a tray of pahos, and the mocking bird was very glad to receive the prayer offerings. This was the fourth day when the mocking bird was called.

After receiving the prayer sticks the mocking bird said, "Yes, I am called a wise bird and one that knows everything, and of the songs I know all. But there is still somebody higher than I and he is above me, and this one is the canary bird, *Si-katsi*. Make no mistakes, call him. If he comes and says for me to help you, then I will, for he is still the wisest of all and his advice we must follow. Now I must go and hide for I do not want him to know and grow jealous because I came first."

The mocking bird left and was gone. Then again they sang their calling song for the canary bird and he came and sat on a nearby bush.

"Welcome," said the men, and he flew and sat down right in the center of them.

"Why do you call me?" he asked. "Why do you want me here?"

"Yes," said the chief, "we called you because we are in trouble and you being the wisest of all, we need your help. With all my heart, truly and honestly I pray you to help us."

"You are right," said the bird, "I am always in all prayer offerings. My feathers are always first. The trouble you are having I know all about. I wondered why you have waited so long to call me."

"My dear bird," said the chief, "it is like this. Our minds are full; we are almost insane and cannot think right, so do not think we mean to pass you by."

"I understand you," said the bird, "so I am here to help you. But I cannot do everything alone. I cannot perform my ceremony without the magic songs. The mocking bird must be with us. Call him at once. We need him."

Again the Hopis sang their calling song and soon the mocking bird was in sight. As he came near everybody said, "Welcome."

"Yes, here I am," said the bird, "Why do you want me?"

"It is I," said the canary. "Without you and your magic songs nothing could be done."

"Certainly, being noted for my songs I feel that it is my duty to be here and help you," said the mocking bird.

Before getting things ready for the ceremony, the two birds flew back around the rocks and there they changed their form into human beings. When they came back, the Hopis saw that they were handsome tall men with long straight black hair.

Now all this time the men were getting the things ready with which the Birdmen were to work and perform their ceremony. In laying the altar they spread out the sand in a small square and in the center they placed a sacred water bowl and for each direction an ear of corn was placed. Each ear of corn was of a different color—yellow for the north, blue for the west, red for the south, and white for the east.

When the altar was set up, they were ready for the mocking bird to take the lead in singing. The first songs were for making up the medicine water in the sacred water bowl. After the medicine water was made, the calling songs were to be next, but the questions arose: who would they call first? Who would have the courage and strength to go out to find a place for these Hopis to go, where they might rest and live in peace? The two Birdmen knowing all things, the Hopis left everything to them that there might be no more trouble. So they first called the eagle, *Kwa-hu*. At the end of every song the sacred water was sprinkled to each direction.

As they were singing the eagle came and sat in the midst of them and said, "Why do you call me? Why do you want me?"

"Welcome," said the men. "You being strong on the wing that is why we call you. We want you to help us. We think that you might find a place for us that we may be saved, and we pray that you will."

"Even though being a bird of the air and strong on the wing it is a hard undertaking. But with all my heart I am willing to help you, so let us hope for the best and pray our gods that I may come back to you alive. To be sure, which way must I go?" asked the eagle.

"We wish you would go up into the skies. There may be an opening and another world up there," said the men.

When the eagle was ready to fly and the prayer feathers were tied around his neck and upon each foot, the eagle said, "Pray that I may find a place up there and bring good news." Then off he went up into the skies. He circled round and round above these men and they watched him as he went up, till he was no more to be seen. At last it was getting late in the day and the people felt rather uneasy about him, but finally he was seen coming down, and now it was very late. It seemed as though he was just dropping down, and sure enough he was. He was hardly alive when he came and dropped in front of them all, exhausted, and they rushed to him and rubbed him till he came to. Soon he was quite well and had come to himself again. Then he was ready to tell the news.

"I know you are anxious to hear how far I have gone and what I have seen. Well, my dear good men," he said, "to tell you the truth, the way up there is rather discouraging. When I left here and kept going higher and higher, not a living thing was to be seen above the clouds. As I went on going higher I began to wonder where I would rest, but there was nothing to light on and nowhere to get a rest. When I looked up, it seems as though there is an opening up there, but I was getting very tired already, and if I didn't start to come back I might not be able to return here alive and tell you this news."

After hearing all this they were very much troubled and deep in sadness,, and they wondered what else must be done. The eagle then received his prize of many prayer offerings and was asked to stay with them to the finish, and, of course, he was glad to be with them.

By this time the two leaders—canary and mocking bird—thought of someone else to call. Again they were singing the calling song, and in singing the song it was mentioned who they wanted. Before the fourth song was half sung, a hawk, *Ki-sa* came and circled above once and sat down in the midst of them and said, "Why do you call me? Why do you want me?"

"We call you because we are in trouble and we need your help," said the men.

"Yes, I do know that you are in trouble," said the hawk. "All who have a heart wish to help and save you, and I am willing to do whatever you will ask of me."

"Very well," said the Hopis, "we want you to search the skies for us. You are strong on the wing and can fly high, so we feel that you might be able to find a way out of this wicked world."

"Very well," said he, "I will try."

So they made ready for the hawk to fly and put prayer feathers on him as was done to the eagle—around his neck and on his feet.

When he was all ready, he said, "Pray with all your hearts that I may find a place for you and bring you good news."

"We will," said the men, "for we want to save our families and many others who have good hearts, so may our gods take care of you while you are on the journey."

Up the hawk went and circled round and round overhead, as the eagle had done. For a long time he could be seen up in the air till he was gone above the clouds. All this time the men were singing prayer and luck songs that nothing would happen to the hawk.

It was getting late and everybody was rather uneasy again, and they kept watching for him very anxiously. Finally, he was seen again, but he did not seem to be alive and the eagle did not wait to be asked but went right up to meet him. Then every heart was troubled because they thought that he was surely dead. Now, before the eagle knew, the hawk had dropped past him, and then he just dived for the hawk, to catch him, and when the eagle did catch him his mouth was wide open but his heart was still beating a little. When the eagle came down with him in his claws he laid him down on a white robe and every eye was full of tears. Soon one of the men started to rub him, while the mocking bird sang the "life returning song." When he came to he was quite weak, and earnest prayers were shown by smoking many pipes for the hawk. Now by this time he was ready to tell his story.

"I know," said the hawk, "you are all anxious to hear what I have found out for you up in the skies. When I left here, the first part about going up is the same as what brother eagle had seen and told you. I had gone as far as he did, then I took the courage upon myself and went on up as far as I could see up there. I am quite sure that there is an opening up there, but I was tired out and was not able to go any further before I knew that I was dropping down. I tried to turn myself over, but could not make it, for I was exhausted. Finally I felt something hurting me on my sides. I opened my eyes and found myself in the sharp claws of brother eagle. Then, I do not know how we got here, but now I thank the gods and you all that I am alive again. But let us not be discouraged, we might find someone that will make it up there and find out for us all about what is up there. I know every heart is in trouble. My heart is in trouble too because of you."

After hearing this story of the hawk, there was very little light in the hearts of the men. But the thoughts with the men were still very deep of what is to be done next, or who would be the third to try the skies for these Hopis. Everything and everybody was very still and quiet—prayers were being said by the smoking of many pipes.

The next morning being the fifth day of their ceremony, the wise Birdmen—canary and mocking bird—called the men to attention, to come around the altar and fill up their pipes by which to say their prayers again to the gods. After this was said and done, they started singing the calling ceremony again, but they did not know who they were calling this time. Before long something came and just went "whip," sounding like a whip over their heads many times and then sat down in the midst of them, and he was a swallow, *Powvowkiaya*.

He said, "Here I am."

"Welcome," said the men.

"Why do you call me? Why do you want me?" said the bird.

"Yes," said they, "we need you. We want you to help us out of the troubles we are having. We want to be saved."

"I know you do," said the swallow. "I was anxious and longed to be called, but I know your minds are full and of course I know the way things have happened, so I have no envy against those who were called first, because I may not be able to equal what they have already done, but do understand that I am willing to help you."

"Yes," they said, "you being strong and swift on the wing, we pray in hopes that you will make it up through the skies to find a place for us, and here we have these prayer feathers made for you to wear on the way."

"Thank you," said he, "I would be happy to have them, but all those might be in the way so I will go without them."

"Very well," said the Hopis, "you know best of how you go in the air. May our gods bless us and have mercy upon us so that nothing will happen to you and we pray that our gods may take care of you on your journey and bring you back safely to us, so pray that no heart may be discouraged."

"You have all said well. I thank you all," said he.

Then he went off and in a little while he was out of sight. The men filled their pipes and were smoking. Those who were not smoking were singing the prayer songs of good luck. Again it was getting late in the day and the men were still strong with smoking and singing, while the eagle and the hawk were looking up into the skies with their sharp eyes. Finally they saw that the swallow was coming and they hesitated not, but flew right up to meet him. When they reached him he was nearly done and with a faint voice he said, "Catch me." They made a dive for him and did catch him and brought him down and right away they gave him some water and started to rub him up till he had come to himself. While he was resting the gift of prayer feathers was given to him.

When the chief handed all this to him, he said, "This is our gift to you, from us all. We are glad that you have returned to us again."

"Yes," said the swallow bird, "and I know you would like to hear what I have seen and done. It is too high up there. What these two brothers and I have seen is too great and wonderful, and to anybody without wings it is dangerous because the wind is strong up there. Going into the opening I got scared of the wind and was afraid to go any higher for fear I may not be able to come back. If I did I might not be alive to tell you this. What all I did see I could not begin to tell you all about it."

Now the Hopis were wondering who would be the next one to fly into the skies for them, so rather hopelessly they filled their pipes again to smoke and to pray some more, and of course they were very silent.

Finally the canary bird spoke up and said, "My dear fellowmen, we will make our last try so we will call brother shrike, *Si-katsi* and see what he can do for us. He is pretty wise too, so cheerfully come to the altar and we will sing again."

They all moved up around the altar and took up a little more courage, hoping down in their hearts for success. Before many calling songs were ended someone came flying very close to the ground and sat down on top of a nearby bush and from there into the midst of them.

"Welcome," said the Hopis.

"Yes, yes, here I am," he said. "Why do you want me in such a hurry?"

"Yes," said the mocking bird. "Here we are in trouble. Brother canary and I have been working here with these Hopis trying and hoping to find a place and a way to save them from this sinful land. These three brothers here have done their best up in the skies and they all seem to be very certain about an opening somewhere up there. This is why we wanted and called you, hoping that you can find another world and save us."

"With all my heart," said the shrike, "I am here to help you. I know and feel that it must be a hard undertaking because these three brothers were not able to make it. But to be sure, you must all tell me if you are all earnest in the hope to be saved. Somebody's heart must be bad here and he is the one that is holding you back and keeping you working so hard. Every heart must be true and honest. Let us all be one if we really want to be saved."

The chief of course was most troubled to think of all that time he had spent and had not yet accomplished anything, for he, himself, had good faith in his men and trusted them. Anyway, he asked the people then if there is any one of them with a false heart and who is intending to forsake them and they declared themselves to their chief and father to be all true men.

"No fault having been found in you, it gives me courage to go on and take the trip," said the shrike, "so pray for the best while I am away." He went off on a slow flight and as he went higher, he kept going faster. Soon he was no more to be seen. The men then took their pipes, filled them up and smoked with all their hearts, while the canary and the mocking bird were singing their prayer songs. The eagle and hawk were keeping their sharp eyes looking up into the skies.

Praying for many days with their pipes, every tongue was burning with the taste of the tobacco, but their courage was still strong for they were hoping for good news with all their anxious hearts. The day seemed very long.

It was very late when the shrike was seen high up in the sky and he was very slowly coming down. The eagle and the hawk saw that he was still strong so they did not go up to meet him for his little wings were still holding him up. As he was coming down nearer everybody was asked to hold their heads down with high hopes that he may land safely. As he landed they felt that their prayers were answered and they were filled with much joy. The shrike was asked to be seated in the center of them and be resting while the men joined in prayer by smoking their pipes.

When this was done the chief said to the bird, "I am more than glad and happy to see you come back to us again and it is not only I, but everybody here who is anxious to hear the news of what you have for us, so let us hear you."

"It is the same story," said the shrike, "from here on up to where these others had gotten to. When I passed that, I could see the opening and from there on the passage looked rather narrow. As I went on higher into the narrow passage, in there I found many a projecting rock on which I could light and rest myself. Then, at last, up through the opening which is just like a kiva you have down here. The light and sunshine is much better than here, but there is no sign of human life, only the animals and birds of all kinds. Now the question is, how are we going to get you up there? Because even the strongest birds carrying you one by one could not get you all up through there."

"So it is," said the chief, "that is another hard proposition, but let no heart be discouraged. Let us all be strong and we will succeed and leave our troubles behind here in this sinful world for I am more than glad and happy to know that there is another and better world up above, so if there is anyone present to give us advice of what is to be done next, I would like to hear him."

"It is I, who am called Kochoilaftiyo (the poker boy) said a boy who was sitting way in the back. They did not even know that he was with them all this time, for he was ranked and considered as of the low class people.

"Come forward to my side," said the chief.

And he was seated on the left side of him. Being only a poor boy it was rather doubtful to the others that he would know of any advice to give, but he was treated like the others and so they smoked their pipes together. When this was done, the chief asked him of what he had in mind.

"It is not much of anything," said the boy. "But I am with you and with all my heart I wish to help you. You know and everybody knows that I am not recognized nor respected half as much as the others."

"You have spoken the truth, but you must forget that now," said the chief. "You who are with me here, I refuse no one."

"I thank you," said the boy with eyes full of tears. "I know a little creature, *kuna* (chipmunk), who lives on the nuts of the pines. I think he knows how to plant and grow those pines and he may have some seeds. If he would come and plant and grow us one of those tall trees it might reach the sky so that we may climb up on it. He lives in the rocks and pines."

"Very well," said the chief, "let us call him." At this he turned to the mocking bird and asked him to sing his calling song for the chipmunk. At the altar the mocking bird picked up his rattle and started to sing. It was not very long before the chipmunk appeared over the rocks with his usual chip-chip voice, and when he did come up he ran in front of the altar.

"Why do you call me, and why do you want me?" he asked.

"It is because we are in trouble. We need your help."

"I am ready," he said.

"As you are noted for your tree planting and know how to make them grow so fast we would like you to plant one for us that will reach up to the sky and into the new world. We have been here many days trying to find out how we can get up there."

"Yes," said the chipmunk, "I do know how to plant trees, but I cannot be very sure and promise you that I could make it grow up to reach the sky, but for your sake I will try, so let us pray to our gods who really have power."

They filled up their pipes and smoked again, to carry their earnest prayers to the gods. After this was done, the little chipmunk reached into his bag for his tree seeds.

"This," he said, "is a spruce. We will try it first." He put it in his mouth and sang four of his magic songs. Then he took it out and set it in the ground in front of him, watching it very closely. Again he reached into his little bag and drew out his little rattle of sea shells with which he sang over his planted seed. Soon the tree began to grow out of the ground, and when it was about three inches high, he spit all over it and around the roots. With that it began to grow faster. Now, he kept this up as he was singing and his mouth began to get awfully dry so he asked for some water to increase the moisture in himself. Finally the tree was as high as a man stood and when it got this high he would run up on it and with his little paws would pull it upward at the very top. With songs and pulling it up, the tree was growing very fast indeed. The little creature kept this up till it had grown to its full height, but it did not reach the sky.

"I have done my best," said the chipmunk. "The tree will grow no more."

The high hopes of the chief sank again because the tree did not reach the opening up in the sky.

"Being called to help you," said the chipmunk, "I will try again, so keep your hopes and do not be discouraged. I think it has weakened this tree making it grow too fast, so this time it will be a little slower."

And he reached into his little bag for another seed which was a fir-pine. This he planted, with the same performance as the first time. Again, the little tree began to grow and the chipmunk repeated his same songs with new and strong hopes that he might make it reach the hole in the sky. Going up on this tree he would take his sacred meal and at the very top, with his prayer, he would throw this meal upward as high as he could, hoping that this would make it grow up through the opening.

While he was busy growing his tree every man was smoking his pipe and they were making their earnest prayers from their very hearts. Finally the chipmunk came back down to the ground again and said, "My tree has stopped growing again, although it has passed the first one by four men's height, but be not discouraged, I will try again. First, I must have prayer."

He reached into his bag and out he brought his little pipe and smoked. While he was smoking he kept a seed in his mouth which was a long-needle pine. When he had finished he set the seed in the ground again, and started his performance in the same manner with all the hopes of making it reach the sky, but this was also in vain, though it did pass the two first trees.

Now not only the chipmunk, but all the rest of the people were very much troubled and crying in their hearts to think that the trees had failed to reach the opening in the sky. The chipmunk, with a broken heart, filled up his little pipe and smoked, thinking very hard of what he could do next, because he thought himself powerless and knew that only his gods had unlimited power so with his smoking he prayed the gods for more wisdom. He could see that every heart was sad for the men were sitting around with their heads down upon their folded arms over their knees.

A thought came to him now, so he slowly raised his head and said, "We are all very sad but I will try again, so I wish to ask you from your very hearts if there is someone here who is not very willing to go and hates to leave behind the ones he loves or there may be some of you that still have evil thoughts in your hearts. All this work and many sleepless nights are getting heavy on our father, our chief. We must confess ourselves to him and to our gods that we will do right and will try to live the right kind of life in the upper world."

"We are all true," said they, "If we were not true we would not have stayed to this day with our chief."

The chipmunk left them and went to a place where the bamboo tree grows. Here he took a little shoot of a bamboo plant and with this he brought a tiny piñon shell full of water. These he set on a small basket tray and smoked his pipe over it, which was his earnest prayer. Others followed in the same manner. When this was done he put the piñon shell of water in the ground, at an arm length deep and on top of it he planted the bamboo shoot and he covered it up. He took his sacred corn meal in his right hand and stood over the plant and said his prayers in silence. Then he threw the meal high up toward the sky. Then the others followed one by one.

"Now," he said, "this being the last plant I know that will grow high we must give all our hearts to our gods that they may believe and answer our prayers and make this tree grow up through the opening in the sky."

When all their preparations were made and their sacred corn meal was thrown up toward the sky, the two birdmen started to sing their magic songs and the rest all joined with them because by that time, they knew the songs so that they could follow along with them. After the songs were ended, the little chipmunk ran up the tree and when he got to the top he pulled on it and he ran back four times up into that tree. Then he came down and filled up his pipe and started smoking.

He was always keeping time with the singing and he knew just when to run up the tree, and he just kept this performance up till the tree was high enough, and still they were singing and then, while they were singing, they asked the four other birds that had made their attempt to go up into the sky to find the opening, to fly up and see how high the tree had gone up, because by that time, the little chipmunk was tired, he couldn't run up the high tree again.

Now these birds, that is, the eagle and the hawk and the swallow bird and the shrike, made their trip up into the sky to the top of this tree four times and each time, when they came back they told the people that it was coming nearer to the opening. Toward the last, it was only the shrike that could go up and he made this trip up four times. But the last trip he made he stayed up on the top limb, and with him on the top limb the tree went through the opening. Of course, the old shrike felt very safe because he knew he could come back down, resting on the limbs of the tree.

When he came down he told the people that the tree had gone through the opening. Now the chipmunk was very glad that it had gone through, and of course you know that he was overjoyed. Then the chipmunk told them that it would be rather impossible to climb up on the tree. He told them that this tree was hollow inside and he started to gnawing on the bottom of the tree to cut an opening into it. While he was gnawing away all the men circled around the little fire and started their prayers again by smoking. After all this was done the chief said that, as it was rather late in the day, [and that] they would start their prayers and songs for the people at dawn. Now they were all very anxious to see the morning come and before it did come the chief had appointed two birds—the eagle and the swallow, to be on the look-out, so that no wicked people might pass.

Now on this day, before they started out, the chief said to the wise men that they must give an order for some kind of a guard that would hold back the bad people and the witches and wizards that would try to steal their way into the reed with the rest of the people. So the chief told the wise men to make their pahos for each four directions. These were to represent the closing of all the different trails from all directions. When these were made he sent out the One Horned Society or priests who were supposed to guard the North and West, and the Two Horned priests to guard the South and East. When they got to the four directions they made four lines out of sacred corn meal about six feet long and on both ends of the lines they set a paho falling backward—not toward the bamboo. Whoever steals their way into the bamboo and crosses this line will perish, which means that they will drop dead. Of course, many people tried to cross from different directions and were found dead.

This is how two of the societies or religions were started; *Kwakant* (One Horned Society) and *A-alt* (Two Horned Society), which are still in existence today. Whoever came to the bamboo by the set path came safely to the chief, to join in going to the Upper World.

The time came for them to sing their calling songs and before they started to sing they renewed their altar on which they had laid their prayer offerings. They made four of these prayer offerings and set them up on four sides of the tree to hold it up. These prayer offerings were about the span of a man's hand. When they started to sing they had to sing around the altar and the two birds were watching the opening at the bottom of the tree so in case the wicked people should start to come through they could drive them away. The two birds were appointed because they had sharp claws. When they started to sing their calling song, being a magic song, it took effect and they found the names of men who were in this ceremony following one another because the calling song as it began, named all the wise men who were serving in the ceremony. Before long the people were coming up one after another—that is, one family after another family.

When the people were gathered there, the chief had his prayer offering ready and at the foot of the tree he set this little prayer offering down in front of it. Then with his sacred corn meal he made a line pointing into it and then he walked in and his family followed and the rest of the royal families came after him, like the family of the village crier and the families of the others who had a high position, such as the high priest.

As they were going up through the tree the shrike started outside, because he was rather light and he could rest on the limbs. They didn't know how far they were going up. It took them quite a long while and the chief was rather anxious to get up to the top and after a long time they finally came up to the opening. When the chief got up there the shrike was waiting for him and when he crawled out of the tree the rest followed and as some of these people came out they started to sing the same songs that they were singing down at the bottom. These songs were limited and they were only to be sung four times, because they were awfully long songs. In a ceremony like this everybody was so anxious to get to the top it didn't seem so long and before all the people were through, the songs were ended and there were still some more people gathered around the tree. Then everywhere there was trouble down below, for those who hadn't been able to get up while the songs were being sung had to stay at the bottom, because the ceremony couldn't be sung any more.

Then the One Horned Priests who remained below had to cut the tree down for fear that someone might steal their way up, so they cut down the tree and this tree still had some people in it, so that is why the bamboo is jointed—because the people in there stuck in the tree and the tree kind of shrunk in between them.

[…]

A Yoruba Story

The Leopard-Man (from the Yoruba)

A HANDSOME stranger once came into a certain village and strolled about among the people in mysterious silence. All the maidens admired him and wished that he would choose one of them for his bride. But he said nothing, and at last walked away into the forest and disappeared from sight.

A month later the stranger came again, and this time one of the maidens fell so much in love with him that she resolved to follow him into the forest, as she could not bear to be separated from him.

When the stranger looked back and saw her coming behind him, he stopped, and begged her to return home; but she would not, and exclaimed: "I will never leave you, and wherever you go, I will follow."

"Beautiful maiden, you will regret it," replied the stranger sadly, as he hurried on.

After a while he stopped again, and once more begged her to retrace her steps; but she made the same reply, and again the handsome stranger said in sorrowful tones: "You will regret it, beautiful maiden!"

They went far into the depths of the forest, and at length reached a tree at the foot of which there lay a leopard-skin. Standing under the tree, the stranger began to sing a melancholy song, in which he told her that though he was allowed once a month to wander about in villages and towns like a man, he was in reality a savage leopard and would rend her in pieces as soon as he regained his natural form.

With these words he flung himself upon the ground, and immediately became a snarling leopard and began to pursue the terrified girl.

But fear gave such speed to her feet that he could not overtake her. As he pursued her he sang that he would tear her in small pieces, and she in another song replied that he would never overtake her.

For a great distance they ran, and then the maiden suddenly came to a deep but narrow river, which she could not cross. It seemed as if the leopard would catch her after all. But a tree, which stood on the river-bank, took pity on her and fell across the river, so that she was able to cross.

At last, nearly exhausted, she came to the edge of the forest and reached the village in safety. The leopard, disappointed of its prey, slunk back into the forest, and the handsome stranger was never seen again.

[…]

How the Native Bear Lost His Tail (An Australian Aboriginal Story)

The native bear and the whip-tail kangaroo were very friendly. They shared the same gunyah, and hunted together, and were very proud of their long tails. At this time a drought was over the land. Water was very scarce, and the two friends had camped by a shallow waterhole which contained some stagnant water. It was very nauseating to have to drink such water after the clear springs of the mountains. Nevertheless, it saved them from dying of thirst. At sunset banks of dark clouds would float low across the sky, and give promise of heavy rain, but at sunrise the sky would be as bright and clear as before, At last even the supply of stagnant water was exhausted, and the two friends were in a desperate plight.

After some time the kangaroo spoke and said: "When my mother carried me in her pouch I remember such a drought as this. The birds fell from the trees, the animals died fighting around dry water holes, and the trees withered and died. My mother travelled far with me, over the mountains and down by the river bed, but she travelled slowly, as hunger and thirst had made her very weak, and I was heavy to carry. Then another kangaroo spoke to her and said: 'Why do you carry such a heavy burden? You will surely die. Throw him into the bush and come with me, for I will travel fast and take you to water.' My mother would not leave me to die, but struggled on, and the other kangaroo left her to die from thirst. Wearied by her heavy burden, she struggled on until she again came to a sandy river bed. She now dug a deep hole in the sand, which slowly filled with cool, clear water. We camped by this waterhole until the rain came. I shall go to the river and see if I can dig and find water, for if we stay here we shall surely perish from thirst."

The native bear was delighted at the suggestion, and said: "Yes! Let us both go down to the river bed. I have very strong arms, and will help you." They made their way to the river, but, before reaching it, stumbled across some of their friends who had died of thirst. This made them very serious and determined. When they reached the river, the sun was very hot and they were very tired. The native bear suggested that the kangaroo should start digging, as he knew most about it. The kangaroo went to work with a will, and dug a deep hole, but no signs of water were visible. The kangaroo was exhausted with his work, and asked the native bear to help him. The native bear was very cunning, and said: "I would willingly help you, but I am feeling very ill; the sun is very hot, and I am afraid I am going to die." The kangaroo was very sorry for his friend, and set to work again without complaining.

At last his work was rewarded. A trickle of water appeared in the bottom of the hole, and gradually increased until it filled it to overflowing. The kangaroo went over to his friend, and, touching him gently on the shoulder, said: "I have discovered water, and will bring some to you." But the native bear was only shamming, and dashed straight to the waterhole without even replying to the surprised kangaroo. When the native bear bent down to drink the water his tail stuck out like a dry stick. The kangaroo, who could now see the despicable cunning of his friend, was very angry, and, seizing his boomerang, cut off the tail of the drinker as it projected above the waterhole. To this day the native bear has no tail as an evidence of his former laziness and cunning.

[…]

A Celtic Story

The Corpse Watchers

There was once a poor woman that had three daughters, and one day the eldest said, "Mother, bake my cake and kill my cock, till I go seek my fortune." So she did, and when all was ready, says her mother to her, "Which will you have—half of these with my blessing, or the whole with my curse?" "Curse or no curse," says she, "the whole is little enough." So away she set, and if the mother didn't give her her curse, she didn't give her her blessing.

She walked and she walked till she was tired and hungry, and then she sat down to take her dinner. While she was eating it, a poor woman came up, and asked for a bit. "The dickens a bit you'll get from me," says she; "it's all too little for myself; and the poor woman walked away very sorrowful. At nightfall she got lodging at a farmer's, and the woman of the house told her that she'd give her a spade-full of gold and a shovel-full of silver if she'd only sit up and watch her son's corpse that was waking in the next room. She said she'd do that; and so, when the family were in their bed, she sat by the fire, and cast an eye from time to time on the corpse that was lying *under* the table.

All at once the dead man got up in his shroud, and stood before her, and said, "All alone, fair maid!" She gave him no answer, and when he said it the third time, he struck her with a switch, and she became a grey flag.

About a week after, the second daughter went to seek her fortune, and she didn't care for her mother's blessing no more, nor her sister, and the very same thing happened to her. She was left a grey flag by the side of the other.

At last the youngest went off in search of the other two, and she took care to carry her mother's blessing with her. She shared her dinner with the poor woman on the road, and she told her that she would watch over her.

Well, she got lodging in the same place as the others, and agreed to mind the corpse. She sat up by the fire with the dog and cat, and amused herself with some apples and nuts the mistress gave her. She thought it a pity that the man under the table was a corpse, he was so handsome.

But at last he got up, and says he, "All alone, fair maid!" And she wasn't long about an answer:—

"All alone I am not,
I've little dog Dog and Pussy, my cat;
I've apples to roast, and nuts to crack,
And all alone I am not."

"Ho, ho!" says he, "you're a girl of courage, though you wouldn't have enough to follow me. I am now going to cross the quaking bog, and go through the burning forest. I must then enter the cave of terror, and climb the hill of glass, and drop from the top of it into the Dead Sea." "I'll follow you," says she, "for I engaged to mind you." He thought to prevent her, but she was as stiff as he was stout.

Out he sprang through the window, and she followed him till they came to the "Green Hills," and then says he:—

Open, open, Green Hills, and let the Light of the Green Hills through;"
Aye," says the girl, "and let the fair maid, too."

They opened, and the man and woman passed through, and there they were, on the edge of a bog.

He trod lightly over the shaky bits of moss and sod; and while she was thinking of how she'd get across, the old beggar appeared to her, but much nicer dressed, touched her shoes with her stick, and the soles spread a foot on each side. So she easily got over the shaky marsh. The burning wood was at the edge of the bog, and there the good fairy flung a damp, thick cloak over her, and through the flames she went, and a hair of her head was not singed. Then they passed through the dark cavern of horrors, where she'd have heard the most horrible yells, only that the fairy stopped her ears with wax. She saw frightful things, with blue vapours round them, and felt the sharp rocks, and the slimy backs of frogs and snakes.

When they got out of the cavern, they were at the mountain of glass; and then the fairy made her slippers so sticky with a tap of her rod, that she followed the young corpse easily to the top. There was the deep sea a quarter of a mile under them, and so the corpse said to her, "Go home to my mother, and tell her how far you came to do her bidding: farewell." He sprung head foremost down into the sea, and after him she plunged, without stopping a moment to think about it.

She was stupefied at first, but when they reached the waters she recovered her thoughts. After piercing down a great depth, they saw a green light towards the bottom. At last they were below the sea, that seemed a green sky above them; and sitting in a beautiful meadow, she half asleep, and her head resting against his side. She couldn't keep her eyes open, and she couldn't tell how long she slept: but when she woke, she was in bed at his house, and he and his mother sitting by her bedside, and watching her.

It was a witch that had a spite to the young man, because he wouldn't marry her, and so she got power to keep him in a state between life and death till a young woman would rescue him by doing what she had just done. So at her request, her sisters got their own shape again, and were sent back to their mother, with their spades of gold and shovels of silver. Maybe they were better after that, but I doubt it much. The youngest got the young gentleman for her husband. I'm sure she deserved him…

[…]

A Native Tale from Siberia

A Shaman Story

In Olzoni, where this story was told, there lived three hundred years ago an old Shaman who could raise the dead. One day when he was in his seventy-fifth year he went on a visit to a neighboring village. The people there were so glad to see him that they killed a number of sheep, roasted them, and all feasted for three days.

On his way home he came to a large gate opening into a field, and there he met three hundred horned cattle. He thought that a butcher was driving them, but soon discovered that they were driven by a woman who was riding on a red ox. The woman was holding an infant in her arms. After the red ox had passed him he met a man whose head was as big as a cock of hay, he was riding on a gray stallion of enormous size.

"From where do you come, flesh merchant?" asked the Shaman.

"I am not a flesh merchant," replied the man, "I am Minga Nudite Milá (Thousand Eyes), and I have just destroyed all the cattle in the country around here."

The Shaman hurried home and found that his cattle were gone, not a cow, sheep, or horse was left. He was very angry, and going to his five brothers, who were all Shamans, he said: "Let us take counsel. Shall we not go in pursuit of Minga Nudite Milá?"

"Of what use?" asked they. "He would not yield to us, for he is subject to no one."

When he saw that his brothers were unwilling to help him, and he must do all with his own magic, the old Shaman went home, made tarasun and drank it; then he went to the corner of the room, got his axe and put it under the pillow on his bed, tied his horse to a post in the yurta and lay down, saying to his wife,

"Do not let my horse out, and do not waken me." Soon he and his horse were sound asleep. But they were not asleep, it was only their bodies which were so quiet. In reality the Shaman was riding swiftly toward the Angara.

Before reaching Irkutsk there is a mountain, Torkoi Tonkoi. From the top of this mountain the Shaman saw that Minga Milá had made a bridge across the river and was beginning to drive his cattle over it. Half of the bridge was silver and half of it was gold.

The Shaman turned himself into a bee, made his axe equally small, and, taking it with him, flew under the bridge and hewed the pillars so that the bridge broke in two. All the cattle fell into the Angara, as well as the woman on the red ox. Minga Milá fell, but he saved himself—at least he did not sink, though he and his gray stallion remained in the water.

The old Shaman threw his gold ring of a Shaman toward heaven, and a dreadful wind sprang up which lasted for three days. Minga Milá sat on the water and was driven back and forth by the wind. After the three days of wind came three days of strong rain. By the end of those six days the hoofs of Minga Milá's horse fell off. When the storm was over Minga Milá came out of the river; his horse followed him, and they began to dry themselves. The horse's hoofs came from the river and went on to his feet.

Enraged by the loss of the cattle and the woman on the red ox, but frightened by the terrible storm, Minga Milá swore a great oath that henceforth he would not go to the Olzoni country. "Should I go there may my one thousand eyes jump out of my head, and my body be cut in three pieces. I will neither kill people hereafter nor destroy cattle," declared he. Hearing this oath the Shaman was greatly pleased, and at once started for home.

On the road he went to his five brothers and told them how he had punished Thousand Eyes. "I have freed myself and you of this monster," said he; "we can now live in peace." When he reached his yurta he rose from the bed, where his wife thought he was sleeping, untied his horse and drove it out to pasture. And all was as if it had not been. But the cattle of Olzoni were never stolen again.

The Shaman began to drink tarasun and visit his friends. In the spring, about a year after his return from the Angara, he was on his way to see friends in Olzonski-Rod when he came upon three men who were burying a dead child. "What are you doing?" asked the Shaman.

"Go thy way, grandfather," answered the men. "Stand not there, for the child is dead. No one is free from death."

They let down the body and began to cover it with earth.

"Take away that earth," commanded the Shaman; "give me the child and do you kill a goat and bury it in this grave." He carried the child to its home, had six stones heated red hot, took off his leggings, danced with bare feet on the red hot stones, and "shamaned" till morning, stepping over the dead child from time to time, until the first cock crowed. That made the blood move in the child's body, and he opened his eyes, but could not talk.

The next night the Shaman had the boy's father and mother tied to a post in the yurta, and again he danced and shamaned until the first cock crowed. All this time the child lay without moving. At sunrise the Shaman blew on the child's head and feet. He sprang up and asked, "What are you doing, father?"

Then the Shaman unbound the father and mother. "Your child is alive and well," said he; "now I will go home."

"No," said the father, "I must reward you; I am rich. I will give you half my money and half my cattle for what you have done."

"I do not need your money or your cattle," replied the Shaman. But the father was too happy over the recovery of his child to let the Shaman go without a reward. "Well," said the Shaman, "all I need is one cock of hay, an arkan rope (skin rope, hide), and nine copecks in money."

The father gave him the money, the rope, and the hay, and loaned him an ox to draw the hay home. The Shaman fed the hay to his cattle, hung up the rope, and kept the nine copecks in memory of the father's gratitude.

The raising of the boy from the dead was the last great act of the Shaman's life, for he died soon after.

[...]

Sun-Worship. The Sources of Hallowe'en

IF we could ask one of the old-world pagans whom he revered as his greatest gods, he would be sure to name among them the sun-god; calling him Apollo if he were a Greek; if an Egyptian, Horus or Osiris; if of Norway, Sol; if of Peru, Bochica. As the sun in the center of the physical universe, so all primitive peoples made it the hub about which their religion revolved, nearly always believing it a living person to whom they could say prayers and offer sacrifices, who directed their lives and destinies, and could even snatch men from earthly existence to dwell for a time with him, as it draws the water from lakes and seas.

In believing this they followed an instinct of all early peoples, a desire to make persons of the great powers of nature, such as the world of growing things, mountains and water, the sun, moon, and stars; and a wish for these gods they had made to take an interest in and be part of their daily life. The next step was making stories about them to account for what was seen; so arose myths and legends.

The sun has always marked out work-time and rest, divided the year into winter idleness, seed-time, growth, and harvest; it has always been responsible for all the beauty and goodness of the earth; it is itself splendid to look upon. It goes away and stays longer and longer, leaving the land in cold and gloom; it returns bringing the long fair days and resurrection of spring. A Japanese legend tells how the hidden sun was lured out by an image made of a copper plate with saplings radiating from it like sunbeams, and a fire kindled, dancing, and prayers; and round the earth in North America the Cherokees believed they brought the sun back upon its northward path by the same means of rousing its curiosity, so that it would come out to see its counterpart and find out what was going on.

All the more important church festivals are survivals of old rites to the sun. "How many times the Church has decanted the new wine of Christianity into the old bottles of heathendom." Yule-tide, the pagan Christmas, celebrated the sun's turning north, and the old midsummer holiday is still kept in Ireland and on the Continent as St. John's Day by the lighting of bonfires and a dance about them from east to west as the sun appears to move. The pagan Hallowe'en at the end of summer was a time of grief for the decline of the sun's glory, as well as a harvest festival of thanksgiving to him for having ripened the grain and fruit, as we formerly had husking-bees when the ears had been garnered, and now keep our own Thanksgiving by eating of our winter store in praise of God who gives us our increase.

Pomona, the Roman goddess of fruit, lends us the harvest element of Hallowe'en; the Celtic day of "summer's end" was a time when spirits, mostly evil, were abroad; the gods whom Christ dethroned joined the ill-omened throng; the Church festivals of All Saints' and All Souls' coming at the same time of year—the first of November—contributed the idea of the return of the dead; and the Teutonic May Eve assemblage of witches brought its hags and their attendant beasts to help celebrate the night of October 31st.

[…]

A Seneca Tale of the Great Bear and the Six Hunters, or…

The Seven Stars of the Dipper

Six men went out hunting, for a long time they found no game. One of their number said he was sick (he was lazy) and they had to make a litter of two poles and a blanket, and four carried him. The sixth member of the party came behind bringing the kettle. Besides this each man had his own load to carry.

At last, when the hunters were getting very hungry, they came upon bear tracks. They were so hungry that when they saw the tracks they dropped their companion and their burdens and each man ran as fast as he could after the bear.

At first the tracks looked old but they thought, "We will overtake the bear sometime."

Later they saw that the tracks couldn't be more than three days old. The farther the men went the fresher the tracks were till the men said, "To-morrow we will overtake the bear."

The man they had carried so long was not tired and when they dropped him and he knew he was going to be left he jumped up and ran on after them. As he was fresher than they were he soon passed them and killed the bear.

The men in their race after the bear didn't notice that they were going up all the time. Many people saw them in the air, as they ran along, always rising.

When they overtook the bear and the lazy man, they had reached the sky and there they have remained to this day and can be seen any starlit night. The man who carried the kettle is in the bend of the Dipper, the middle star in the handle and a small star which is the only one near any other of the Dipper stars is the kettle. The Bear is at the lower outside corner. Every Autumn, when the first frost comes, one can see on the leaves of the oak-tree drops of oil, not water, and this is the oil and blood of the Bear.

On seeing it the Indians say, "The lazy man has killed the Bear."

[...]

A Tale from Southern Nigeria

The Story of Lightning and Thunder

In the olden days the thunder and lightning lived on the earth amongst all the other people, but the king made them live at the far end of the town, as far as possible from other people's houses.

The thunder was an old mother sheep, and the lightning was her son, a ram. Whenever the ram got angry he used to go about and burn houses and knock down trees; he even did damage on the farms, and sometimes killed people. Whenever the lightning did these things, his mother used to call out to him in a very loud voice to stop and not to do any more damage; but the lightning did not care in the least for what his mother said, and when he was in a bad temper used to do a very large amount of damage. At last the people could not stand it any longer, and complained to the king.

So the king made a special order that the sheep (Thunder) and her son, the ram (Lightning), should leave the town and live in the far bush. This did not do much good, as when the ram got angry he still burnt the forest, and the flames sometimes spread to the farms and consumed them.

So the people complained again, and the king banished both the lightning and the thunder from the earth and made them live in the sky, where they could not cause so much destruction. Ever since, when the lightning is angry, he commits damage as before, but you can hear his mother, the thunder, rebuking him and telling him to stop. Sometimes, however, when the mother has gone away some distance from her naughty son, you can still see that he is angry and is doing damage, but his mother's voice cannot be heard.

[...]

A Polynesian Tale

The Two Sorcerers

Kiki was a celebrated sorcerer, and skilled in magical arts; he lived upon the river Waikato. The inhabitants of that river still have this proverb: 'The offspring of Kiki wither shrubs.' This proverb had its origin in the circumstance of Kiki being such a magician, that he could not go abroad in the sunshine; for if his shadow fell upon any place not protected from his magic, it at once became *tapu*, and all the plants there withered.

This Kiki was thoroughly skilled in the practice of sorcery. If any parties coming up the river called at his village in their canoes as they paddled by, he still remained quietly at home, and never troubled himself to come out, but just drew back the sliding door of his house, so that it might stand open, and the strangers stiffened and died; or even as canoes came paddling down from the upper parts of the river, he drew back the sliding wooden shutter to the window of his house, and the crews on board of them were sure to die.

At length, the fame of this sorcerer spread exceedingly, and resounded through every tribe, until Tamure, a chief who dwelt at Kawhia, heard with others, reports of the magical powers of Kiki, for his fame extended over the whole country. At length Tamure thought he would go and contend in the arts of sorcery with Kiki, that it might be seen which of them was most skilled in magic; and he arranged in his own mind a fortunate season for his visit.

When this time came, he selected two of his people as his companions, and he took his young daughter with him also; and they all crossed over the mountain range from Kawhia, and came down upon the river Waipa, which runs into the Waikato, and embarking there in a canoe, paddled down the river towards the village of Kiki; and they managed so well, that before they were seen by anybody, they had arrived at the landing-place. Tamure was not only skilled in magic, but he was also a very cautious man; so whilst they were still afloat upon the river, he repeated an incantation of the kind called 'Mata-tawhito,' to preserve him safe from all arts of sorcery; and he repeated other incantations, to ward off spells, to protect him from magic, to collect good genii round him, to keep off evil spirits, and to shield him from demons; when these preparations were all finished, they landed, and drew up their canoe on the beach, at the landing-place of Kiki.

As soon as they had landed, the old sorcerer called out to them that they were welcome to his village, and invited them to come up to it: so they went up to the village: and when they reached the square in the centre, they seated themselves upon the ground; and some of Kiki's people kindled fire in an enchanted oven, and began to cook food in it for the strangers. Kiki sat in this house, and Tamure on the ground just outside the entrance to it, and he there availed himself of this opportunity to repeat incantations over the threshold of the house, so that Kiki might be enchanted as he stepped over it to come out. When the food in the enchanted oven was cooked, they pulled off the coverings, and spread it out upon clean mats. The old sorcerer now made his appearance out of his house and he invited Tamure to come and eat food with him; but the food was all enchanted, and his object in asking Tamure to eat with him was, that the enchanted food might kill him; therefore Tamure said that his young daughter was very hungry, and would eat of the food offered to them; he in the meantime kept on repeating incantations of the kind called Mata-tawhito, Whakangungu, and Parepare, protections against enchanted food, and as she ate she also continued to repeat them; even when she stretched out her hand to take a sweet potato, or any other food, she dropped the greater part of it at her feet, and hid it under her clothes, and then only ate a little bit. After she had done, the old sorcerer, Kiki, kept waiting for Tamure to begin to eat also of the enchanted food, that he might soon die. Kiki having gone into his house again, Tamure still sat on the ground outside the door, and as he had enchanted the threshold of the house, he now repeated incantations which might render the door enchanted also, so that Kiki might be certain not to escape when he passed out of it. By this time Tamure's daughter had quite finished her meal, but neither her father nor either of his people had partaken of the enchanted food.

Tamure now ordered his people to launch his canoe, and they paddled away, and a little time after they had left the village, Kiki became unwell; in the meanwhile, Tamure and his people were paddling homewards in all haste, and as they passed a village where there were a good many people on the river's bank, Tamure stopped, and said to them: 'If you should see any canoe pulling after us, and the people in the canoe ask you, have you seen a canoe pass up the river, would you be good enough to say: "Yes, a canoe has passed by here"?—and then, if they ask you: "How far has it got?" Would you be good enough to say: "Oh, by this time it has got very far up the river"?'—and having thus said to the people of that village, Tamure paddled away again in his canoe with all haste.

Some time after Tamure's party had left the village of Kiki, the old sorcerer became very ill indeed, and his people then knew that this had been brought about by the magical arts of Tamure, and they sprang into a canoe to follow after him, and puffed up the river as hard as they could; and when they reached the village where the people were on the river's bank, they called out and asked them: 'How far has the canoe reached, which passed up the river?'—And the villagers answered: 'Oh, that canoe must [have] got very far up the river by this time.' The people in the canoe that was pursuing Tamure, upon hearing this, returned again to their own village, and Kiki died from the incantations of Tamure.

Some of Kiki's descendants are still living—one of them, named Mokahi, recently died at Tau-ranga-a-Ruru, but Te Maioha is still living on the river Waipa. Yes, some of the descendants of Kiki, whose shadow withered trees, are still living. He was indeed a great sorcerer: he overcame every other sorcerer until he met Tamure, but be was vanquished by him, and had to bend the knee before him.

Tamure has also some descendants living, amongst whom are Mahu and Kiake of the Ngati-Mariu tribe; these men arc also skilled in magic: if a father skilled in magic died, he left his incantation to his children; so that if a man was skilled in sorcery, it was known that his children would have a good knowledge of the same arts, as they were certain to have derived it from their parent.

Credits

Edwin Arnold, trans., Selections from *The Bhagavad Gita*. Copyright in the Public Domain.

Buddha; Paul Carus, ed., Selections from *The Word*. Copyright in the Public Domain.

Confucius; James Legge, trans., Selections from *Confucian Analects*. Copyright in the Public Domain.

Lao-tzu; James Legge, trans., Selections from *Tao Te Ching*. Copyright in the Public Domain.

Selections from the *Old Testament*, King James Version. Copyright in the Public Domain.

Selections from the *New Testament*, King James Version. Copyright in the Public Domain.

E.H. Palmer, trans., Selections from *The Qur'an*. Copyright in the Public Domain.

Edmund Nequatewa, Selections from *Truth of a Hopi*. Copyright in the Public Domain.

M.I. Ogumefu, "The Leopard Man," *Yoruba Legends*, pp. 18-20. Copyright in the Public Domain.

W.J. Thomas, ed., "How the Native Bear Lost His Tail," *Some Myths and Legends of the Australian Aborigines*. Copyright in the Public Domain.

Patrick Kennedy, "The Corpse Watchers," *Legendary Fictions of the Irish Celts*. Copyright in the Public Domain.

Jeremiah Curtin, "A Shaman Story," *A Journey in Southern Siberia*. Copyright in the Public Domain.

Ruth Edna Kelley, Selection from *The Book of Hallowe'en*. Copyright in the Public Domain.

Jeremiah Curtin, ed., "The Great Bear and the Six Hunters, or The Seven Stars of the Dipper," *Seneca Indian Myths*, pp. 503-504. Copyright in the Public Domain.

Elphinstone Dayrell, "The Story of the Lightning and the Thunder," *Folk Stories from Southern Nigeria*. Copyright in the Public Domain.

Sir George Grey, "The Two Sorcerers," *Polynesian Mythology & Ancient Traditional History of the New Zealanders*. Copyright in the Public Domain.

CPSIA information can be obtained
at www.ICGtesting.com
Printed in the USA
BVOW08s0359050817

491154BV00005B/39/P